MONEY, MARKETS, AND SOVEREIGNTY

MONEY, MARKETS, AND SOVEREIGNTY

Benn Steil and
Manuel Hinds

A Council on Foreign Relations Book
Yale University Press
New Haven & London

Printed in the United States of America

Library of Congress Control Number: 2008045623
ISBN 978-0-300-14924-1 (cloth : alk. paper)

A catalogue record for this book is available from the British Library.

This paper meets the requirements of ANSI/NISO Z39.48-1992 (Permanence of Paper). It contains 30 percent postconsumer waste (PCW) and is certified by the Forest Stewardship Council (FSC).

10 9 8 7 6 5 4 3 2

THE COUNCIL ON FOREIGN RELATIONS

The Council on Foreign Relations (CFR) is an independent, nonpartisan membership organization, think tank, and publisher dedicated to being a resource for its members, government officials, business executives, journalists, educators and students, civic and religious leaders, and other interested citizens in order to help them better understand the world and the foreign policy choices facing the United States and other countries. Founded in 1921, CFR carries out its mission by maintaining a diverse membership, with special programs to promote interest and develop expertise in the next generation of foreign policy leaders; convening meetings at its headquarters in New York and in Washington, DC, and other cities where senior government officials, members of Congress, global leaders, and prominent thinkers come together with CFR members to discuss and debate major international issues; supporting a Studies Program that fosters independent research, enabling CFR scholars to produce articles, reports, and books and hold roundtables that analyze foreign policy issues and make concrete policy recommendations; publishing *Foreign Affairs*, the preeminent journal on international affairs and U.S. foreign policy; sponsoring Independent Task Forces that produce reports with both findings and policy prescriptions on the most important foreign policy topics; and providing up-to-date information and analysis about world events and American foreign policy on its website, www.cfr.org.

FOR GLORIA

*FOR MY DAUGHTERS—CARMEN BEATRIZ,
ELEONORA, AND EVA MARIA—AND FOR MY
GRANDCHILDREN*

CONTENTS

ACKNOWLEDGMENTS

We are extremely grateful and indebted to six talented and highly motivated young people who provided critical research support in the writing of this book: Jesse Schreger, Adam Fleisher, James Bergman, Danielle Gilbert, Eli Nagler, and Oren Ziv. We were also privileged to have had ongoing feedback and sage advice from our Council on Foreign Relations study group, and would like to express our warmest thanks to each of the members who so generously dedicated their time and shared their expertise: Jonathan Chanis, W. Bowman Cutter, Robert Dinerstein, Anthony Faillace, Tim Ferguson, Sergio Galvis, Peter Gottsegen, D. Blake Haider, George Hoguet, Peter Kenen, Marc Levinson, John Makin, John Mbiti, Richard McCormack, Walter Russell Mead, Richard Medley, Jeffrey Rosen, Robert Rosenkranz, Amity Shlaes, Paul Schott Stevens, Ian Vásquez, and, in particular, the chairman of the group, Charles Calomiris. We also benefited greatly from detailed comments on draft text from Sebastian Mallaby and two anonymous referees. Finally, we would like to thank Gary Samore, director of the David Rockefeller Studies Program at the Council on Foreign Relations, and Richard N. Haass, the Council's president, for their support and encouragement. Errors and other failings are, of course, ours and ours alone.

1

THINKING ABOUT MONEY AND GLOBALIZATION

The word *globalization* has a manifold paternity, but its modern coinage has been popularly ascribed to former *Harvard Business Review* editor Ted Levitt, who in a 1983 *Review* article argued that new technology had "pro-letarianized" global communication, transportation, and travel.[1] On a more visceral level, its popular tableau is captured in Rory Stewart's travelogue of his walk across Afghanistan, one of the least globalized parts of the globe, immediately following the fall of the Taliban, in which he observes men in Herat unloading Chinese tablecloths and Iranian flip-flops marked "Nike by Ralph Lauren."[2]

The *idea* of globalization, however, the notion that commerce and technology were bringing powerful foreign influences to bear on established ways of life, for good or for ill, goes back centuries, in a form fully recognizable even in the Internet age. "When has the entire earth ever been so closely joined together, by so few threads?" asked the German philosopher Johann Gottfried von Herder in 1774. "Who has ever had more power and more machines, such that with a single impulse, with a single movement of a finger, entire nations are shaken?"[3] And this was seventy years before the first public use of the telegraph.

Ideas about the idea of globalization also go back centuries, and they parallel remarkably the views passionately expressed on both sides of the divide today. For every Adam Smith and Baron de Montesquieu embracing a commerce-driven cosmopolitanism, there was an Adam Müller or a Jean-Jacques Rousseau condemning it with equal fervor and eloquence.

Both sides recognized technology as a powerful force impelling industrial and social change, and both sides saw politics as critical to determining whether society evolved well or badly in technology's slipstream.

Contemporary critics of globalization argue that money and markets are today operating outside timeless norms relating to the sovereign powers of governments. Their condemnations of trade and capital flows go well beyond allegations of negative economic effects, extending to questions of political legitimacy.

The question of effects is a perpetual moving target, as anti-market arguments have been for centuries. The success of pro-globalization policies in China and India has, for example, merely shifted the allegations of anti-globalizers from increasing poverty to increasing inequality to *perceptions* of increasing inequality.[4] But charges that financial markets and institutions, such as the International Monetary Fund (IMF), are violating fundamental rights of states remain largely unchallenged and have a natural and growing appeal to organized interests who are only too willing to harness the powers of state organs in the name of reclaiming lost sovereignty.

Our discussion in chapter 2 of the history of Western law and its relation to both states and private commerce is intended to address these challenges to globalization's legitimacy directly. To the extent that we are correct in arguing, as we do in chapter 3, that the most prominent negative critiques of globalization are fundamentally reprisings of history's most prominent arguments against markets generally, the potential consequences of state organs arrogating more powers to confront economic liberalism in the cause of reasserting sovereignty are considerable. The vastly divergent political and economic fortunes of nations that have embraced liberalism and those where it has been suffocated in the name of cultural preservation, or fairness to one or another social, ethnic, or religious group, suggest real dangers in political leaders successfully tarring globalization with charges of sovereign usurpation.

Why should a book on globalization which aims to be of practical relevance spend so much ink discussing the history of political and legal thought? In the words of Bertrand Russell, "To understand an age or a nation, we must understand its philosophy."[5] The remarkably rapid (by historical standards) progress of science since the mid-nineteenth century has conditioned Westerners to think of history in linear terms, as a forward march of progress. But the history of philosophy is not like this. The new circumstances in which each generation finds itself stimulate the emergence of philosophical ideas appropriate to them. Thus Greek ethical thought down through Aristotle focused on the life lived as a *citizen* of a small city-state. The "good life" was one lived in a context that was in the deepest sense political. But once the Greeks, from the late fourth century BC onward, became subject first to Macedonian and then to Roman authority, such ideas lost all practical meaning. The Hellenistic philosophies which emerged—bracingly cosmopolitan in comparison to their Hellenic precursors[6]—were appropriate to the new world in which their adherents had no role in government[7] but vastly greater contact with foreigners. Very similar ideas, we argue, are in ascendance today, in a context in which dramatic declines in communication and transportation costs are enabling unprecedented global interaction among people, wholly outside any formal political context over which they have meaningful influence.

Critics of globalization do not generally object to such interaction, provided it does not involve commerce. But this is like approving of marriage while objecting to childbearing. The former is certainly possible without the latter (and vice versa), but most pursue the former because of their intention to pursue the latter. Likewise, most of the people with whom we come into contact outside our small local circle of family and friends are commercial acquaintances, or at least purely so at first. When we travel, we do not generally expect to be fed and sheltered by grace of the kindness of strangers. We take it for granted that, to the extent that we have money to exchange, others whom we have never before met will more or less cheerfully provide us with what we want. Globalization, like travel outside our network of immediate friends and family, is a fundamentally commercially driven experience, and only *facilitated* by technologies like air transport and the Internet.

Few of the pro- and anti-globalizers discussed in this book are philosophers. They come from many disciplines, and only a minority are academics. But, to paraphrase Keynes, they, like us, are in considerable part intellectual slaves of defunct academic scribblers. We are all firsthand witnesses to powerful new social and technological phenomena, but we process their meaning through secondhand thought. And in the words of Istvan Hont, author of a book on the politics of trade in the eighteenth century, "The history of political thought is at its most helpful when it unmasks and eliminates repetitive patterns of controversy."[8]

To the extent that pro-globalizers acknowledge an intellectual lens, it is eighteenth-century cosmopolitan liberalism. This, however, we will argue, is itself a revival of thought two millennia older; specifically, Stoic political thought of the Hellenistic world emerging in the late fourth century BC. Stoic thought sought to situate men in some natural relation with all other men, absent any assumption of common ends. It owed at least as much to Alexander's armies as to Mediterranean thinkers, in the sense that the destruction of boundaries between Greek and barbarian necessitated a new philosophy of human coexistence.[9] The early liberalism of England and Holland was also founded on such a need, brought to the fore by the horrendous religious wars that tore Europe apart in the sixteenth century. The notion that "all men are created equal," enshrined in the American Declaration of Independence, is eminently Stoic in its individualism, cosmopolitanism, and underpinning of "natural law," or law which was held to be valid by "Right Reason" rather than by virtue of emanation from some well-armed authority. Its conspicuous popular revival in our age is driven, yet again, by the emergent need for a philosophy of coexistence, this time in an environment in which a well-cultivated twentieth-century mythology of unlimited state sovereignty confronts the daily reality of a wired world oblivious to geographic jurisdictions.

What is so striking about contemporary anti-globalist thought, whether from political philosophers like John Gray or media messiahs like Lou Dobbs, is its rank lack of originality, given that it aims to diagnose and treat ills proprietary to our age. It calls for a bold new public policy agenda that will return us to a past in which commerce and finance were fairer and less culturally disruptive. But this past never existed. Going back hundreds of years, each successive generation has produced a cadre of reactionary intellectuals who have held forth on the unprecedented economic evils of their age and called for the intervention of enlightened rulers to restore the tranquility of yesteryear. The moral foundation of their program has always been distinctly national, even if they frequently maintain that foreigners would also benefit by our refusal to buy and borrow from them, or sell and lend to them.

Anti-globalizers generally reject classical liberalism on both practical and idealistic grounds. Practically, what seems not just to anti-globalizers but even to many classical liberals as a compelling indictment of globalization is the proliferation of devastating national currency crises since the 1980s. We devote much space to confronting the argument that private capital flows, rather than governments defending "sovereignty," are to blame. Idealistically, the alternative world visions of anti-globalizers harken back to the Romantic reaction to liberalism, best represented by Rousseau and Hegel. Romantics were contemptuous of commerce and finance (even private property), suspicious of science, and ardent in their nationalism— nations having, in their view, a collective soul. Bertrand Russell characterized the political aspects of such thought as "the doctrine of State worship, which assigns to the State the position that Catholicism gave to the Church, or even, sometimes, to God."[10] Extreme twentieth-century manifestations of such thought produced the catastrophes of fascism and communism. Whereas only the reactionary fringes of today's anti-globalism express the slightest sympathy with such ideologies, they all demand new, and often very robust, assertions of state sovereignty, which they defend as mere *re*assertions of a sovereignty lost to anthropomorphicized "markets." They tend to paint liberalism as a version of radical individualism. Historically, however, this is wholly inconsistent with the belief in the fundamental harmony of public and private interests which is characteristic of liberalism. Liberalism as a doctrine is a conscious attempt to escape the cycle of political oscillation between tyranny and anarchy, the latter fostered by truly radical individualist religious ideologies of the distant past.[11]

Whereas anti-globalizers typically paint classical liberals as being utopian, or "fundamentalist," in their faith in market forces, failing to acknowledge inherent corruption and shortsightedness guiding the pursuit of wealth, they tend to see no such evils at work in the state sector. Like Plato, they see government and moneymaking as radically different, and indeed incompatible, enterprises. Not only is identification of the common good unproblematic, in their view, but its practical pursuit through government is as well. Stoic thinking differed radically. The third and most illustrious head of the school, Chrysippus, saw politics pragmatically as one mode among many of earning a living. Chrysippus was, however, neither cynical (in the modern rather than Greek sense) about public service nor materialistic. He saw humans as by nature social animals, and saw natural law—objective, derivable from human nature, and discovered rather than created—as the only moral basis for governing interaction among people.[12]

This concept of natural law, which came to form the foundation of Roman cosmopolitan jurisprudence, has been fundamental to the development of commercial culture in the Western world over two millennia. The hugely important medieval *Lex Mercatoria*, the international "laws merchant," which developed spontaneously and laid the legal foundation for Europe's commercial fairs and sea trade over eight centuries ago, lives on today as true law, governing the conduct of business both within and across national borders. The thread connecting Roman law to the modern-day globalist commercial mindset is eloquently captured by historian Jerry Muller:

> There was no room—or little room—for commerce and the pursuit of gain in the portrait of the good society conveyed by the traditions of classical Greece and of Christianity, traditions that continued to influence intellectual life through the eighteenth century and beyond. Yet when discussion turned from outlining an ideal society to regulating real men and women through law, accommodating commerce and the pursuit of gain inevitably played a larger role. Roman civil law, with its origins in the empire and its emphasis on the protection of property, served as a reservoir of more favorable attitudes toward the safeguarding and accumulation of wealth. The hot and cold wars of religion that marked the early modern period were a turning point in the relations between these traditions. For as men judged the cost of imposing a unified vision of the common good too high, they increasingly took their bearings from the Roman civil tradition, which focused upon giving each his own, without subordinating all to some vision of the common good they no longer shared.[13]

Law and commerce were indelibly linked in the thought of David Hume, who argued that it is *commerce itself* that gives rise to notions of justice between people and peoples. Although commerce is today typically seen as something which is proactively enabled by law, it is much more accurate historically to see law as something which emerges because of its vital importance in commerce — and particularly commerce involving foreigners. Within the Roman Empire, it was the *ius gentium*, the "law of nations," derived from custom rather than legislation, and applying specifically to noncitizens, that governed most types of commercial transactions.[14]

The modern notion that law is inseparable from the will of a ruler or ruling body, antithetical to the idea of a universal natural law or a ius gentium, has, in parts of the world and during epochs where it has actually been applied, been devastating to economic development. The Soviet Union was only the most conspicuous example of the economic consequences of the state arrogating legal powers from the private sphere. "With us," in contrast to the West, Lenin declared in 1921, "what pertains to the economy is a matter of public law, not private law."[15] Today, economic "sovereignty" has become the rallying cry of the anti-globalization movement. Commerce, contracting, and investment across borders are increasingly subjected to a sovereign legitimacy test which they are held to fail not because they are illegal but rather because they are "alegal" — not enabled by a state body that has determined their desirability in advance.

Of course, commerce and politics have rarely operated in isolation anywhere. International trade and national politics have been locked in a volatile and often highly destructive embrace since the Renaissance period, when European governments first began to see themselves in a struggle for survival against others for commercial success in trade. As national self-defense came to be seen as the highest calling of the state, trade, as a means of financing wars, became a component of the doctrine of "reason of state," first popularized in a 1589 book *Ragione de Stato* by Italian political theorist and statesman Giovanni Botero, who drew heavily on Machiavelli. It took on its greatest political importance in the seventeenth century, when the rise of the two maritime powers, England and Holland, drew the large continental monarchies, France in particular, into an increasingly intense rivalry for European trade supremacy. "Commerce," wrote Louis XIV's economic minister, Jean-Baptiste Colbert, in a memorandum to the king, "is a perpetual and peaceable war of wit and energy among all nations."[16] What made trade warlike was the image of states as sellers in an increasingly desperate search for markets and profits. To be sure, thinkers such as Montesquieu and Voltaire argued strenuously against the use of commerce as a tool of Machiavellian international politics, stressing that it was bound to lead to ruinous real war. Adam Smith railed against the influence of merchants over the politics of trade, stressing their baleful effects and urging that the interests of consumers instead be paramount in pursuit of "reason of state." But mercantilist politics and international commerce have never since been successfully disentangled, even as innovations in sovereignty such as the European Union have diluted the toxicity of the mix considerably.

The most potent threat to globalization is not the backlash against trade, however. Multilateral trade liberalization agreements may indeed be harder to fashion in the future, but this is largely a measure of how far trade liberalization has come in the past fifty years. The remaining hot-button issues, like intellectual property protection and removal of the last vestiges of agricultural trade barriers and distortions, were always bound to be political landmines. But even as the World Trade Organization stalls, robust global trade growth continues. Anti-globalizers have not shut down the ports, nor have governments brazenly abrogated existing multilateral commitments.

If anything is likely to throw globalization into reverse, it is not trade itself, but the money that facilitates it. National monies and global markets simply do not mix; together they make a deadly brew of currency crises and geopolitical tension and create ready pretexts for damaging protectionism. Political leaders in both poor and rich countries are fashioning new policy agendas grounded in this growing, if as yet inchoate, realization. But most of these are addressing symptoms rather than causes, and are doing so in a manner that will only add to, rather than reduce, global economic and political tensions.

As we discuss in chapter 3, virtually every major argument leveled against globalization has been made against markets generally for hundreds of (and in some cases over 2,000) years, and can be demonstrated to be misconceived. But the argument against capital flows is fundamentally different. It is highly compelling, so much so that even globalization's most eminent intellectual supporters treat it as an exception, a matter to be intellectually quarantined until effective crisis inoculations can be developed.

Since the early 1980s, dozens of developing countries—even the most successful among them, such as South Korea—have been buffeted by severe currency crises. The economic and social damage wrought by the rapid and massive selling of developing country currencies has been enormous. And the economics profession lacks anything approaching a coherent and compelling response. IMF staff have endorsed all manner of national exchange rate and monetary policy regime that has subsequently collapsed in failure. They have fingered numerous and disparate culprits, from loose fiscal policy to poor bank regulation to bad industrial policy to official and private corruption. We have for ten years now been in the midst of a roaring bull market in academic financial crisis literature.

From a historical policy perspective, our current age of globalization is highly unusual. Typically, trade protectionism and monetary nationalism have coincided, as have free trade and a universal monetary standard. Since the 1970s, however, the world has moved robustly toward liberalization of both trade and capital flows while governments have asserted a historically unprecedented sovereign right, and indeed responsibility, to control the supply and price of national money unfettered by any external standard against which people measure value across borders—whether that be a precious metal, like gold, or another currency, like the U.S. dollar. That the result has been significant growth in living standards across those countries that have integrated into the global marketplace, side by side with devastating national currency crises that have periodically wiped out much of such progress, should not be surprising. Monetary nationalism dramatically alters the way capital flows operate. During the previous great period of globalization, in the late nineteenth and early twentieth centuries, capital flows were enormous, even by contemporary standards. Yet currency crises were brief and shallow, and capital flows were a *stabilizing* factor, wholly unlike today. The difference is in the change in the nature of money. Back then, global trade and capital flows went hand in hand with global money. "When the scope of trading expands," wrote the eminent German sociologist and philosopher Georg Simmel in 1900, "the currency also has to be made acceptable and tempting to foreigners and to trading partners."[17] Today, however, trade and capital flows go hand in hand with national monies that are, with few exceptions, not in the least bit acceptable or tempting to foreigners.

Throughout most of the world and most of human history, money was gold or silver or another intrinsically valued commodity, or a claim on such a commodity. It is only during the most recent three decades that monies flowing around the globe have been claims on—well, nothing at all. All of these monies are conjured by governments as pure manifestations of sovereignty. And the vast majority of such monies are unwanted. People are unwilling to hold them as wealth, something which will buy in the future at least what it did in the present. Governments are able to oblige their citizens to hold national money by requiring its use in domestic transactions, but foreigners exempt from such compulsion choose not to do so. And as we will document at length in the second half of this book, in a world in which people choose to accept only dollars and a handful of other monies from foreigners in lieu of gold or other intrinsically valuable commodities, the mythology tying money to sovereignty is a costly and sometimes dangerous one. Monetary sovereignty is incompatible with globalization, understood as integration into the global marketplace for goods and capital. It has always been thus, but it has become blindingly apparent only over the past three decades of human history.

Our diagnosis will doubtlessly be bracing to many, but we must emphasize that economists of the 1930s and 1940s would by and large have considered it rather obvious. And this would not have been a matter of ideology. Writers with vastly different views of global capitalism, such as Friedrich Hayek and Karl Polanyi, took it as given that globalization required gold, or something accepted as money by all. The remarkably foresighted Simmel did anticipate the emergence of an international fiat money—one not tied to anything of intrinsic value—but stressed that it would be the *result* of an organic process of global economic and social integration, and not something that any authority could engineer. The marked recent rise in global angst over whether fiat dollars conjured by the U.S. government can continue playing that role highlights the need to view globalization in the context of a long history in which money and sovereignty have aligned and misaligned in ways that have deeply affected the lives of people around the world.

2

A BRIEF HISTORY OF LAW AND GLOBALISM

> The further backward you look, the further forward you can see.
> —Winston Churchill

Globalism—broadly speaking, the view that increasing economic and cultural interconnections across the globe are a positive development, to be advanced rather than resisted—has a much older and historically esteemed pedigree than is widely recognized. In the context of the contemporary debate over the legitimacy of globalization, particularly as it relates to the sovereign powers of states vis-à-vis individuals, the historical development of Western law has been very much consistent with globalist thought; in particular, the notion that individuals have certain natural universal rights that transcend the will of rulers.

The Philosophy of Globalism

> [T]here is . . . a broader need to wrench globalization from all the
> dry talk of markets penetrated, currencies depreciated, and GDPs acceler-
> ated and to place the process in its proper political context: as an exten-
> sion of the idea of liberty and as a chance to renew the fundamental rights
> of the individual. . . . The first principle [of liberalism] is that rights be-
> long to individuals rather than to governments or to social groups.
> The second is that the essence of freedom lies in individual
> choice.
> —John Micklethwait and Adrian Wooldridge[1]

As with John Micklethwait and Adrian Wooldridge, authors of *Future Perfect: The Challenge and Hidden Promise of Globalization*, Martin Wolf identifies his convictions as being those of the "classical liberal." He ends his book *Why Globalization Works* not with "dry talk" on economics, but with a defense of the Popperian liberal open society.[2] Deepak Lal, in a similar critical analysis of globalization, calls for a revival of "classical liberalism in the twenty-first century."[3] Tom Friedman begins his 2005 bestseller explaining optimistically that "what the flattening of the world means is that we are now connecting all the knowledge centers on the planet together into a single global network, which—if politics and terrorism do not get in the way—could usher in an amazing era of prosperity, innovation, and collaboration, by companies, communities, and individuals."[4] In his earlier globalization treatise, he even strays into what might be termed a classical liberal "theology" of global cyberspace: "God celebrates a universe of such human freedom, because he knows that the only way He is truly manifest in the world is not if He intervenes, but if we all choose sanctity and morality in an environment where we are free to choose anything."[5] In other words, globalization may or may not turn out well, but the only moral way to approach it is to allow individuals to seek each other out on their own terms.

Writers of the most prominent pro-globalization screeds do not simply applaud commerce. Rather, they celebrate technological and political forces advancing and deepening interaction among people across national boundaries for their consistency with, and advancement of, older ideas about human nature and society of which they approve. Generally speaking, these are the ideas of eighteenth- and nineteenth-century Scottish and English cosmopolitan liberals such as Adam Smith and John Stuart Mill.[6] We would argue, however, that the idealistic roots of globalism actually go much deeper in history, and that much of what seems new and radical about the changing relationship between states and societies actually reflects a movement *back* to the way in which concepts such as law and sovereignty were widely understood in the West from the time of the deaths of Aristotle and Alexander to at least the late nineteenth century. What is truly new in Friedman's flat world is the technological change in communications and transport encouraging a revival of the world's oldest systematic body of cosmopolitan political thought.

Stoicism and the Rise of Natural Law

CREON: Now, tell me thou—not in many words, but briefly—knewest thou that an edict had forbidden this?

ANTIGONE: I knew it: could I help it? It was public.

CREON: And thou didst indeed dare to transgress that law?

ANTIGONE: Yes; for it was not Zeus that had published me that edict; not such are the laws set among men by the justice who dwells with the gods below; nor deemed I that thy decrees were of such force, that a mortal could override the unwritten and unfailing statutes of heaven. For their life is not of today or yesterday, but from all time, and no man knows when they were first put forth.

—Sophocles, *Antigone*, 442 BC[7]

Whereas it is commonplace today to think of law as nothing more than the will of a legislator, such thought has been mightily resisted by great thinkers each time it has emerged throughout history. Such resistance is perhaps nowhere more eloquently displayed than by Sophocles' female heroine Antigone, who refuses to obey her king's edict against burying her brother, asserting that such an edict, which is contrary to morality and custom, cannot possibly be law, and therefore cannot be obeyed.

In the Western tradition, "good law"—law worthy of the name, worthy of obedience—has always been law that was eternal, in the sense that it was rooted in human nature, or a divine design for mankind. The earliest coherent formal philosophy of law so understood can be traced back to ancient Hellenistic society. Widely known as "natural law," this philosophy is embedded in the ideas that inspired the American Declaration of Independence and Constitution. It is also a philosophy that is indelibly linked with the development of commerce and trade over millennia.

Two great bodies of thought are commonly held to lie behind the development of Western civilization, one deriving from classical Greece and the other from Christianity. Phillip Cary likens their roles to the left and right legs of the human body.[8] The right, stronger leg represents the conservative moral tradition deriving from Judeo-Christian thinking. The left leg represents the ever-questioning, ever-critical older secular tradition deriving from Socrates, Plato, and Aristotle in fifth- and fourth-century-BC Athens. (We relegate the rest of the anatomy of intellectual history to a footnote.[9]) Globalization can be said to have an important foundational philosophy, but it is not to be found in either the classical Greek or Christian traditions. Commerce and the pursuit of wealth—the driving forces behind globalization, even in its cultural manifestations—have no place in the portrait of the good society represented by either. The philosophy underlying the intellectual passion in pro-globalization thought is to be traced back to the historical period between the decline of classicism, with the death of Aristotle in 322 BC, and the emergence of Christianity. This interregnum is the high era of Stoicist thought, which, while its founding fathers, in particular Zeno and Chrysippus, have lacked the cachet of Socrates or Jesus, has been critical in the development of Western legal philosophy and tradition.

The fundamental changes taking place in Greek social and political relations in the course of the late fourth and third centuries BC bear an important parallel with those taking place in global social and political relations today. The notion of man as a fundamentally political animal, a component of a self-governing city-state, the *polis*, steadily lost meaning after the death of Aristotle. Alexander the Great, who died a year before Aristotle, had ushered in a new era of much larger political units and distant rulers. Roman legions destroyed the distinction between Greek and barbarian, and broke down local and tribal loyalties. Political life could no longer be conducted on an intimate scale, and Greek thinkers struggled to redefine the understanding of man as an individual; one who was now more conscious of his isolated role in the universe, and simultaneously of his need to relate to many distant others whose values and motivations he did not know. Whereas the intimacy of the polis is today virtually unknown, it is the *relative* intimacy of the nation-state which is being challenged for our attention by foreigners with whom we trade, share, correspond, and mingle with ever greater frequency and intensity.

Stoicism emerged from the flux of the early Hellenistic Age. It elevated reason as the only way to comprehend the order of the universe; an order which no longer seemed apparent in social and political life. At the base of Stoic moral theory was the vision of the individual as a world citizen; an early Davos man. It posited the value of each person and simultaneously the importance of a common human nature, so that all were bound to respect the intrinsic worth of others. For most contemporary Westerners, such an outlook is so ingrained as perhaps to seem banal, but it was not an integral part of the ethics of Aristotle's world, where the significance of an individual derived from his specific function and status as a citizen of the polis.[10] But function and status are absent when the individual relates to the wider world, and so he must claim an *inherent* right if he wishes respect as an autonomous being from those residing outside the moral intimacy of the polis. Such a claim requires reciprocality, and therefore lends ethical meaning to the idea of universality.

As a moral philosophy, Stoicism is exceptionally well suited to a social and political space in which agreement on common ends cannot be assumed, and therefore locates ethics wholly in the *means* through which people interact rather than the ends they seek. This is where the Stoic doctrine of natural law becomes critically important, particularly in a globalizing world. Men can have their own purposes, but their fundamental moral equality, whether "Greek" or "barbarian," is manifested in all being subject to the highest possible authority, the law of nature, which is the product of universal reason and above the multiplicity of local customs. In the striking words of Stoicism's most influential thinker, Chrysippus of Stoa (280–206 BC), "Law is the ruler over all the acts both of gods and men. It must be the director, the governor and the guide in respect to what is honorable and base and hence the standard of what is just and unjust. For all beings that are social by nature the law directs what must be done and forbids what must not be done."[11] The parallels between the thinking of Chrysippus and the Dutch father of modern international law, Hugo Grotius, nearly 1,900 years later is remarkable. When U.S. politicians today invoke the notion that theirs is "a nation of laws and not of men," they are reprising thought that is distinctly Stoicist.

Stoic philosophy became part of normal life in the Hellenistic world. Arbitration developed into the accepted practice for adjudicating disputes across cities and kingdoms, which necessarily involved a comparison of customs and an appeal to a common standard of equity. The idea of natural law thus emerged as far more than a body of philosophical utopian principle; it emerged as a critical, practical means to promote harmony among civilizations, based on establishing common justice rather than common ends. Importantly, international private commercial arbitration, having all but disappeared during the age of the nation-state ideology of the nineteenth century,[12] saw a massive revival during the 1980s, *The Economist* in 1992 declaring arbitration "the Big Idea set to dominate legal-reform agendas into the next century."[13] The social and commercial forces which led to the emergence of international arbitration in the Hellenistic world are identical to those which are driving its conspicuous revival today.

It was the accomplishment of Panaetius of Rhodes (ca. 180–109 BC) to restate Stoicism as a less austere philosophy of humanitarianism, one that was attractive to the Roman aristocratic class, which coveted the learning of Greece but knew little of philosophy. Stoicism appealed to the native Roman virtues of self-control, devotion to duty, and public spiritedness, and lent some universalist idealism to the gory business of imperial conquest. Stoic legal thinking also lent itself perfectly to the task of accommodating the proliferation of foreign traders in Rome, which required a new body of law based on what private business convention regarded as fair dealing, rather than one based on local custom and ceremony. Lawyers referred to this emerging body of law as *ius gentium*: the law of nations, or that law which natural reason establishes for all men.

Consistent with the commercial imperative behind its germination in republican Rome, ius gentium has been invoked throughout the ages in the context of trade. The famous sixteenth-century Dominican theologian and international jurist Francisco de Vitoria (1480–1546), for example, justified Spanish trading rights in the Americas on the basis of the law of nations: "It is an apparent rule of the *ius gentium* that foreigners may carry on trade, provided they do no hurt to citizens. . . . Neither may the native princes hinder their subjects from carrying on trade with the Spanish; nor, on the other hand, may the princes of Spain prevent commerce with the natives."[14] The great Spanish philosopher and theologian Francisco Suarez (1548–1617) argued that "it has been established by the *ius gentium* that commercial intercourse shall be free, and it would be a violation of that system of law if such intercourse were prohibited without reasonable cause."[15] The period's greatest natural law thinker, Hugo Grotius (1583–1645), saw morality, law, and trade as indelibly intertwined. "Under the law of nations," he argued, "the following principle was established: that all men should be privileged to trade freely with one another." This "freedom of trade is based on a primitive right of nations which has a natural and permanent cause; and that right cannot be destroyed, or at all events it may not be destroyed except by the consent of all nations." Rulers could not prevent subjects from trading with subjects of other states, as the "right to engage in commerce pertains equally to all peoples." This was self-evident in that "God has not willed that nature shall supply every region with all the necessities of life; and furthermore, He has granted preeminence in different arts to different nations."[16] It is not surprising that thinkers living in sixteenth- and seventeenth-century maritime powers like Spain and the Netherlands should see free trade as a dictate of natural law, much as thinkers in cosmopolitan republican Rome saw commerce generally in this light.

Free trade is not, of course, an idea etched in the eternal fabric of the cosmos. Such historical thought is important, however, as it highlights the fact that today's trade mythology—that autarky is the natural state of affairs, and that people should not buy from foreigners except with dispensation from the state—is hardly one with a compelling pedigree.

The Romans distinguished ius gentium from *ius civile*, or the civil law peculiar to one state or people. Drawing such a distinction naturally led to the ius gentium being seen as higher law, which must through reason, the common faculty of humanity, be perceived as valid and just for all peoples. Although ius gentium had no particular philosophical meaning, it came naturally to fuse with the Stoic idea of natural law, translated into Latin as *ius naturale*, which lent the former an association with substantial justice, above and beyond mere ratification of observed practice.[17] The latter had a revolutionary impact in bringing enlightened criticism to bear on custom and ceremony, and promoting the notion of all being equal before the law.[18]

Stoicism's conception of natural law became the foundation of Roman jurisprudence, as it developed from the first century BC onward. It also came to provide a new political theory of the state which was radically different from that of the classical Greek tradition. The idea of *legalism*—the state itself being a *product* of law, circumscribed by it, and separate from questions of the content of ethical good—was fundamentally a Roman one, and one which has profoundly influenced Western political thought right up to the present. This idea, as we will discuss, is also directly challenged by the Romantic and anti-Enlightenment thought of Rousseau and Hegel, in particular, as well as contemporary anti-globalist thinkers, who aim to elevate the moral status of the nation-state and to reclaim what is seen as its lost authority to impose law on commerce.

It is first and foremost to the great Roman statesman, lawyer, scholar, and writer Cicero (106–43 BC) that we owe the transformation of Stoicism from philosophical ideal to political blueprint. Cicero is the earliest influential expositor of the notion that men should be governed by the rule of law: "For as the laws govern the magistrate, so the magistrate governs the people, and it can truly be said that the magistrate is a speaking law, and the law a silent magistrate."[19] The philosophical ideas expounded by the Stoics and Romanized by Cicero underpinned the development of Roman jurisprudence, the great compilation of which was brought to publication as the *Digest* by the Emperor Justinian in 533 AD. Whereas the *Digest's* authors were lawyers and not philosophers, their body of thought owed everything to the Stoical philosophy of law, and was unaffected by the growth of the Christian communities. (Christian influence in the development of law after Constantine is typically seen in pragmatic efforts to establish the legal position of the church and assist in advancing its policies.) Great Christian scholastic thinkers came, however, to adopt natural law thinking, and were to argue on that basis that rulers could not "make" law. The most important scholastic theologian, Thomas Aquinas (1224–1274) saw natural law as part of a hierarchy of laws, beneath the "eternal law" by which God creates living beings and imprints them with a divine purpose, but, in its linking of human reason with God's creative will, standing morally above the civil law of states, which are circumstantial and valid only insofar as they are consistent with natural law. Thus, according to Aquinas, "we can only accept the saying that *the ruler's will is law*, on the proviso that the ruler's will is ruled by reason; otherwise a ruler's will is more like lawlessness."[20]

Whereas the Napoleonic practice of codifying national law based on the Roman inheritance is today dominant in continental Europe and Latin America, Roman law itself shares with uncodified English common law a genesis wholly outside the realm of political legislation. The modern notion that law is nothing more than the expression of will of an authorized legislative body is of recent historical origin, having established itself in the popular consciousness over the course of the nineteenth century. This notion underlies much of the shock and awe visible in the anti-globalization movement today over the spread of transnational private commerce and financial contracting, which is commonly but confusingly often labeled "anti-democratic" specifically because it is not "authorized" by a competent lawmaking body. This is in spite of the fact that it is in "the practices of the ports and fairs that we must chiefly seek the steps in the evolution of law which ultimately made an open society possible."[21]

It is in a very tangible sense that law first took on great importance in allowing societies to expand because of the commercial need to accommodate outsiders. In the common law tradition, it is precisely the spread of new interactions among people that is held to form the basis of the establishment of reasonable expectations, which is then extrapolated by judges to determine what the law "must be."

It is startling to note that Chrysippus and Cicero, in their conviction that a man must be treated as an end and never a means, are much closer to Kant and Hume than to Aristotle and Plato: "Society is made for man, not man for society. . . . The individual is both logically and ethically prior," according to George Sabine, summarizing the moral basis of natural law.[22] Many contemporary anti-globalists, John Gray perhaps the most philosophically literate among them, clearly find a common law model for globalization repugnant precisely insofar as it leaves the emergent spontaneous social order, rather than a legislated general will, in the driver's seat.[23]

Though Christian writers through the late Middle Ages never denied or even doubted the existence of a fundamental natural law, intrinsically just and therefore binding on all peoples, Christian doctrine did not provide stable ground for maintaining its validity. With the violent schism that emerged in the sixteenth century between the Catholic and Protestant peoples, neither the authority of the church nor appeals to Scripture could provide any basis for law inherently binding on both. Protestants in particular came, with justification, to fear that scholastic natural law would be used to undermine the legitimacy of Protestant rulers on the basis that their laws were inconsistent with Catholic theology and metaphysics, and the rulers themselves therefore heretics.[24]

Law so grounded was, obviously, even less compelling as a basis for governing relations between Christian and non-Christian rulers. In detranscendentalizing and rejustifying natural law, and positioning it as the foundation of international law, or law regulating relations between sovereign states, its greatest Renaissance expositor, Hugo Grotius, therefore appealed back beyond Christianity to the Stoic notion of law; law which was valid because it sustained "the social order," an order which, as man has "an impelling desire for society," is an inherent and necessary good. In stark contrast, however, to modern invocations of the term *social justice* as a marker for any particular distribution of wealth adjudged beauteous by the beholder, Grotius's notion of the just social order was that order which emerged *spontaneously* from the application of essential principles of just, voluntary interaction among people: "To this sphere of law belong the abstaining from that which is another's, the restoration to another of anything of his which we may have, together with any gain which we may have received from it; the obligation to fulfil promises, the making good of a loss incurred through our fault, and the inflicting of penalties upon men according to their deserts."[25]

Although this postscholastic idea of natural law still had religious overtones, Grotius actually placed such law above and beyond God. Natural law would be valid "even if we were to suppose . . . that God does not exist or is not concerned with human affairs." And "Just as even God . . . cannot cause that two times two should not make four, so He cannot cause that which is intrinsically evil be not evil."[26] As man is intrinsically a social animal, an observation Grotius traced back to the Stoics, natural law was to be identified with the maintenance of the social order. It is a "dictate of right reason," to be discovered, as it could in no sense be invented by anyone. As God, should he exist (which Grotius passionately believed he did), cannot make true a proposition that is logically false, religious sanction can neither make edicts into natural law nor negate it.[27]

The development of natural law thinking in the seventeenth century was, as in the sixteenth century, fundamentally shaped by major contemporary political and social movements. In particular, there was a widely and deeply felt desire among philosophers to accommodate, first, moral principle; second, the political need to found an intellectual basis for justifying sovereign powers in the coalescing nation-states; and, third, the practical imperative of stopping religious wars. In the English context,

Richard Cumberland (1631–1718) attempted the accommodation by asserting that it was impossible to have metaphysical insight into God's willing of natural law, thereby undercutting the absolute authority of the priests, while asserting that human reason could only allow acquisition of "probable" knowledge of its essence, thereby undercutting claims of absolute moral authority by an Hobbesian sovereign to impose all law.[28] The moral balance between the spheres of church and state was therefore perilously fragile in this thinking, but its maintenance was nonetheless essential to limit the social dangers of either the church or the state attempting to crush dissent.

David Hume (1711–1776) argued for an understanding of the laws of nations based on utility, rather than any principles of justice that could be derived either from so-called natural theology or sentiments intrinsic to human nature. Governments come to interact with each other according to certain principles because they find it in their interest to do so. But this conception of the laws of nations shared with Grotius's conception of natural law among nations the notion that it was the contribution to the maintenance of a certain *social order* that defined the content of such laws. In Hume's thought, this content became apparent only after the rise of commerce between nations, as it was only then that principles of just conduct became useful. He noted that when nations go to war, these laws are routinely violated, as the order and therefore principles undergirding it are no longer useful, and violations therefore no longer excite any sentiment of opprobrium. The implication is clearly that it is *commerce itself* that gives rise to notions of justice between peoples, and that attempts to establish enduring principles of just interaction prior to the emergence of mutual commercial interest are wholly inconsistent with human nature as observed over millennia. To the extent, then, that we wish to inculcate enduring international law, commercial ties among people must be permitted to develop.

The first half of the twentieth century marked a dramatic turning away from Stoic ideas of universality. Enlightenment thinking had undermined natural law as a moral system, replacing that system with a utilitarian logic that rendered departures from behavior consistent with natural law mere symptoms of a change in the incentives of international actors, rather than censorable departures from Stoic "right reason." This moral vacuum in political philosophy left considerable intellectual *lebensraum* to Romantic nationalist thinkers like Hegel, a virulent critic of natural law, who shifted the unit of moral analysis from the individual to the state, and in so doing altered the basis for evaluating ethical action. The nation-state became the guiding principle of the historical development of civilization, with each nation-state having a unique telos toward which it tended according to historical "necessity." However confused was Hegel's notion of the dialectic as a logical law underlying history, the idealized state at its apex proved a potent vehicle for twentieth-century reactionary nationalism. It took two world wars for Western Europe to turn its back on this dark development.

From Natural Law to Global Commercial Law

Between contracting parties there is a closer society than the common society of mankind.
—Hugo Grotius[29]

Throughout recorded history new forms of trading have disturbed the established political order. Through all the groupings and regroupings of peoples, the shifts in power and the development of political ideas, the trader has woven and rewoven his web of international economic integration.
—J. B. Condliffe[30]

Stoicism, in the words of a classic 1937 text on political theory, "had boldly undertaken to reinterpret political ideas to fit the Great State,"[31] essentially the whole Mediterranean world. Pro-globalists today are making similar, if as of yet inchoate, attempts to refashion political ideas to fit the modern Great State. James Bennett's *The Anglosphere Challenge* is the most direct in seeing the growth of cross-border forms of organic law as being fundamental to generating international "harmony without homogenization."[32] He sees the English-speaking world as being the most natural laboratory in which such a process would develop, owing to a shared heritage of ever-evolving, nonstatute-based common law. Indeed, the tradition of English common law shares much with the natural law notion of legitimate law being "discovered" by judges rather than "created" by rulers. Historically, the most influential statement of the primacy of common law over legislation is the decision of the chief justice of England's Common Court of Pleas, Sir Edward Coke, in *Bonham's Case* of

1610: "In many cases the Common Law will control Acts of Parliament and some times adjudge them to be utterly void; for when an Act of Parliament is against common right and reason, or repugnant, or impossible to be performed, the common law will control it and adjudge such Act to be void."[33]

In the common law tradition, life comes first, and law follows in train according to the expectations established by repeated social interactions. Former French foreign minister Hubert Védrine sees common law as one of globalization's essential principles; "principles that correspond neither to the French tradition nor to French culture." Védrine sees globalization, not surprisingly, as inconsistent with a French identity "built upon a strong central state [that] was painstakingly built by jurists."[34] It is indeed difficult to reconcile a state so characterized to the spread of organic forms of law.

Even outside the realm of common law systems, commercial practice has throughout history driven the codification of systems of law, and not vice versa. "[T]he merchants who began the process of transforming European feudal society into the commercial, democratic, international trading world of our day," argued historian J. B. Condliffe, "were merchant adventurers in the crudest sense. Unless we realise this fact, we cannot understand the continuous struggles between them and the church in its efforts to apply the doctrines of Canon law."[35]

The Rise of the Lex Mercatoria

Contract law has long and largely been driven by the shared needs of international traders.[36] The hugely important *Lex Mercatoria*, or the international "laws merchant," which developed privately and spontaneously to govern commercial transactions, dates from the twelfth century, before the consolidation of states.

In Europe's prenational stage, the Lex Mercatoria consisted of a "body of truly international customary rules governing the cosmopolitan community of international merchants"[37] on the high seas and at commercial fairs.[38] Its emergence corresponded with a rapid expansion of European agricultural production, the accompanying dramatic increase in city size, and the consequent rise of a new class of professional merchants that marked the eleventh and twelfth centuries. Europe's urban population grew roughly tenfold from 1050 to 1200, while its general population per-haps doubled, and its merchant class grew from a few thousand to several hundreds of thousands. "Outsourcing" was already emergent nearly a mil-lennium before Lou Dobbs declared it treason. English merchants bought wool from local manors and, instead of processing it locally, sold it on to Flemish merchants. They in turn distributed it to Flemish spinners and weavers to be worked into cloth, which was then reimported back into England to be sold at international fairs. All aspects of the commerce, from transport to insurance to financing to sale, were governed by the transnational Lex Mercatoria.[39]

Merchant law as it evolved was based on the customs of maritime port cities and inland fairs and markets. It came to be codified in a number of different forms. The Amalfitan Table of 1095, a collection of maritime laws, was an example of merchant custom becoming written legislation. Adopted by the Republic of Amalfi on the Italian coast, its authority spread throughout all the city republics of Italy. A compilation of mar-itime judgments by the court of Oléron, an island off the French Atlantic coast, became a form of judge-made common law. It was adopted by sea-port towns of the Atlantic Ocean and North Sea, including those of En-gland, around 1150. Norms of merchant practice also evolved into written commercial instruments of standardized character, disputes over which came to be adjudicated in specialized mercantile courts, presided over by elected representatives of the merchants themselves.[40]

The importance of the Lex Mercatoria as transnational law was re-flected in the fact that by the late eleventh century, transnational trade, generally conducted at large international fairs held at regular intervals throughout Europe, or more regularly in the leading market towns and cities, predominated over local trade across much of Europe. Its universal character is stressed in much early writing on it. For example, the Chan-cellor of England wrote in 1473 that foreign merchants who brought suits before him would have them determined "by the law of nature in chancery . . . which is called by some the law merchant, which is the law universal of the world." Gerard Malynes, author of the first English book on the Lex Mercatoria, wrote in 1622: "I have entitled the book according to the ancient name of Lex Mercatoria . . . because it is customary law ap-proved by the authority of all kingdoms and commonweals, and not a law

established by the sovereignty of any prince." Its enduring nature is attested to by Lord Blackstone writing in the mid-eighteenth century: "The
affairs of commerce are regulated by the law of their own called the Law
Merchant or Lex Mercatoria, which all nations agree in and take notice of,
and it is particularly held to be part of the law of England which decides
the causes of merchants by the general rules which obtain in all commercial matters relating to domestic trade, as for instance, in the drawing, the
acceptance, and the transfer of Bills of Exchange."[41]

The Lex Mercatoria became part of national law, while maintaining its
transnational character and authority, through the patronage provided to
it by emerging national political authorities. The Magna Carta of 1215 provided that "All merchants shall have safe conduct to go and come out of
and into England, and to stay in and travel through England by land and
water for purposes of buying and selling, free of legal tolls, in accordance
with ancient and just customs." Such ideas came to be reflected in recip-
rocal rights of individual property holding and commerce provided for in
treaties, such as those which evolved among Italian cities from at least the
twelfth century on. So-called *staple towns* in fourteenth-century England,
Wales, and Ireland—where trade in wool, leather, lead, and other staple
products was conducted—were required to apply the Lex Mercatoria in
all matters relating to the staple, and granted resident foreign merchants
political rights which today would be considered incredible. Such foreigners were legally entitled to vote in elections for the local mayor, who was
required to have knowledge of the Lex Mercatoria, and comprised half the
jury in all trials involving a merchant stranger and an Englishman.[42]

The Lex Mercatoria was absorbed into English common law in the seventeenth century, where judges, who were paid out of litigation fees, initially treated it with some contempt. Competition from continental civil
law countries, however, which frequently proved more accommodative to
the Lex Mercatoria, ultimately forced English judges to recognize commercial custom in international trade in order to attract cases.[43] In the
United States, widespread early adoption of the practice of commercial arbitration, as well as the history of state jurisdictional competition, contributed to greater acceptance of the Lex Mercatoria than in England. The
U.S. Uniform Commercial Code thus reflects the fact that business practice and custom are the primary source of substantial law.[44] "The positive

law of the [American] realm," Leon Trakman notes in his history of the Lex Mercatoria, "was forced to conform to the mandate of the merchants, not vice-versa."[45]

The Modern Lex Mercatoria

The Lex Mercatoria, even in today's world of autonomous nation-states, still has vital importance as a form of commercial law. The Lex Mercatoria today is a combination of trade usages, model contracts, standard clauses, general legal principles, and international commercial arbitration, underpinned by a body of expert legal writing intended to facilitate its coherence and precision. It is arguably of considerably more consequence today than it was in medieval times, as nonsimultaneous trade was much rarer then, owing to difficulties of enforcement where international merchants interacted only infrequently.

Of the modern Lex Mercatoria's components, trade usages are the most important. Defined in the U.S. Uniform Commercial Code as "any practice or method of dealing having such regularity of observance in a place, vocation or trade as to justify an expectation that it will be observed with respect to the transaction in question,"[46] its importance lies in the fact that commercial behavior considered normal in a given industry will guide the application of both private arbitration and public common law litigation. In other words, today, as throughout Western history, the way in which people freely choose to conduct commercial transactions with each other across borders is examined by both private and public tribunals in order to *discover* what the commercial law must be.

To what extent is the Lex Mercatoria truly "law"? Legal scholars holding an "autonomist" view of the governance of international commerce maintain that the fact that traders conduct cross-border business in a consistent manner and act as if bound by behavioral precedents is evidence of an autonomous legal order in operation[47] — a "Grotian regime," in the vocabulary of International Relations scholarship. Those holding a "positivist" view agree that the modern Lex Mercatoria is effectively law, but insist that this is so *because* it has become codified in national laws.[48] They share with autonomists the conviction that international custom and standard forms of contract effectively create law unto themselves, and note that private commercial parties routinely choose the law under which their relations will be governed and utilize international commercial arbitration—through bodies such as the London Court of Arbitration, the International Chamber of Commerce in Paris, and the World Bank's International Center for the Settlement of Investment Disputes—in lieu of state courts. Furthermore, commercial trade law has become substantially harmonized across nations through conventions on international commercial arbitration, institutional rules for arbitral tribunals, and legislation recognizing awards based on the Lex Mercatoria. The French Arbitration Decree of 1981, for example, forbids French courts reviewing arbitration awards from interfering with arbitrator decisions regarding applicable rules, provided that they are consistent with the choice of the parties. The decree reflects the fact that governments today compete to have both business and arbitration conducted within their jurisdictions—just as medieval lords did, generating revenues from sales levies and entry tolls associated with merchant fairs.[49] The force of the cosmopolitan principles of the Lex Mercatoria ultimately relies, however, according to the positivists, on the willingness of states to confront noncompliance with coercive sanction.[50] But this fact is entirely consistent with the centuries-old argument of law scholars, such as Grotius, that rulers traditionally obtained their legitimacy through their commitment to *enforcing* the law—law being coeval with society itself—and only undermined it through attempts to impose law which was not already recognized as such by the populace.

People around the globe today have been conditioned to see *governments* as the creators of cross-border commerce, in agreeing with other governments to remove trade barriers which their predecessors imposed to assert sovereignty. State prohibition of trade with foreigners is widely seen as the natural state of affairs, leading to the inference that globalization of business is being deliberately created by trade liberalization policies, rather than being ratified by them. But the development of the Lex Mercatoria, as with its conspicuous revival today, was driven from below by traders—stimulated, for example, by the rapid expansion of European agricultural productivity in the eleventh and twelfth centuries—rather than from above by rulers decreeing some hitherto unknown right to trade. And just as medieval trade could not have expanded and flourished without the foundation of a cosmopolitan private commercial law—standing in for conflicting and inappropriate local public laws—so globalization of trade today would never be possible on the basis of agreements among governments simply to allow private trade or to reduce taxes on it. A legal framework for the actual conduct of trade is necessary, and that framework is a spontaneous private creation.

Many anti-globalists see the deliberate creation of new law as necessary precisely to preempt the organic development of common international commercial practice and expectations, and instead to dictate ex nihilo the form and scope of permissible facets of globalization. Political philosopher John Gray goes so far as to argue that the actual content of such law is less important than the fact that there be a regime capable of imposing it: "A regime of global governance is needed in which world markets are managed so as to promote the cohesion of societies and the integrity of states. Only a framework of global regulation—of currencies, capital movements, trade and environmental conservation—can enable the creativity of the world economy to be harnessed in the service of human needs. The specific policies that should be implemented by such institutions are less important, for the purposes of the present inquiry, than the recognition of the need for a new global regime."[51] If Gray were to be taken seriously, the coercive power that would have to be bestowed upon this new regime—regulating "currencies, capital movements, trade and environmental conservation" with the express purpose of "promot[ing] the cohesion of societies and integrity of states"[52]—would be such that it is difficult to imagine what aspects of private interaction with foreigners could any longer be considered the prerogative of individuals themselves. Gray's thinking embodies the primal constructivist belief, which he fiercely derided two decades ago, that only actions that deliberately aim at purported common purposes can serve common needs. There is perhaps no realm of global social interaction in which such thinking is so demonstrably mistaken as in that of money, to which we dedicate chapters 4–7. Historically, governments observing the political and economic importance of money have chosen in consequence to monopolize it, and in the process have wreaked far more damage on people's livelihoods than any private economic behavior condemned by Gray. As a matter of historical experience, it is also critical to understand that Gray, and not the globalists, is the radical in calling for the legal cart to be put in front of the commercial horse.

Global Private Law with Private Enforcement

In an article entitled "Private Justice in a Global Economy: From Litigation to Arbitration," Oxford political economy professor Walter Mattli traces the reemergence of private nationless law, which is a striking and almost wholly neglected aspect of globalization. "Today's scene," Mattli observes, "calls to memory the flourishing era of arbitration practices and institutions associated with the international trade fairs of medieval Europe." British Lord Justice Kerr in 1990 described the rise of international arbitration as "something of a world movement."[53] Roughly 90% of all cross-border contracts now contain a private arbitration clause.[54] Scholarly neglect of the phenomenon is largely a reflection of the myopic focus of international relations writing on what *governments* do, under the assumption that the way in which private actors manage their commercial relations cross-border must necessarily have been deliberately enabled by governments.

The number of commercial arbitration forums has grown about tenfold since the 1970s, to over one hundred today. One of the most popular of these, the International Court of Arbitration (ICA), releases basic data, though infrequently, on the volume of cases coming before it. ICA saw 580 filings in 2003, up from 450 in 1997, 333 in 1991, an annual average of 272 between 1977 and 1987, and an annual average of 55 between 1923 and 1977. The 1,584 litigants in 2003 came from 123 different countries. The organization has over 7,000 member enterprises across these countries.[55]

Just like the medieval merchant courts which sat in fairs, markets, and seaport towns, today's private tribunals provide arbitrators with specialist industry knowledge to resolve commercial disputes. In the absence of an agreement between the parties on the applicable rules of law, the arbitral tribunal determines them on the basis of the specific contract provisions and, importantly, general trade practice. In other words, the law *follows* accepted behavior in the industry, rather than *dictating* it. Tribunals often deal with highly technical matters, such as intellectual property in software, where applicable public law can be very limited, as illustrated in a seminal 1983 case involving IBM and Fujitsu. The privacy, speed, and flexibility of arbitration, relative to public courts, are major attractions for commercial enterprises, just as they were in medieval private courts: medieval sea merchants, for example, typically demanded that cases be settled "from tide to tide according to the ancient law marine and ancient customs of the sea . . . without mixing the law civil with the law marine."[56] And just like the medieval merchant courts, arbitration forums like ICA rely on reputation and commercial ostracism as enforcement tools. ICA decisions have a strong record for implementation, with only about 6% of awards being challenged by the losing party in a national court, and 0.5% ultimately being set aside by such a court.[57]

As successful as arbitration has been in the private sphere, states have proven exceptionally reluctant to use it—or where they have used it, they have typically asserted absolute immunity when it comes to enforcement. Hostility to arbitration is sustained by the doctrine of inviolable state sovereignty.

Global Private Law with Public Enforcement

Public common law courts are also used to adjudicate and enforce private law, particularly where the question is well defined, the law is clear, and the benefits of clarity outweigh those of flexibility. This is typically the case in the international financial markets, where the subject of dispute is typically whether one party has defaulted on an obligation.

There is no better example of James Bennett's international common law in operation than the global market in financial instruments. As far back as 1842, U.S. Supreme Court Associate Justice Joseph Story wrote that "the law respecting negotiable instruments may be truly declared in the language of Cicero, adopted by Lord Mansfield . . . to be in great measure, not the law of a single country only, but of the commercial world."[58] Today, it is the over-the-counter (OTC) derivatives market that is the embodiment of global private law.

The OTC derivatives market is an interbank market for two types of financial contract in particular, known as *swaps and options*—promises to trade one set of future financial flows for another, in a given currency or across currencies. At the end of 2007, the notional value of interest rate swaps, cross-currency swaps, interest rate options, credit default swaps, and equity derivatives outstanding was $454 trillion, or 26 times what it was in 1995 and 525 times what it was in 1987.[59] OTC derivatives account for 83% of aggregate derivatives trading, the remainder being traded on organized exchanges.

Whereas $454 trillion is a staggeringly large number, it is important not to overstate its economic significance. Notional values vastly exceed the actual risk exposure that market participants take. For example, a swap of a variable interest rate for a 5% fixed rate on a $10 million notional amount commits the parties to annual payments to each other of about $500,000, with differences in future payments depending on how interest rates move in the future. Consequently, the typical derivative involves a credit exposure equal to only a small fraction of its notional value.[60] Nonetheless, booming portions of this market, in particular credit default swaps, have seen a dramatic increase in counterparty risk, which will inevitably oblige major participants to collaborate in the establishment of centralized trade netting and clearing facilities, of the type found on organized exchanges.

What is remarkable about the size of this market and its growth is the fact that it has no territory; it is not a U.S. market or a U.K. market, or even an "offshore" market. Its legal foundation is a privately produced document of about thirty-two pages—unimaginably brief by the standards of U.S. statutory regulation—laying out the common rules for each derivatives transaction, and specifying that any dispute resulting from the transaction will be adjudicated by a common law English or New York state court, as per the specified preference of the parties. This ISDA Master Agreement can be downloaded for free from the website of the International Swaps and Derivatives Association,[61] a global industry body founded in 1985, with about 840 member institutions located in fifty-six countries.

The fact that people from around the globe, the vast majority of whom have never met, would agree routinely to exchange millions of dollars in financial assets based on thirty-two downloadable pages of Anglo-American market and legal jargon, unauthorized by any sovereign body, and to subject any disputes arising there from to a U.K. or New York court is nothing short of an astounding sociological phenomenon. Just how astounding was brought to life in the mid-1990s, after passage of the French language law colloquially called "*la loi Toubon*," after the name of the French culture minister. The law (subsequently partially struck down by the French constitutional court) caused a brief panic in the French financial markets in appearing to undermine the legal validity of English-language contracts such as the ISDA Master Agreement. Whereas one might suppose that French bankers would prefer French-language contracts, at least among themselves, this is not the case where a common understanding of the legal meaning of French contract provisions is absent. An ISDA contract is understood, in the deepest sense, by virtue of a global pattern of behavior having established itself around the contract's repeated bilateral exchange, and has been reinforced by decisions of common law U.K. and New York courts.[62]

This phenomenon of global private law developing around financial contracts has been virtually ignored by legal scholars,[63] which is testimony to the degree to which the profession has been trained to think of law as being the exclusive handiwork of governments. The effect of this mindset is that there is little general knowledge of the degree to which growing international exchange is producing enduring patterns of common behavior and expectation, which are in turn forming the basis for new law.

What is striking about the financial markets in an age of instant global communication is that they could only have been created and sustained internationally on such a scale to the degree that all the primary elements of Grotius's natural law among peoples had come to be widely accepted among the myriad dispersed participants, irrespective of their cultural upbringings: the sanctity of private property, contracting in good faith, accepting responsibility for harm to another, and sanction in accordance with harm done. The banker in London and Dubai may have vastly different understandings of the "Good Life" and the origins and purpose of existence, but they must nonetheless adopt a common commitment to fair dealing in order to participate in the same global commercial network. Those that do not are invariably obliged to depart, as no one will deal with them.

Past and Future Linked

> The view that law transcends politics — the view that at any given moment, or at least in its historical development, law is distinct from the state — seems to have yielded increasingly to the view that law is at all times basically an instrument of the state, that is, a means of effectuating the will of those who exercise political authority.
> —Harold Berman[64]

The technology of modern globalization is clearly new and consequential, socially as well as economically. Computerization and the Internet in particular have vastly lowered communications and production costs, enabling the creation of new global markets and supply chains, and changing the way each of us lives his or her life in consequence. Innovations in telegraph and shipping technology in the late nineteenth century were comparably important in expanding global commerce and changing lifestyles.

Dubious, however, is the popular notion that modern globalization is new in its challenging of timeless tenets of state sovereignty and authority. The constructivist mythology that law worthy of the name must be, and must have been, consciously *designed* to achieve specific ends, which emerged in the seventeenth and eighteenth centuries, has in our time come to dominate popular thinking, and has been bluntly confronted by the spontaneous, "unauthorized" emergence of economic and social orders across national legal jurisdictions. Scholars and the public intelligentsia who reflect on the palpable manifestations of globalization are typically struck by its emergence in an institutional vacuum—national law appears impotent, and supranational law is yet to emerge. Therefore, the implication is frequently drawn that there is something fundamentally illegitimate about globalization.

Yet the history of law in the Western world, going back to ancient Greece, shows clearly that it is not possible to separate the activity of private exchange from the evolution of law, and the evolution of thought about law. It is property that first gives rise to established notions of justice among people. Trade is much older than states; indeed, it is older than agriculture itself.[65] Principles of just interaction emerge only after sentiments of mutual commercial interest take hold—and it is specifically in dealings with foreigners that it was necessary for law to develop which was independent of any ruler's will. Good law was always old law, and old law is what emerged by dint of its consistency with what people came to expect as just behavior from others. Legitimacy is the cornerstone of stable government, and rulers established legitimacy by demonstrating appropriate reverence for the law and the ability to enforce it.

The glue that melded the Greek and barbarian peoples under the Macedonians and Romans was commerce. The creation of the Hellenistic world, the earliest "globalization," was founded on an historically remarkable degree of economic freedom, underpinned by the development of a Roman civil law which was almost entirely the product of law-finding by jurists, rather than legislation.

The fact that belief in a "natural law" rooted in the intrinsic social nature of human existence, true irrespective of even the wishes of God or gods, persisted from Chrysippus to Grotius with few credible intellectual challenges, is testimony to a powerfully enduring conviction that a healthy society cannot be governed by the unfettered will of legislators. But what relevance can that have to our day and age, when practical people know full well that legislators can and will use their powers to control international commerce as they wish? The answer lies in Hume's observation that it is *commerce itself* that gives rise to symmetrical sentiments among people of different nations that there are identifiable principles of just conduct between them. Legislation does not give rise to such sentiments. New rules may or may not be enforceable, but they do not change what people view as being just or unjust behavior between them.

Sovereign legislatures are, of course, generally empowered to ban virtually any and all forms of exchange with foreigners. Irrespective of current passions against "outsourcing" to foreigners or receiving capital flows from them, however, an art director in New York will never see it as just for her government to stop her contracting a website designer in Buenos Aires, nor will the designer see it as just for his government to restrict his access to foreign money. As Hume believed of all international law, any sustainable bonds of cooperative human behavior will ultimately be fashioned on shared feelings of economic interest. Globalization is simply what we choose to call the ongoing spontaneous creation of such bonds of shared interest across borders.

3

THE ANTI-PHILOSOPHY OF ANTI-GLOBALISM

> It may be remarked that Santayana's maxim "those who do not remember the past are condemned to repeat it" is more likely to hold rigorously for the history of *ideas* than for the history of events. The latter, as we all know, never quite repeats itself; but *vaguely similar* circumstances at two different and perhaps distant points of time may very well give rise to *identical and identically flawed* thought-responses if the earlier intellectual episode has been forgotten.
> —Albert O. Hirschman, *The Passions and the Interests*

What unites the pro-globalization literature is the way in which its authors appeal explicitly to an established philosophy of liberal cosmopolitanism. As we illustrated in chapter 2, the roots of such thought are actually two millennia older than their tracts recognize, originating in the Hellenistic world of the late fourth and third centuries BC. The body of Stoicist political philosophy has deeply infused the development of Western law, two branches of which, Anglo-Saxon common law and the Lex Mercatoria, have organically reincarnated themselves as foundations for modern international commerce and finance.

Anti-globalization writers, in contrast to their pro-globalization counterparts, do not tether their arguments to the history of ideas. They do not defend a philosophy; they endorse no particular principles of just conduct or lawmaking. Rather, their arguments are largely based on defending visions of a sublime past, now being supplanted by what are alleged to be new and illegitimate forces.

In *The Politics of Cultural Despair*, historian Fritz Stern analyzes three prominent anti-globalizers who "thought of themselves as prophets, not as heirs. They were proud of their originality, proud of their intuitive sense of the crisis of their times. In fact, however, they had been much more influenced by past traditions than they realized, and without knowing it they served as cultural middlemen, transmitting old ideas in new combinations to later generations. They acknowledged no intellectual masters and rarely mentioned earlier thinkers at all."[1]

Yet Stern was not writing about today. He was writing about three important German reactionary intellectuals—Paul de Lagarde, Julius Langbehn, and Moeller van den Bruck—whose lives spanned from the mid-nineteenth century to the rise of Hitler. What is remarkable is that he was also describing with great accuracy the intellectual character of today's most prominent anti-globalizers, from the high brow of John Gray to the low brow of Ralph Nader.

Consider John Gray. Gray tells us that today's international marketplace is historically unique in its destabilizing social effects: "The corrosion of bourgeois life through increased job insecurity is at the heart of disordered capitalism. Today the social organization of work is in a nearly continuous flux. It mutates incessantly under the impact of technological innovation and deregulated market competition."[2] But has Gray truly identified a new "disordered" capitalism? Consider what Karl Marx told us about his own epoch:

> The bourgeoisie cannot exist without constantly revolutionising the instruments of production, and thereby the relations of production, and with them the whole relations of society. Conservation of the old modes of production in unaltered form, was, on the contrary, the first condition of existence for all earlier industrial classes. Constant revolutionising of production, uninterrupted disturbance of all social conditions, everlasting uncertainty and agitation distinguish the bourgeois epoch from all earlier ones. All fixed, fast-frozen relations, with their train of ancient and venerable prejudices and opinions, are swept away, all new-formed ones become antiquated before they can ossify. All that is solid melts into air.[3]

The only difference between Gray and Marx on disordered capitalism is that "bourgeois life" is victim rather than perpetrator in Gray's account. Yet Gray assures us that "capitalism today is very different from the earlier phases of economic development on which Karl Marx and Max Weber modeled their accounts of capitalism."[4] We can thus presumably take comfort that when the "global free market" is shortly "swallowed into the memory hole of history,"[5] as Gray ordains, the revolution will turn out much better this time.

Ralph Nader, for his part, tells us that today's international marketplace is historically unique in its destabilizing political effects: "Best described as corporate globalization, the new economic model establishes supranational limitations on any nation's legal and practical ability to subordinate commercial activity to the nation's goals."[6] And Karl Marx told us the same about his epoch: "The establishment of Modern Industry and of the world market, conquered for itself, in the modern representative State, exclusive political sway. The executive of the modern state is but a committee for managing the common affairs of the whole bourgeoisie."[7]

Truly rare, however, is the anti-globalization writer who pays intellectual homage to Marx. On the contrary, Gray is fond of mocking Marx in the company of Jefferson, Mill, Voltaire, Smith, and Bentham as just another Enlightenment thinker naively wedded to the notion of a single, world civilization based on Western institutions and values. Gray characterizes "global capitalism" as yet another dangerous utopia, like Communism. He lauds states for their socially protective function, "achiev[ing] modernity by renewing their own cultural traditions."[8] In terms of past thought, Gray praises only the Romantic Counter-Enlightenment critique of "cultural imperialism"—"a criticism of Enlightenment universalism that is no less salient today."[9] Again, the parallels with Stern's account of pre–World War II German anti-liberal thinkers is notable. "[Rousseau's] followers," Stern wrote, "particularly in Germany, linked his criticism to an attack on what they called the naïve rationalism and the mechanistic thought of the Enlightenment."[10] Gray's anti-Marx anticapitalism is also wholly consistent with Bertrand Russell's account of why Romantic thinking on economics differs fundamentally from socialist thinking, a distinction central to understanding the broad spectrum of contemporary anti-globalization thought. "[T]he romantic outlook, partly because it is aristocratic, and partly because it prefers passion to calculation, has a vehement contempt for commerce and finance," wrote Russell. "It is thus led to proclaim an opposition to capitalism which is quite different from that of the socialist who represents the interests of the proletariat, since it is an opposition based on dislike of the economic preoccupations. . . ."[11] It is precisely this visceral antagonism to commerce generally which accounts for the absence of Marx in contemporary anti-globalization writing, in spite of the anti-capitalist animus they so clearly share.

In what follows, we take a critical look at the major anti-globalist claims against globalization: that it violates fundamental tenets of sovereignty, that it undermines culture, that it distributes wealth unfairly, that it destroys nations, and that its alleged benefits are theoretical rather than real. These claims, we will show, are actually time-honored negative notions about *markets generally*. The practical importance of this observation lies in the fact that the status quo which anti-market tracts defend against market forces is a rolling one, and the anti-market policies trumpeted to great acclaim at one point in time tend almost invariably to be widely seen as naïve or fundamentally misguided a decade or two hence. Few, for example, wish any longer to defend through economic policy the 1940s status quo in which nearly a fifth of the U.S. population was employed in agriculture, and virtually no one will defend the eighteenth-century Austro-Hungarian status quo in which the entire peasant class were feudal serfs, having no right of movement, freedom of marriage, or choice of profession. Yet both in their time had prominent, passionate intellectual defenders who, had they been successful in keeping men tied to farms would have ended up universally pilloried supporters of reactionary economic and cultural stagnancy in their countries. Twentieth-century Communism is only an extreme case of the societal dysfunction that results from governments setting out to halt commerce-driven social change and to impose ruler-friendly change in its stead. Thus, if the major claims against contemporary globalization are not actually to do with globalization, but rather with markets as they have existed for centuries, there are obvious risks in implementing anti-globalization political agendas which merely repackage the anti-market policy programs of the past.

"Globalization Violates Sovereignty"

The idea of lost sovereignty emerges time and again in the globalization literature. From the perspective of globalization's critics, the sovereignty of national governments is generally represented as a natural and beneficent ordering of human affairs—political, economic, and cultural—that is threatened by foreign forces. As characterized by former World Bank chief economist and Nobel Prize winner Joseph Stiglitz,

> Globalization has entailed a loss of national sovereignty. International organizations, imposing international agreements, have seized power. So have international capital markets, as they have been deregulated.[12]

> Countries are effectively told that if they don't follow certain conditions, the capital markets or the IMF will refuse to lend them money. They are basically forced to give up part of their sovereignty, to let capricious capital markets, including the speculators whose only concerns are short-term rather than long-term growth of the country and the improvement of living standards, "discipline" them, telling them what they should and should not do.[13]

> And there are a variety of indirect ways in which globalization has impaired the effectiveness of the nation state, including the erosion of national cultures.[14]

In Stiglitz's portrait, the foreign forces threatening sovereignty can be either consciously designed institutions ("international organizations") or similarly malevolent anthropomorphically imbued social constructs ("international capital markets" or alien "cultures"). If a national government cannot persuade "the capital markets" or the International Monetary Fund to lend it money on terms it finds convivial, the country has lost sovereignty. If citizens change their tastes and behaviors to mimic those of foreigners, the "effectiveness of the nation state" itself has been impaired.

But what then is sovereignty, and what are its natural limits? Stiglitz offers no help, but globalization critics writing within the discipline of international relations typically appeal to the so-called Westphalian model of sovereignty. Named after the famous Peace of Westphalia, which ended the Thirty Years War in 1648, it is held to mark the emergence of an international system based on states which are sovereign in the sense that their governments maintain exclusive authority within their respective territories. They are autonomous arbiters of legitimate domestic behavior. Jan Aart Scholte, like many of those adopting the Westphalian perspective on sovereignty, asserts that under globalization "the state survives, but it has lost its previous claims to supreme, comprehensive, absolute and exclusive rule."[15] Such "claims" may be understood as manifesting a sort of strong-form conception of sovereignty. It contrasts, for example, with the understanding of international legal scholars, who focus on the right of certain governing actors to enter into international agreements—agreements which frequently reduce their autonomy, and are thus inconsistent with Westphalianism.

Sovereignty in the Westphalian sense is indeed violated frequently in the modern world. The emergence of the European Union (EU) represents a particularly flagrant violation of Westphalian national sovereignty, as it has involved the development of powerful authority structures operating outside national territorial boundaries. The fact that member state governments can be said to accede to this arrangement willingly does not make it less of a violation, as Westphalian sovereigns have no right to compromise their own autonomy. The EU's mutual recognition regimes, which allow firms in certain sectors to operate cross-border under their home-state law, are a particularly conspicuous example, as entities operating within one state can be governed by the laws of another state.[16]

Stiglitz has never, to our knowledge, expressed opposition to the internal operations of the EU, but the Bretton Woods international economic organizations are another matter. The World Trade Organization (WTO), the World Bank, and, in particular, the International Monetary Fund (IMF) have, in his view, illegitimately "seized power."[17]

There can be no doubt that conditionality in IMF lending, for example, which has been part of the IMF's Articles of Agreement since 1969, alters national institutional structures and compromises autonomy in borrowing countries, in violation of Westphalian sovereignty. Conditions attached to IMF lending have covered items such as government spending, aggregate credit expansion, subsidies for state-owned enterprises, government employment, levels of taxation and consumption subsidies, exchange rate regimes, and trade policies.[18] They have explicitly altered the power of targeted actors and institutions in recipient countries in ways which significantly limit government autonomy. Other international financial institutions such as the World Bank and the European Bank for Reconstruction and Development have also acted to restrict the autonomy of client governments. Dispute settlement within the WTO has conspicuously reduced the autonomy of member governments in areas as diverse as fiscal policy and environmental policy. Ralph Nader and Lori Wallach's self-justifying condemnation of the WTO is that in joining it "the [Clinton] administration voluntarily sacrificed U.S. sovereignty."[19]

The important question is not, however, whether participation in the international institutions associated with globalization involves violations of the Westphalian conception of sovereignty. It clearly does. The important question is whether this tells us anything useful about the relationship between globalization and sovereignty.

It does not. This is because the Westphalian model has been subject to so many egregious violations over the past 358 years—including in the areas of money and sovereign lending in the century prior to the creation of the Bretton Woods institutions—that it simply bears no relation to historical fact. The Peace of Westphalia, actually comprising two separate treaties of Munster and Osanbruck, *itself* violated the "Westphalian model." The Westphalian peace patently contradicted the right of governments to do as they please within their territories, instead imposing obligations on rulers regarding religious toleration which were seen by the Habsburg monarch, who deplored Protestantism, as wholly undesirable but merely preferable to further war.[20] In the twentieth century, provisions regarding minority and universal human rights in international agreements from Versailles (1919) to Helsinki (1975) followed the Westphalian Peace template in violating the "Westphalian model" of sovereignty.

But what about the international economy? Surely globalization has forced states to accept far more sovereign intrusion into their economic policies and institutions than at any time in the past?

Not at all. Sovereign borrowing is an ancient practice. The compromises on autonomy which sovereign borrowers today reach with the IMF were in the past reached directly with foreign governments. And in the nineteenth century, these compromises cut far more deeply into national autonomy. Throughout the Balkans and Latin America, sovereign borrowers subjected themselves to considerable foreign control, at times enduring what were considered to be egregious blows to independence. Following its recognition as a state in 1832, Greece spent the rest of the century under varying degrees of foreign creditor control. On the heels of default on its 1832 obligations, the entire finances of the country were placed under French administration. In order to return to the international markets after 1878, the country had to precommit specific revenues from customs and state monopolies to debt repayment. An 1887 loan gave its creditors the power to create a company that would supervise the revenues committed to repayment. After a disastrous war with Turkey over Crete in 1897, Greece was obliged to accept a Control Commission comprised entirely of representatives of the major powers which had absolute power over the sources of revenue necessary to fund its war debt. Protests were raised in the Greek parliament that the commission effectively suspended the country's independence. Greece's experience was mirrored in Bulgaria, Serbia, the Ottoman Empire, Argentina,[21] and Egypt.[22]

In short, Stiglitz's notion that globalization has meant the loss of national sovereignty at the hands of foreign creditors—international organizations and international capital markets—is simply unfounded. Sovereign borrowing is not a phenomenon of contemporary globalization. Countries have always borrowed, and when offered the choice between paying high interest rates to compensate for default risk (which was typical during the Renaissance) or paying lower interest rates in return for sacrificing some autonomy over default (which was typical in the nineteenth century) they have typically chosen the latter, in violation of Westphalianism. As for the notion that the IMF today possesses some extraordinary power over borrowing countries' exchange rate policies, this too is historically indefensible. Adherence to the nineteenth-century gold standard, with the Bank of England at the helm of the system, severely restricted national monetary autonomy, yet governments voluntarily subjected themselves to it precisely because it meant cheaper capital and greater trade opportunities.

What about "culture," which, though it be in the possession of no one or nobody, is still a yardstick for Stiglitz of "the effectiveness of the

nation-state"? Sovereignty does not mean and has never meant, even under the Westphalian model, state omnipotence. Grotius, widely considered to be the father of international law, grounded his famous argument
for freedom of the high seas not on any religious or metaphysical principle, but on the simple observation that legal claims which were effectively unenforceable could not be sovereign claims. An "erosion of
national cultures,"[23] which Stiglitz condemns and ascribes to loss of sovereignty, similarly has nothing to do with sovereignty, as *culture*—"the
civilization, customs, artistic achievements, etc., of a people"[24]—is not a
viable object of law. Culture derives from a social order which Grotius
defined as "the source of law properly so called,"[25] and logically such law
cannot define culture. Nor should it try. As Jeremy Rabkin, an ardent
supporter of national sovereignty, has argued,

> The very idea of a state implies a distinction between its govern-
> ing authority and the private lives of citizens, in what came to be
> seen as "society" in contrast to the state. Enlightenment thinkers
> who championed the doctrine of sovereignty took it for granted
> that a sovereign state could not, and should not, want to control
> all aspects of society. By the 19th century, when sovereignty was at
> the height of its prestige as a political doctrine, most European
> governments interfered far less in social life than they had in the
> past—or would seek to do in the twentieth century. . . . Borders
> were more open to immigration and cultural exchange than they
> have been since then. Few people seriously imagined that govern-
> ments were therefore lacking in sovereignty.[26]

In short, Stiglitz's notion that national sovereignty requires that governments have the power to stop cultural change is wholly contrary to any
traditional understanding of legitimate sovereignty.

"Globalization Undermines Culture"

The economical benefits of commerce are surpassed in importance by those of
its effects which are intellectual and moral. It is hardly possible to overrate the
value, for the improvement of human beings, of things which bring them into
contact with persons dissimilar to themselves, and with modes of thought and
action unlike those with which they are familiar . . . it is indispensable to be

perpetually comparing [one's] own notions and customs with the experience
and example of persons in different circumstances . . .
—John Stuart Mill, 1848[27]

When steam power will be perfected, when, together with telegraphy and
railways, it will have made distances disappear, it will not only be commodities which travel, but also ideas which will have wings. When fiscal and
commercial barriers will have been abolished between different states, as
they have already been between the provinces of the same state; when different countries, in daily relations, tend toward the unity of peoples, how
will you be able to revive the old mode of separation?
—François-René de Chateaubriand, 1841[28]

That Stiglitz misunderstands or misuses the concept of sovereignty does
not mean that he has necessarily failed to identify an effect of globalization
that is intrinsically negative. Great European thinkers going back to ancient
Greece have decried cultural change, and in prose considerably more re-
flective than Stiglitz's "if McDonald's triumphs, so be it."[29] (McDonald's
is a ludicrous red herring, as local authorities around the globe routinely,
and wholly legally, bar their franchises.) The critical question is whether
the contemporary cultural critique of globalization has anything to say
about the effects of international markets that were not said with equal or
greater force in the distant past.

Enlightenment thinkers such as Voltaire (1694–1778) and Adam Smith
(1723–1790) celebrated the cosmopolitan vision of the market as a social institution promoting peace and mutually enriching exchange among people who otherwise led very different ways of life. Enlightenment thinking
above all else emphasized the centrality of individual autonomy and opportunity, as well as their consistency with the common good. This vision,
of course, has its equally passionate adherents today. Likewise, many of
the most prominent eighteenth-century civil servants and scholars, particularly in German-speaking Europe, were every bit as ardent as their contemporary counterparts in their desire to standardize and rationalize laws
and regulations as widely as possible in order to overcome the stultifying
effects of custom and historical local law and to encourage the organic
growth of markets.

Johann Heinrich Gottlob von Justi (1717–1771), one of the most prominent eighteenth-century German *cameralists*—scholars and bureaucrats
devoted to enhancing national wealth and the revenue of the state—

celebrated the traditionally despised roles of merchant, peddler, and financier for their contributions to harmonizing the creations of society's productive groups. Sounding every bit the modern libertarian policy analyst, he wrote that "if we wish to regulate the nature of economic movement correctly, then we must imagine how it would be if it perfectly followed its natural processes and found not the slightest hindrance from the state."[30] Such thinking was far from just commercial or utilitarian, but moral. For Voltaire, local institutions needed to be reformed and laws unified in the light of universal reason.

Stiglitz champions the role of national governments in correcting international market failures. Liberal Enlightenment thinkers championed the role of markets in correcting government failures. Montesquieu celebrated the way in which medieval Jews not only overcame violence and extortion at the hands of nobles and kings, but helped liberate the wider populace from their malevolent control through their contribution to the development of bills of exchange[31] and obliterating the shackles on commerce imposed by prohibitions on interest:

> . . . and through this means commerce could elude violence, and maintain itself everywhere; for the richest trader had only invisible wealth which could be sent everywhere without leaving any trace. . . . In this manner we owe . . . to the avarice of rulers the establishment of a contrivance which somehow lifts commerce right out of their grip. Since that time, the rulers have been compelled to govern with greater wisdom than they themselves might have intended; for, owing to these events, the great and sudden arbitrary actions of the sovereign have been proven to be ineffective and . . . experience itself has made known that only good government brings prosperity.[32]

But as globalization has its discontents, celebrated in Stiglitz's post–World Bank confessional,[33] the Enlightenment most surely had its own. Perhaps none of these encapsulated the rejection of Enlightenment and cameralist cultural values as robustly as Justus Möser (1720–1794). A central political and intellectual figure in the 125,000-inhabitant west German town of Osnabrück, Möser condemned the growing German commercial culture and foreign trade that were undermining the traditional guild-based modes of production and the rigid and hierarchical social and political structures in which they were embedded. He despised itinerant peddlers, eighteenth-century agents of globalization, for spreading foreign ideas, creating new wants, and undermining "the good morals"[34] of rural peoples. Möser scoffed at the notion that law could be derived from simple principles, and eloquently argued that capitulating to demands for universal law would "depart from the true plan of nature, which reveals its wealth through its multiplicity, and would clear the path to despotism, which seeks to coerce all according to a few rules and so loses the richness that comes from variety."[35]

A century after Möser wrote, conservative writers in imperial Germany continued to express the same fears, only writ larger—the fears "that the German soul would be destroyed by 'Americanization' [*"Amerikanisierung*," in late nineteenth-century German writing], that is by mammonism, materialism, mechanization and the mass society."[36] And today, two centuries after Möser wrote, Naomi Klein, in a remarkable exhibition of *plus ça change, plus c'est la meme chose*, declares that "market-driven globalization doesn't want diversity; quite the opposite. Its enemies are national habits, local brands and distinctive regional tastes. Fewer interests control ever more of the landscape."[37] Similarly, William Greider decries "commerce . . . disturbing ancient cultures with startling elements of modernity."[38]

Justus Möser passionately defended the illiberal and inegalitarian values of his native Osnabrück—serfdom; discrimination against illegitimate offspring; protection of artisans against importing shopkeepers and peddlers; an indelible bond between ownership of land, which could not be sold, and political power—applying the touchstones of Enlightenment thinking, happiness and utility, to argue against Enlightenment values. As Stiglitz's hero-discontents rail against local culinary tastes being sullied by McDonald's, Möser similarly condemned the supplanting of indigenous tastes by international ones. The market, for Möser, created wants that disrupted custom and expectations, and thereby undermined respect for the traditional social order. It was the very duty of those such as himself, who wielded political power in the public interest, to protect the people against the terrible temptation to acquire what they clearly did not need.

Whereas Möser's social and political values will be an affront to most modern readers, it is important to recognize that the values being defended against globalization today by developing country rulers are rarely those which Western supporters of such "sovereign" rights would ever wish to live under. We, and we include Professor Stiglitz in "we," take it for granted that the market should and will bring us foods, gadgets, fashion, music, art, literature, and lingo from foreign shores. Lowbrow and high. Yet defenders of sovereignty in developing countries are all too frequently seeking to keep these out specifically to sustain politically congenial barriers to social change, abetted by widespread local ignorance of alternative ways of life. Their agendas are backed by Western supporters of cultural "diversity" who, paradoxically, oppose the increase in diversity *within* countries that naturally arises from the growth of trade with foreigners. Tyler Cowen trenchantly chastises the desire of rich Westerners for poorer societies to serve as "diversity slaves," allowing the former, as "collectors and museum-goers," to enjoy more of the latter's cultural products by denying them diversity of choice.[39]

Stiglitz's claim that in the cultural realm "contrary to Adam Smith's claims, especially in this arena, individual choices may not lead to socially desirable outcomes,"[40] proffered in his case against globalization advocates, is an open invitation to authoritarianism. It is, not surprisingly, heartily endorsed by Chinese state censors. As one such official explained to Reuters after banning a popular weekly journal, the intervention was necessitated by an article that had "severely hurt the national feelings of the Chinese people, creating malicious social consequences."[41]

"When politicians complain that globalization is changing society, they are correct," note Micklethwait and Wooldridge, "but they seldom bother to ask whose society it is."[42] Stiglitz certainly does not. Whereas he would presumably condemn Chinese-style censorship, he can do so on no firmer basis than personal predilection, as his principle that the cultural needs of the national collective trump individual freedom is no less subject to authoritarian abuse than was the far more emotionally compelling Romantic nationalist thought of the eighteenth and early nineteenth centuries. In Rousseau's stirring words from *The Social Contract*, "In order then that the social compact may not be an empty formula, it tacitly includes the undertaking . . . that whoever refuses to obey the general will shall be compelled to do so by the whole body. This means nothing less than that he will be forced to be free. . . . This alone legitimizes civil undertakings, which, without it, would be absurd, tyrannical, and liable to the most frightful abuses."[43] Coercion is thus not truly coercion, in Rousseau's thinking, because one who desires other than what the social order allows him is at best capricious and at worst a cultural subversive. The contrast between Rousseau's conception of the social order and that of Smith, Stiglitz's target, could not be more stark. For Smith, the notion of men being "forced to be free," to conform to a "general will," is a logical and moral monstrosity. Rather than bringing order to society, Rousseau's social compact guarantees disorder. In Smith's words,

> The man of system . . . is apt to be very wise in his own conceit, and is often so enamoured with the supposed beauty of his own ideal plan of government, that he cannot suffer the smallest deviation from any part of it. He goes on to establish it completely and in all its parts, without any regard either to the great interests or the strong prejudices which may oppose it: he seems to imagine that he can arrange the different members of a great society with as much ease as the hand arranges the different pieces upon a chessboard; he does not consider that the pieces upon the chess-board have no other principle of motion besides that which the hand impresses upon them; but that, in the great chess-board of human society, every single piece has a principle of motion of its own, altogether different from that which the legislature might choose to impress upon it. If those two principles coincide and act in the same direction, the game of human society will go on easily and harmoniously, and is very likely to be happy and successful. If they are opposite or different, the game will go on miserably, and the society must be at all times in the highest degree of disorder.[44]

The practical distinction between Enlightenment and Romantic social thought is of utmost political consequence. The logical ends of Romantic thinking were graphically illustrated in the Nazi embrace of Hegel in the 1930s, wherein the state arrogated full powers to impose the social order upon the basis of a new ethics, one deliberately divorced from that which members of society applied to themselves.

It is only the banality of Stiglitz's apology for restricting individual choice on the basis of cultural externalities that masks its decidedly anti-Enlightenment heritage. However unconsciously, it shares with the Romantic tradition the principle that underpinned the emergence of twentieth-century reactionary nationalism and the ruthless persecution of those labeled cultural outsiders.

It is critical to note that much economic, social, and political liberalization in the developing world today is driven explicitly by a concern among the elites in those countries that they will become marginalized by faster-growing, high-trading nations. The backlash which then frequently emerges from those in the population that lose traditional protections against competition, domestic as well as foreign, is blamed on globalization and a loss of sovereignty. The IMF, World Bank, and WTO become particularly convenient targets in such cases. Yet reform is a sovereign choice, and the fact that it may be motivated by what foreigners think or do does not make it less so.

This phenomenon of dramatic liberalization being driven by foreign developments is hardly a feature unique to modern globalization. The early nineteenth-century Prussian king, Friedrich Wilhelm III, for example, instituted a vast program of political, social, and economic liberalization under the express belief that more individual freedom was essential to enabling the kingdom to withstand the challenge from France. The entire feudal agrarian society was dismantled, the monopoly power of guilds broken, and economic and social restrictions on Jews relaxed. After Napoleon's defeat at Waterloo, however, the external stimulus was extinguished, and reactionary Romantic philosophers such as Adam Müller provided the cultural arguments against social change—the depersonalization of human relations driven by the "universal despotism of money"—which bolstered the aristocrats in their opposition to the extension of the rule of law to all and to the separation of private property from political power.[45] This Prussian cultural drama was every bit as disorienting as anything seen in the developing world today, yet the birth of the globalization bogeyman was still nearly two centuries away.

To conclude, today's cultural critique of globalization is misplaced along three dimensions.

First, whether indigenous "traditional values" are better or worse than imported ones, they are not being changed by outside forces impinging on the legal autonomy of states. Thus, this is not an issue of sovereignty. Globalization critics lamenting alleged cultural homogenization, such as Benjamin Barber,[46] are wrong in pinning their arguments to the mast of sovereignty. As Stephen Krasner has argued, they see sovereign violations everywhere merely because they have "fail[ed] to distinguish between challenges to control and challenges to authority."[47]

Second, political programs aimed at enfranchising previously subordinated or nonprivileged groups, such as those undertaken by many developing countries over the past two decades, have throughout history been motivated by foreign ideas and challenges, and have invariably led to resistance from those who did not benefit. Thus, this is not a story about contemporary globalization.

Third, the cultural critique is at best a hollow echo of history's most vibrant and important critiques of the social costs and benefits of individual economic freedom, and is not fundamentally to do with foreigners or foreign trade, the purveyors of globalization. "By creating an imaginary past," in Krasner's words, one in which states had sovereignty over cultural change, "observers have exaggerated contemporary changes."[48] And whereas great thinkers will never agree on the degree to which the market is a benign or malignant social force, it is eminently clear in which direction history has been moving since the eighteenth century, when production for trade first became more important than production for subsistence—the twentieth-century Communist speed bump notwithstanding. Powerful historical traditions dating back to Christian asceticism, and even classical Greek republicanism, have influenced and still influence critical thinking over whether people *should* pursue wealth over nonmaterial aims,[49] but the popular will has rarely been divided when confronted with the ability to acquire greater wealth.

"Globalization Makes the World Unequal"

If one holds that people's utility functions include not only their absolute level of income but their relative position in income distribution too, then globalization must, by changing the reference point upward, make people in poor countries feel more deprived.[50]

Globalization . . . by itself contributes to the sharpening of the perception of inequality regardless of whether inequality is in fact increasing or not. It does so by heightening people's awareness of, on the one hand, differences in income and wealth, and, on the other, showing a fundamental human similarity between them.[51]
—Branko Milanovic

Globalization probably mitigated the steep rise in income gaps between nations. The nations that gained the most from globalization are probably those poor ones that changed their policies to exploit it, while the ones that gained the least did not.
—Peter H. Lindert and Jeffrey Williamson[52]

[I]f the result of individual liberty did not demonstrate that some manners of living are more successful than others, much of the case for it would vanish.[53]

However human, envy is certainly not one of the sources of discontent that a free society can eliminate. It is probably one of the essential conditions for the preservation of such a society that we do not countenance envy, not sanction its demands by camouflaging it as social justice, but treat it, in the words of John Stuart Mill, as "the most anti-social and evil of all passions."[54]
—Friedrich Hayek

Nobel Prize winner in economics Amartya Sen has called inequality "the central economic issue related to globalization."[55] Note that he refers to inequality, and not to poverty. Few commentators blame globalization for actually making people poor, with conspicuous exceptions such as Ralph Nader and Lori Wallach.[56] But even where studies refute the charge that globalization causes inequality, observers like the World Bank's Branko Milanovic still give it a black mark for generating the "perception of inequality."

The elevation of the anti-inequality agenda has neatly tracked the rise of China and India as economic powers. Following conspicuously pro-globalization strategies over the past decade, their exceptional progress in bringing hundreds of millions out of poverty has forced critics of outward-oriented economic policies to shift their focus away from poverty and toward the wealth gap between rural and urban populations.[57]

Migration from rural to urban areas is a long-running global trend, driven by greater and faster growing economic opportunities in the latter. But has globalization as such actually increased inequality? The case that it has is weak to nonexistent. The evidence suggests that international income gaps generally widened from the sixteenth to early twentieth centuries, with no discernible "globalization" effect; that inequality across countries accelerated between 1914 and 1950, when governments imposed trade and factor market barriers with the intention of counteracting globalization forces;[58] and that global inequality among individuals has actually fallen since the 1970s.[59] Claims by Stiglitz and others that inequality, as well as poverty, increased during the 1990s[60] have been shown by former World Bank economist Surjit Bhalla to have been based wholly on a statistical artifact: the World Bank radically changed the way it calculated its poverty figures in the early 1990s, yet the underlying data needed to ferret this out were only recently put into the public domain.[61]

But let us grant, for the purposes of discussion, that a perception of globalization-induced inequality exists today, and that it is wholly lamentable. We shall do so even though vignettes such as the rapturous reception received in Vietnam by Bill Gates—one of the world's greatest personal sources of income inequality, and its greatest-ever philanthropist—suggest a muddier message. What should be done about it?

Milanovic wants massive globally progressive transfers—not just from rich countries to poor countries, but specifically from rich households in rich countries to poor households in poor countries. His vision is to inculcate a North European "redistributionist philosophy"[62] on a global scale.

Milanovic's critique of global inequality, or the perception of it, has the merit of being clearer and more specific than the vast majority of popular critiques. For Milanovic, interdependent utility functions are part of human nature, in that personal pleasure and misery depend on the observed wealth of others. If CNN shows its global audience a rich man losing a dollar down a manhole, the world is so much happier for the resulting decline in inequality. Should he be filmed retrieving it, suffering revives. Envy and schadenfreude in Milanovic's analysis are not emotions to be condemned, as per John Stuart Mill, but compensated.

More global income equality may indeed be a good thing along many dimensions. But this does not mean that the policies necessary to effectuate it will be consistent with more morally compelling principles, or that the benefits of more equality will not be outweighed by costs.

Reducing global inequality as a principle of state action, however suggestive of an impeccable moral conscience, may well require curtailing fundamental rights underpinning free societies; free societies generally being one and the same with rich ones. Justice in a free society means treating individuals according to identical rules of conduct. If we are to supplement or replace the classical principle of justice, which applies to *individual* conduct, with one of global "social justice"—or more precisely, "distributive justice"—wherein no one shall acquire more benefits than a designated authority deems justified by the prevailing distribution of global wealth, the authority will of necessity need to treat individuals according to vastly *different* rules of conduct.

If the earth were merely a pile of commodities from which we could each effortlessly take a share, an equal global distribution would doubtlessly be both just and effective in maximizing the wealth of the poor (as there would be no meaning to rich and poor). But the earth is not like this. Many of the world's wealthiest countries are, in fact, commodity impoverished. Most wealth is created de novo in the process of applying ingenuity to comparatively worthless commodities, and the benefits flowing from consumers to providers in a free society bear no relation to any distributive or merit-based calculus. There can exist no principles of just conduct—which necessarily imply free choice—that would produce a pattern of wealth distribution which could also be called just. It is logically impossible to have a game in which both the actions of the players *and* the final score can be subject to rules of fairness. If it is unfair for one team to outscore another by more than a certain margin, the behavior of the players will have to be directed by the umpires. But if the players are to be free to act within rules of fair play, the outcome logically cannot be said to be unfair. Likewise, if citizens following all the rules of just conduct become wealthy, there is no basis on which to condemn the resulting distribution of wealth as "unjust." If no one actually commits an injustice, then no moral principle can reconcile justice to individuals with social justice after the fact. Only in centrally directed social systems, such as the military, can social justice even make sense, as there are no rules of just conduct in settings where individuals are *instructed* what to do.[63]

Many may still object on the basis of the Stiglitzian corollary that "contrary to Adam Smith's claims . . . individual choices may not lead to socially desirable outcomes."[64] If individual choice implies that some societies will become much richer than others and thereby engender global conflict, are there not compelling grounds for restricting it? The fact that many people may, with the best of moral intentions, believe in the importance of certain claims to global social justice does not mean that there exist rules that can effectuate them without producing *more* global conflict rather than less. This fact is starkly illustrated by the passion with which advocates of greater national import and immigration barriers, such as Lou Dobbs, emphasize the *moral* basis of a preference for domestic over foreign labor; preferences which are inconsistent with the competing moral objective of greater global income equality.

Wholly absent from Milanovic's analysis is even a discussion of what is driving wealth creation in the rich countries of North America, Europe, and Asia, and particularly the now rapidly growing poorer ones such as China and India. Milanovic takes a few crude swipes at the legacy of Western colonialism, but makes not a mention of the fundamental role of private commerce in lifting hundreds of millions from the absolute poverty which would have been their certain fate in its absence. In fact, it is precisely the elevation of social justice agendas in many poor countries, asserting the rights of politically powerful groups to existing wealth over the rights of individuals to create and invest it, that has kept them poor. It is their absence from the vast and growing network of global commerce that explains their stagnation.

Consider sub-Saharan Africa, which, according to the 2007 International Monetary Fund *World Economic Outlook*, has lately witnessed a falling income gap. Should this fact be celebrated? As trade economist Gordon Hanson has pointed out, the dominant cause may well be the recent civil wars that have decimated the wealthy classes. This is certainly not a recipe for economic development.

Consider, on the other hand, India. Having for decades pursued equity through anti-growth policies—such as regulations to keep firms outside designated "core" industries small, and therefore incapable of export— India's about-face is now showing real results in alleviating poverty. Thus to suggest taxing globalization to compensate the growing awareness of its success is to countenance and reward the very policies which sustain failure. Clearly, the more effective policy remedies for global inequality lie in bringing the world's poorest countries *into* globalization.[65]

None of this is in any way to question the desirability of rich nations funding poverty alleviation efforts in poor nations. Whereas poverty and inequality are typically invoked in the same breath, they are conceptually very different matters. Even as impassioned and controversial an anti-poverty campaigner as Columbia's Jeffrey Sachs is only at root advocating better aligning aid to need, whereas Milanovic does not even discuss need. His concern is to reduce global envy, as proxied by statistical wealth dispersion measures. These measures are silent on the importance of eradicating malaria, for example, which has no determinate effect on global inequality, but signal success every time the Dow falls, as the stock-owning wealthy thereby become less so.

So many rich-world innovations are now beginning to improve the lives of the world's poor dramatically. For example, mobile communications devices contribute more to the living standards of fishermen in poor remote coastal villages than to most urban bankers, who cannot even imagine life without them. Genetic crop modification technology is already revolutionizing agriculture in a number of poor countries, and arguably holds out even greater prospects for wealth creation in the poorer rather than richer parts of the globe. Of the roughly six million farmers legally growing genetically modified crops in 2002, more than three-quarters were small-scale cotton farmers in developing countries, particularly China and South Africa.[66]

Yet there can be no moral claim to technology that would not exist except for the free decision of others to commit their efforts and risk their resources to create it. Material benefits in a free society flow among individuals not according to the relative efforts, intellects, or intentions of the members, but according to whatever prices must be paid to call forth the specific, freely dedicated efforts and resources necessary to satisfy revealed and emerging wants. The fact that the creators and financiers of mobile and crop technology are so richly rewarded, and in consequence generate more global income inequality in the short run, is precisely the reason *why* such technologies exist in the first place. To the extent that policies are put in place to prevent such rewards, or to redistribute enough of them so as to disallow any rise in measures of global wealth dispersion, it should be clear that the incentives driving these innovations may have to be obliterated. Therefore, policies such as nationalization, barriers to competition, high marginal tax rates, and ex post wealth taxes can certainly stop people from accumulating wealth, but they will also ensure that less global wealth is created, that many poor will be poorer than they otherwise would be, and that many forms of inequality will be greater, as numerous technologies which help the poor disproportionately will be unavailable or priced beyond their reach.

"Globalization Destroys Nations"

> . . . in the numerous countries around the world with a market-dominant
> minority, the simultaneous pursuit of free markets and democracy has led
> not to widespread peace and prosperity, but to confiscation, autocracy, and
> mass slaughter. Outside the industrialized West, these have been the wages
> of globalization.
> —Amy Chua[67]

One of the major themes in the anti-globalization literature is that globalization destroys nations, particularly poorer ones. No text in this genre is more lurid and bracing than Amy Chua's bestseller *World on Fire*.

Chua's argument links globalization with the spread of ethnic hatred, violence, and political instability through a causative chain which can be broken down as follows:

1. The expansion of private enterprise in developing countries typically leads to the emergence of "market-dominant" ethnic minorities—such as Chinese in Indonesia and Jews in Russia—who accumulate wealth faster than the majority ethnic group.
2. This emergence leads to resentment among the majority ethnic group.
3. The introduction of "democracy" in these countries then leads to the majority ethnic group seizing political power and using it to "pursue aggressive policies of confiscation and revenge."[68] "Democracy" is defined as unrestrained majoritarian rule resulting from public elections.
4. "Globalization" is defined as the global spread of "free market democracy."[69] It is therefore globalization that produces ethnic hatred and violence in the developing world.

5. The United States is primarily responsible for exporting "democracy and capitalism," and therefore globalization.

6. As the United States is itself a market-dominant minority on the global stage, the globalization it has exported therefore "more than anything else, accounts for the visceral hatred of Americans that we have seen expressed in recent acts of terrorism."[70]

Chua's semantics disguise some critical loose logical threads in the argument. Pulling these threads leads to the appearance of deep flaws in the storyline as the garment unravels.

First, Chua defines globalization in terms of the adoption of "free market democracy" in the developing world, but makes no argument that its alleged bad effects derive specifically from international trade, investment, or any other form of heightened economic interaction with foreigners. Thus her problem is simply with her understanding of "free market democracy" in the developing world, and not with anything wider. We can therefore drop globalization from her argument entirely.

Second, Chua defines democracy wholly in terms of majoritarian politics. She explicitly divorces constitutionalism or any kind of legally enshrined individual rights from democracy: " 'Democratization' will refer principally to the concerted efforts, heavily U.S.-driven, to implement immediate elections with universal suffrage," she tells us.[71] Her actual problem, however, is with majoritarian rule per se, and has nothing to do with democracy, however defined, as her stories about anti-Chinese riots in predemocratic Indonesia and anti-Jewish propaganda in the nondemocratic Arab Middle East clearly attest. In fact, she bewilderingly chides the United States for being "notoriously lax" in promoting Middle Eastern democracy, and instead highlights the problem of "minimal democratization in the Arab Middle East, [and] an intense, majority-based Arab ethnonationalism."[72] We can therefore drop democracy from her argument entirely, and simply replace it with majoritarian politics.

In short, Chua's story is neither about democracy or globalization. She is doing no more than observing that internal pressures for liberalism in traditionally authoritarian multiethnic countries tend to produce social upheaval. Hers is a story about national failures of transition to liberalism, or, more often, political failures to accommodate such transition in the face of popular demands for it.

Her story tell us nothing at all about democracy, which cannot be divorced from constitutionalism, in spite of her tortured effort to erect democracy as a straw man by equating it with voting and rule by an ethnic majority.[73] Her story likewise tells us nothing about globalization. Her observations on failed and aborted transitions to liberalism are no different than those which were widespread eighty years ago in Germany and Austria during the period of the Weimar Republic—a parallel curiously drawn by Chua herself.[74]

Hayek's major professor at the University of Vienna was Friedrich von Wieser, whose characterization of "the Jewish problem"[75] in the German world jibes perfectly with Chua's stories of a number of developing countries today. Wieser argued that the rise of the capitalist economy and Jewish legal emancipation allowed the Jews, given their particular cultural characteristics, to dominate German trade, industry, and the educated professions. This led to a backlash, a natural and healthy one in his view, among the "Aryans"[76]:

> The stratum of Jews who have risen to power . . . form an ethnically united stratum of power, and seek to advance in closed ranks, similar to the way in which the Normans at one time inserted themselves into the body of the Saxons, even if the Jews have not been able to take over the entire apparatus of domination. No wonder, then, that the Aryans, for their part, united in order to triumph in the struggle for power. They have every right to do so as individuals pursuing their personal interests, and are obligated to do so by their national consciousness (*Volksgefühl*) when they are convinced that the Jewish leadership is leading the *Volk* away from its heritage and history.[77]

Whereas Chua would obviously be appalled by Wieser's support for Aryan reactionaries, Wieser would have had little problem with Chua's diagnosis of the period. Chua tells us that "in Germany after World War I, the pursuit of free market democracy fueled an ethnonationalist conflagration of precisely the kind that threatens much of the non-Western world,"[78] and that today "it will be essential to try to devise measures and create institutions restraining the worst excesses of markets and democracy—excesses that in the presence of a market-dominant minority often lead to confiscations, authoritarian backlash, and mass slaughter."[79] Thus, in Chua's version of history, Nazism represents the product of unrestrained economic freedom and democracy. And in her version of the present, globalization is tragically breaking down these restraints in poor countries. The responsibility of the United States is somehow to help keep the restraints on, at least until their governments can figure out how to become like Canada, whose "ethnically based affirmative action programs" directed at secessionist Quebec are her model for global development.[80]

In the standard version of history, Nazism represents the *repudiation* of Weimar, a fourteen-year period bracketed by hyperinflation and the Great Depression. A political party claiming the mantle of the majority ethnic group destroyed the country's fledgling democratic institutions and any means of peaceful opposition. Nazi "ethnonationalist conflagration" is no more a product of free market democracy than is Janjaweed genocide in today's Sudan. Yet Chua sees the rise of the Nazis as a cautionary tale for those positively inclined toward globalization. We, in contrast, cannot imagine a message more welcome to despotic rulers of poor nations and less conducive to the interests of their people.

"Globalization's Benefits Are 'Just Theory' "

We actually know the answer as to how things are going because of our personal experiences, observations and intuition.
—John Ralston Saul[81]

Thanks be to Heaven, we are thus freed from all this terrifying apparatus of philosophy; we can be men without being learned; dispensed from wasting our life in the study of morals, we have at less cost a more assured guide in this immense labyrinth of human opinions.
—Jean-Jacques Rousseau's fictional Savoyard Vicar[82]

Sorrow is knowledge; they who know the most
Must mourn the deepest o'er the fatal truth,
The Tree of Knowledge is not that of Life.
—Lord Byron[83]

John Ralston Saul's *The Collapse of Globalism* is a passionate, triumphalist, snarling, and largely incomprehensible[84] celebration of the coming "end

of the Western rationalist period and its obsessions with clear linear structures on every subject."[85] Saul shares with Rousseau and Byron a longing
for a world guided by sensibilities rather than abstractions. There is no element of Western rationalism for which Saul has more contempt than
economics, which he lambastes as the centerpiece of "our obsession with a
certain kind of austere, abstracted measurement."[86]

Summarizing an impeccably balanced book-length intellectual history
of the debate over free trade, Douglas Irwin concludes that "free trade . . .
remains as sound as any proposition in economic theory which purports
to have implications for economic policy is ever likely to be."[87] Explaining
the enormous popular opposition to free trade cannot be accomplished,
however, by appealing either to ignorance of this conclusion or even belief
that it is false. The implacable nature of the opposition derives from the
fact that the "economic theory" which Irwin situates as the touchstone for
deciding the merits of free trade is widely rejected as an acceptable basis
for free trade arguments. The roots of such thinking are very much eighteenth-century Romanticism, and in particular Rousseau, for whom "science and virtue . . . are incompatible."[88] Saul, for example, tells us that the
infamous 1930 U.S. Smoot-Hawley tariffs were a mere bogeyman, having
nothing to do with the Great Depression. This was merely a myth invented by free trade theorists.

Why are the gains from trade and the losses from protectionism so easily
dismissed as "just theory"? In the words of Aventis Prize–winning scientist
David Bodanis, for nonscientists, as with noneconomists, all too frequently "only evidence that is immediately obvious is truly important."[89]

Job losses owing to trade—and particularly outsourcing, the hot-
button trade issue at the root of much anti-globalization sentiment in the
United States—tend to be highly visible. When customer orders move to
Chinese suppliers, or when call centers move to India, job losses are conspicuously linked to trade. Business closures can be filmed for the evening
news and the stories of the newly unemployed recounted in daily news-
papers.

Job loss from protectionism, on the other hand, is virtually invisible.
Ditto for the widely spread gains in living standards from greater productivity, which are never popularly connected with foreign trade and investment. The capital preserved in the process of cheaper production must

ultimately flow home, creating new companies, products, and jobs, to supplement the lower cost of living from cheaper end-products. Yet there is no public celebration of new businesses created from the capital saved by old businesses. Few ever see the thread connecting the dollar saved with the dollar invested, in spite of the fact that producing more with less is the very foundation of rising living standards. Likewise, few ever see the thread connecting the loss of a manufacturing job with the higher cost of steel inputs resulting from steel tariffs. The benefits of trade and the costs of protection are, therefore, however real and demonstrable, hidden from public view. They tend all too often, therefore, to be dismissed by the public, like the products of the evolutionary forces of natural selection, as "just theory."

There is perhaps no more influential expositor of this line of thinking than globalization's nightly nemesis Lou Dobbs. Consider this quote from his book, *Exporting America*: "Even if the result is more profits for multinational corporations, do we truly believe that exporting those jobs will lead to a better life in this country, for our workers? . . . Or should we rely on public policy, regulation, tariffs, and quotas to protect our standard of living? Or should we share the blind faith of many in Corporate America and Washington, in the power of a free market to resolve these questions?"[90] Dobbs's fulminations against the alleged ruinous effects of American free trade with poor countries are doubtlessly founded on his belief that he is observing historically unprecedented phenomena. But against the backdrop of the acrimonious debates in late seventeenth- and early eighteenth-century England over the national economic risks of trading with low-wage Ireland and Scotland,[91] there is simply nothing new in Dobbs.

Dobbs's mocking of the notion that a "free market" could produce better outcomes than a protected one is, however, not merely a statement about trade and globalization. It reflects a more deeply held belief about the unreliable nature of "theory" to explain causal connections which cannot be seen. Consider what he says about evolutionary theory: "Faith is required in all views regarding the beginning of life, whether scientific, so-called, or whether religious. . . . The fact is that evolution, Darwinism, is not a fully explained or completely rigorous and defined science that has testable results within it."[92] In other words, evolution, like free trade, is "just theory."

In this regard, economists share a curmudgeonly kinship with evolutionary biologists. They are partners in a seemingly endless struggle to persuade others that impersonal and unseen forces shape our world in predictable ways which, though far from obvious, are eminently demonstrable. This resistance—we call it Dobbsism—can be seen as a form of primal consciousness through which people impute what they observe to intention. The notion of globalization producing higher living standards without a conscious, guiding force, or natural selection producing tremendous adaptive complexity without an Intelligent Designer, is for Dobbsists absurd.

To be clear, no biologist would claim that conscious design cannot improve on unguided evolution. Thousands of years of deliberate human genetic modification of animals and plants attest otherwise. Likewise, no economist would claim that economic outcomes cannot be improved by policy interventions. Governments that spend money and allocate and enforce property rights wisely are essential to private wealth creation. However, it is exceptionally well established that enormous and highly adaptive biological complexity can emerge, and has emerged, over periods of time that are well beyond what humans can intuitively grasp, through processes which are entirely unguided by a deliberate, thinking force. Evolution is indeed "a theory." Gravity is as well. But evolution is a theory strongly supported by the fossil record, comparative anatomy, the distribution of species, embryology, and molecular biology. Likewise, the foundation of the doctrine of free trade, that there is an inherent gain in production specialization along the lines of comparative competence, is far from obvious but logically impeccable and empirically sound. Of this theory of comparative advantage, Nobel Prize winner Paul Samuelson wrote: "That it is logically true need not be argued before a mathematician; that it is not trivial is attested by the thousands of important and intelligent men who have never been able to grasp the doctrine for themselves or to believe it after it was explained to them."[93]

Consider steel tariffs, such as those imposed with great fanfare by President Bush in March 2002, about which Dobbs commented enthusiastically "that the president had decided he had a far more important constituency to serve than the members of the WTO, the EU, and the so-called free traders: namely, working men and women in this country."[94]

Unfortunately for the "so-called free traders," the argument that President Bush helped American working men and women with steel tariffs can only be rebutted with "theory."

Whereas it is a simple task to count the number of American steel workers at two points in time and to ascribe any decline to trade (even if much of it resulted instead from new domestic technology), considerably more abstraction—more data and higher math—must be employed to estimate the effect of steel tariffs on workers, as the vast majority of them are not employed in the steel industry, even though their livelihoods must be affected by steel prices. Yet since statistical estimation techniques are not nearly as comforting in their concreteness as counting steel workers, Dobbsists will readily dismiss as "theory" the studies suggesting that tariffs produced tens of thousands of job losses in steel-*using* industries and corporate earnings losses about twice the size of the gains reaped by steel producers.[95] These earnings losses themselves represent real lost investment and consumption, even if such concepts are mere abstractions to Dobbsists. The workers who lose their jobs due to higher steel costs are conveniently ignored as hypothetical artifacts of statistical regression analysis. This is the case even where theory testing tells us, reliably, that such men and women have been neither intelligently designed nor accounted for in tallying the losses of protectionism.

The hardest sell for economists defending globalization is almost certainly the positive impact of the growth of international financial markets. Any demonstration of the impact of financial markets on wealth creation of necessity involves the highest degree of abstraction, given the nature of contemporary money and securities, which exist primarily as glowing digits on computers. They are not tangible, like barbecue grills, even if they are vitally important to our standard of living. Questions such as "does stock trading make a nation richer?" can only be answered with econometrics, a form of statistical analysis of economic relationships.

One of the present authors has, for example, studied the effect of stock exchange trading costs on the cost of capital for listed companies. Domowitz and Steil found that in the late 1990s each 10% decline in trading costs saved large U.S.- and European-listed companies about 1.5% on their cost of raising capital. This is an important relationship to understand, as the computerization and growth of stock markets over the past three decades has lowered trading costs dramatically, over 50% in the United States in the late 1990s alone, and therefore enabled companies to raise funds much more cheaply than they otherwise would have.[96] This in turn has enabled them to produce products and services more cheaply, raising living standards across the economy.

Yet once econometrics are dismissed as "just theory," nothing but imagination remains to explain the economic relevance of stock markets. No productive dialogue is even possible between the economist who says that "the data suggest x" and the Dobbsist who rejects data in deference to his sensory experience of stock trading, suitably tinged to assure consistency with his broader views on the nature of economy, politics, and society. As David Korten opines, "The world of finance itself has become a gigantic computer game. In this game the smart money does not waste itself on long-term, high-quality commitments to productive enterprises engaged in producing real wealth to meet real needs of real people."[97] No need for data here. Korten's senses tell him everything he needs to know. And most assuredly, his eyes and ears testify to no link between "the world of finance" and "real wealth." It is the philosophy of Rousseau's fictional Savoyard Vicar,[98] "according to which true religion comes from the heart, not the head, and all elaborate theology is superfluous," in the words of Bertrand Russell. "It is, essentially, a rejection of Hellenistic intellectualism."[99]

Often, it must be emphasized, the simplest of theory is sufficient logically to debunk the more grievous instances of Dobbsism, yet it persists unfazed, often calling forth sequels of even greater popular appeal. William Greider's *One World, Ready or Not*, a 473-page tome weaving an impressive collection of numbers and anecdotes with reams of ferocious adjectives, is the pinnacle of Dobbsist confusion. In his review of the book, Paul Krugman shows that Greider's cri de coeur for an end to technology-induced global overcapacity and impoverishment is as silly as arguing that a hypothetical economy consisting of the complements hot dogs and buns could not possibly survive a doubling in bun productivity, as unemployed bun workers must necessarily starve. The underlying assumptions—that consumption would fail to increase along with productivity, and bun workers would not move to the hot dog sector—are logically and empirically preposterous (the U.S. economy added 45 million jobs in the quarter century preceding Greider's book), yet these are the foundational prem- ises of Greider's call "to re-create a national governance that asserts its power to regulate players in the global market."[100] Krugman is no doubt right, however, to conclude that Greider would only respond to such a critique by insisting that Krugman was "talking mere theory,"[101] whereas he, Greider, had travelled the globe observing the truth.

Whereas specific phenomena such as computer-enabled global outsourc- ing may be unique to contemporary globalization, apocalyptic warnings about the effects of new technology and commerce on employment are of weathered pedigree. With the "multiplication and variety of machines," the Viscount de Chateaubriand asked rhetorically in 1841, "what will you do with the human race, unemployed?"[102] But the revival of such warn- ings today is impressive for the cast of Cassandras that have been swept into its fold. John Gray, writing two decades ago in a panegyric to Hayek, lamented the "dominant interventionist and constructivist temper" of the early twentieth century—a temper which he, in his current incarnation as an anti-globalist, now displays with a convert's fervor. The early Gray con- demned socialist intellectuals such as Karl Mannheim, Harold Laski, and Sidney and Beatrice Webb for their influence "in representing the free so- ciety as a sort of chaos, which only rational reconstruction on an ideal pat- tern could save from disabling inefficiency, inequity and eventual crisis."[103] Today's Dobbsists, while accepting that society can be left gen- erally free without inefficiency, inequity, and crisis, see all three emerging once foreigners become part of the template.

Throughout history, mankind has steadily if reluctantly accommodated to the critical observation that coherent order may emerge from physical or sociological processes that are not consciously directed by gods or gov- ernments. Globalization presents yet another challenge for such accom- modation, as the level of economic abstraction necessary to link the organic growth of trade with improvement in living standards is consider- able. Sensory experience and passion are not effective substitutes for such abstraction. Yet in Hayek's words, "Activities that appear to add to avail- able wealth, 'out of nothing', without physical creation and by merely re- arranging what already exists, stink of sorcery" for much of the public.[104] Visceral resistance to such abstraction, or "sorcery," among intellectuals as with the wider public, is considerable, as it was with the great Romantic writers. Our fear is that globalization may be undermined by the misguided global mythology associating money with sovereignty, a problem to which we dedicate the remainder of this book, before globalization can establish its public credentials as a logical and desirable further extension of liberalism.

4

A BRIEF HISTORY OF MONETARY SOVEREIGNTY

The Birth of Money

> As *each* economizing individual becomes increasingly more aware of his economic interest, he is led by this *interest, without any agreement, without legislative compulsion, and even without regard to the public interest,* to give his commodities in exchange for other, more saleable, commodities, even if he does not need them for any immediate consumption purpose. With economic progress, therefore, we can everywhere observe the phenomenon of a certain number of goods, especially those that are most easily saleable at a given time and place, becoming, under the powerful influence of *custom,* acceptable to everyone in trade, and thus capable of being given in exchange for any other commodity.
> —Carl Menger, *Principles of Economics*

Carl Menger's account of the process by which money emerged, while wholly supported by the archaeological and historical evidence, appears strange to the modern mind, conditioned as it is to seeing money as a creation of states. This now-indelible association between money and states was first fashioned by powerful men 2,500 years ago not to promote economic activity, but to profit from it. And today the imposition of national monies remains one of the most potent tools available to governments to extract wealth from their populations and to exercise political control over them.

Throughout virtually all of human history, up until 1971, money was some form of valuable and durable commodity, or a claim on such a commodity. The use of specific commodities to measure or value the worth of things is actually built into many languages. The Latin word *aes*, copper, is the foundation of the English verbs "to esteem" (*aestimare*) and "to estimate." The use of copper to esteem or to estimate worth goes back to at least the thirteenth century BC, when the earliest evidence of the value of items being expressed in terms of copper was found in Middle Eastern tomb records. Gold, silver, bronze, iron, and copper were the principal metals used as mediums of exchange, replacing more ancient units of value—principally, the ox—which were far less suitable for commercial transactions. (The Latin word *pecuniarius*, pecuniary, means "wealth in cattle," and the Roman *as* coin's value was actually fixed at 1/100 of a cow.) Gold was well suited as money because of its intrinsic value to people, particularly for use in ornaments, and a simple melting process could transform gold money into gold ornaments, and back again, as demand warranted. Copper was similarly valued for creating tools and weapons, and became particularly popular as early money in Europe owing to gold (and silver) being too precious for settling small transactions. Before coining became widespread, metals were often worked into useful items, such as knives of a conventional size, and circulated as money in that form.

Ancient money was valued by weight, the measure of its intrinsic value, rather than by "tale"; that is, by counting out units, as money is valued today. One of the earliest and most important uses of scales was to measure quantities of precious metals, and scales thus became a vital tool of commerce in the great empires of Egypt, Crete, Babylon, and Assyria. The impact of the spread of coin usage in the ancient world on the organization of all subsequent societies which adopted its use in commerce cannot be overstated. Coins freed people of dependence on their local tribe, allowing them to roam ever farther with confidence that they would have and be able to acquire the means to feed, clothe, and protect themselves. People who knew nothing of each other found a basis for cooperation, and therefore vastly wider social networks. Coins destroyed ancient aristocracies by creating new means of acquiring wealth. The fact that the Spartans and the Chinese rejected coining may have had much to do with the desire of their leaders to protect the existing order.[1]

Once exchanging metals by weight became the normal means of set-tling transactions, the next logical improvement in the process was to affix "seals" on metal pieces to indicate authoritatively their weight and purity. The first clear evidence of seals being used to certify currency metals ap-pears in the seventh century BC, in the eastern Mediterranean. The great variation in types of, and symbols on, the oldest Lydian coins suggests that they were likely of private issue, which was commonplace until the early years of the sixth century BC.[2] From Lydia, the practice of coining metals — that is, sealing them — spread to Asia Minor and the Greek main-land; thereafter to the Greek colonies in Italy, Sicily, and, later, Carthage.

The early efforts by rulers to monopolize the currency certification pro-cess are today typically explained in a manner consistent with the near-universal contemporary conflation of money production with the natural sovereign power of states. The government, according to this account, is playing an essential role in the creation of markets by acting as a disinter-ested, honest broker, guaranteeing both parties to a private transaction the weight, and therefore value, of the money being exchanged. By this account, money and the state are a necessary and benign pairing.

This "textbook fiction," as Robert Mundell has characterized it,[3] is con-tradicted historically by the fact that the artificial electrum, a mixture of gold and silver, used by the earliest coining Lydian kings was of widely varying fineness, from 5% to 95% gold,[4] making stamping for weight a commercially useless exercise. Rulers were driven by the same crass com-mercial objectives that drove their subjects: profit. The gold content of coins was progressively reduced, resulting in ever-increasing seigniorage revenue for the issuers.

The seventh and sixth centuries BC were, as historian A. R. Burns put it, "the age of tyrants"[5] in the Greek world, and coinage and tyrants emerged in tandem. The greater uniformity in appearance, content, and types of coins which appeared in the early sixth century BC was the first sign of a shift toward state monopoly of minting, and the beginning of an enduring association between money and state sovereignty. Lydian tyrants, in the words of classicist P. N. Ure in a treatise on the origins of tyranny, "were the first men in their various cities to realize the possibili-ties of the new conditions created by the introduction of the new coinage, and . . . to a large extent they owed their positions as tyrants to a financial or commercial supremacy which they had already established before they had attained to supreme political power in their several states."[6]

Once in power, the tyrants of the Greek world, like the Lydian ruler Gyges (reigned 687–652 BC), assumed monopoly of coining. This was critical to fending off rivals. To maintain overvaluation of coins, rulers typically asserted exclusive control over gold and silver mines, and their successors suppressed private, episcopal, and baronial mints throughout all subsequent ages. And to create a mystique premium on their coins, whose face value significantly exceeded their intrinsic value, rulers typically adopted religious symbols in their stamps. The less gold, the more God. In fact, "In God We Trust" was added to American dollar bills only after their gold backing was dropped in 1862. Republican Greece and Rome used images of the divinities on their coins as a means of inducing loyalty; the imperial powers of Persia and post-Caesar Rome adopted the leader's effigy as a means of commanding it. In the words of sixteenth-century comptroller of the Paris mint Jacques Colas, "it belongs only to the Prince to give Money to his subjects, because the effigy and arms which are there engraved gives them a witness of the superiority which God has given him over them."[7]

The Persian conquerors of Lydia in the fifth century BC had no prior experience of money management, but readily adopted the policy of the defeated regime, and spread money-based trading into Asia. Darius (reigned 522–486 BC), according to Herodotus, being "anxious to leave such a memorial of himself as had been left by no other King, having refined gold to the utmost perfection, he struck money,"[8] and maintained strict control over its issue. Gold Persian *darics* were for two centuries the principal gold currency of the ancient world, extending well beyond Persian frontiers into the cities and islands of Asia minor, and to a considerable extent the mainland of Greece. Philip and Alexander of Macedon issued prodigious amounts of money in the late fourth century BC, which was instrumental in the spread of coins into Gaul and Britain, and subsequently to Ireland and Scandinavia.

The internationalization of money in the ancient world was shaped by many factors. Gold bars were widely used in the seventh and sixth centuries BC to settle transactions across frontiers. Once coining became widespread, both economic and political factors influenced which coins circulated where. Seals which developed a reputation for reliable quality, and became familiar through ample supply, extended their domain through foreign trade. "Tortoise" coins from Aegina became the most widely used in the Aegean in the sixth century BC through reputation and trade. But politics and might came to hold sway as well. The Persian gold daric and the Athenian silver "owl" dominated in Asia Minor in the fifth and fourth centuries BC within the two powers' respective areas of control. Athenian weights, measures, and coins were forced upon tributary cities. Improvements in mint technique wrought in Athens brought much more regularity to coins, and made it possible for them to begin circulating by tale rather than by weight.

Monetary unions developed throughout the Greek world following the collapse of the Athenian Empire at the end of the fifth century BC, but these disappeared as the Romans established central authority in areas where it had not previously existed. It is fascinating to note that A. R. Burns, writing in the mid-1920s, lamented the post–World War I "parochial nationalism, which has expressed itself in a variety of new monetary units," and presaged the creation of the euro three-quarters of a century later by suggesting the possibility that "these small units will wisely turn for assistance to the Greek device" of monetary union.[9]

The expansion of the Roman dominion from the third century BC on was accompanied by the suppression of mintage rights in conquered territories, with the first emperor, Augustus (reigned 31 BC–14 AD), declaring Roman weights, measures, and coins the only ones in which transactions were legally enforceable. The first three centuries of the empire witnessed the progressive elimination of local issues in gold, silver, and bronze, as such issues became a central element of imperial authority.

It was the Roman emperors who, having presided over a bimetallic (gold and silver) monetary system for centuries, eventually established gold as the primary material of money. That status—having previously been held by copper, bronze, and, at or before the introduction of coining, silver—has been maintained by gold throughout most of history ever since. It was also the Roman emperors who, beginning with Nero (reigned 54–68 AD), conducted the first systematic experiments in currency debasement, mixing increasing amounts of base metals into coins to generate revenues and reduce their debts, creating economic chaos and political unrest in so doing. Burns concludes his magisterial history of early money with the observation that the Romans "gave the world the inestimable curse of practical knowledge of all possible methods of inflation apart from the issue of paper money."[10] Perfection of the method of inflation by issue of paper money would have to wait until the ascendancy of the eminent rulers of the latter part of the twentieth century AD.

Medieval Meditations

We take it for granted today that monetary policy is not only the prerogative of the government but one of its primary responsibilities. After all, having no monetary policy is anarchy, and having it dictated from abroad is imperialism.

The medieval mind did not see things this way. Money was imbued with personal moral obligation, and as such was outside the scope of a ruler to manipulate. To debase a coin was to steal from a creditor. Rulers could mint coins, since a central authority could usefully certify the weight and fineness of the precious metals used, but they could no more legitimately profit from it than they could pilfer livestock.

Popes weighed in on monetary policy, from questions of debasement to seigniorage. In 1199, Innocent III granted the request of the new king of Aragon, Pedro I, to be relieved of his accession oath to "maintain the currency"[11] he subsequently discovered to have been secretly debased. Innocent IV backed his predecessor's decree, proclaiming debasement to be fraud and condemning rulers seeking seigniorage profits, through underweighting of coins, in excess of production costs.

Canonists, authorities on church law, disapproved of all currency manipulations. Treading boldly in the secular sphere, cardinal bishop of Ostia and canon lawyer Hostiensis (1190–1271) proclaimed the illegitimacy of debased coins in satisfying debts, asserting that a debtor must "return money of the same kind and weight, and the same value in weight, even if the coin is current for less (*diminuta quo ad cursum*), unless otherwise specified, because contracts have force of law out of convention."[12] Drawing on the doctrine of satisfaction of monetary debts expounded by jurists specializing in Roman law, or "romanists"—that "the debtor is not allowed to return a worse object of the same nature, such as new wine for old wine,"[13] which they applied to money by insisting it be of the same kind (for example, silver for silver) and fineness—canonists sought to outlaw debasements as a violation of public law by arguing that it necessarily led to violations in the sphere of private (that is, contract) law. Fundamentally, then, money was to both canonists and romanists a matter in which rulers were categorically *not* sovereign, but rather guardians of the people's rights to contract with one another on the basis of "like for like." In the words of Innocent IV, "when [the king] wants to diminish a money already made, we do not believe that he can do so without the consent of the people."[14]

Such "consent" was considered to be manifested by "the majority of the notables,"[15] a ruling which recognized seigniorage as a form of taxation, legitimated only through some form of democratic process. Romanists took a harder line on seigniorage, holding that it should be zero, and thus requiring the government to subsidize minting. In the words of Bartolo da Sassoferrato (1313–1357), one of the great "post-glossators," or authorities on applying revived Roman law to the fourteenth-century Italian cities, "by common law coin must be made such that it brings as much usefulness in coin as in kind, and as much in kind as in coin. . . . And thus the expenses of minting must be borne by the public."[16]

The romanist view dominated in practice, in the sense that the "notables" were frequently wise enough to accept only transparent taxation to support the costs of minting. For example, the Estates of southern France agreed to pay taxes to Jean II in return for the king's promise not to debase the currency—a practice that was known as "monetagium." In the north, where the Estates failed to cut such a deal, the currency was routinely debased, and so they were taxed by stealth.[17] It is his observation of the effects of such repeated debasements in fourteenth-century France which led the illustrious economist, mathematician, physicist, and bishop Nicole Oresme (ca. 1320–1382) to conclude that "an exaction is the more dangerous the less obvious it is"[18] and to warn of the tendency of a king's exercise of power to degenerate into tyranny.

Medieval French philosopher Jean Buridan (ca. 1295–1358) placed the question of debasement squarely within the frame of religion and morality, stating that through debasement "the king would be committing a sin, and unfairly profiting from the common people; unless he were excused of sinning because of a war involving the people, or some other public necessity."[19] Neapolitan jurist and professor Andrea d'Isernia (ca. 1230–1316) qualified this war exception by stating that once the emergency had passed, the king was obliged to compensate the holders of vile money, accepting it in exchange for good money.[20] In other words, war could justify temporarily debased money if the ability to mint good money were impaired, but the king could not profit from the debasement; it was to be solely for "the common good."[21] German economist, philosopher, and Scholastic theologian Gabriel Biel tied the legitimacy of money directly to the value ascribed to it by the people, as "the form of money is a testament to its genuineness and legality, namely that it is of genuine substance and weight."[22] Attempts by rulers to circumvent the correspondence among the value, form, and substance of a coin was a form of perjury.[23]

Renaissance Revisionism

> The Bank is to make us a New Paper Mill
> This Paper they say, by the Help of a Quill
> The Whole Nation's Pockets with Money will fill.
> —Jonathan Swift[24]

Renaissance thinking on money distinguished itself from earlier thinking in explicitly recognizing that money could have value above and beyond the value of its constituent metal by virtue of its utility as a medium of exchange. This body of thought, known as "nominalism," is at the root of the simultaneously wealth-enhancing and ruinous potential of paper (or computer-blip) money. Commodity money is inherently wasteful, as it ties up valuable resources which could otherwise be put to productive use. On the other hand, money untethered to a commodity gives rise to inflation when managed by corrupt, irresponsible, or incompetent rulers.

A seminal thinker in renaissance monetary theory, French jurist Charles Dumoulin (1500–1566) was one of the first to argue influentially that a coin (or a bill) was, for the purposes of contracting, worth its "assigned value,"[25] rather than any intrinsic value as measured by its metallic content. Dumoulin's doctrine was at least partially based on the attractions of its legal simplicity: legal disputes were frequent where the value of coins could be held by one or another party to be other than what the ruler laid down. Yet Dumoulin did not follow his nominalism to its logical conclusion, that the value of money could be entirely divorced from its physical content—the essence of fiat money, which has dominated our world since the early 1970s. Dumoulin rejected the notion that a ruler could assign value to money arbitrarily, but was instead obliged to act in accordance with ius gentium, the Roman "law of nations," which was law held to be fundamentally valid and just across all nations. The ruler's discretion in assigning value to coins was to be intrinsically restrained by "the consent and usage of the people, and the practice of trade."[26] If the ruler's valuation departed significantly from intrinsic content, or if it changed so frequently that the coins became useless as a standard of value, Dumoulin held that medieval rules on debt repayment then applied. Dumoulin held further that rulers could not justly debase coins as a means of generating wealth from seigniorage.

As for fiat money, it was "irrational and ridiculous: why, by the same token, it would be possible to make money out of printed paper, and that is just as ludicrous and ridiculous as a children's game, and not only contradicts the origin and definition of money, but also experience and common sense."[27] Our modern paper monetary regimes would, to Dumoulin, be conceptually "irrational and ridiculous." And for much of the less developed world over the past quarter century, paper monies have in fact fully lived down to Dumoulin's conception of them.

Dumoulin was effectively straddling two boats that were bound to head off on divergent courses. Justice in money valuation was to be found either in consensual popular practice or in the edicts of rulers; there was no way to meld the two. The decade of the 1570s, during which Dumoulin's views on debt contracts were the law of the land in France, pitted the people against the ruler in a battle over monetary sovereignty which would be replayed again and again in subsequent centuries.

French creditors suffered large losses as gold écu coins rose in market value vis-à-vis "billon," underweighted copper pennies, which, having been designated by the king legal tender and official units of account for the écu, were used by debtors to settle obligations. Small change quickly became scarce. Billon went out of general circulation as importers shipped it abroad to avoid the losses they would suffer by paying in gold and silver, which had become much dearer in France than abroad, and taxpayers happily dumped it to settle liabilities. This was an early-model currency crisis, complete with speculators who rapidly melted money and minted it, and imported and exported it as market valuations rose and fell. A creditor revolt eventually led to the collapse of the legal tender regime for billon, resulting in a 1577 Estates General decision legally to denominate all sums in excess of an écu solely in écus, and converting existing billon debts into écus at a fixed rate. The new system, the sort of hard-money regime which invariably follows the collapse of a soft one, survived a quarter century, prefiguring the late nineteenth-century gold standard, albeit with significant technical flaws.[28]

If Dumoulin was unwilling to make the full intellectual leap from money-as-metal to money-as-medium, contemporaries were. Italian jurist Girolamo Butigella (1470–1515) was a target of Dumoulin's scorn for insisting that money could be made of "lead, indeed even of wood or leather," so long as it was "publicly approved," meaning authorized as money in law.[29] Thinkers like Butigella; French legal scholar and poet Étienne Forcadel (1534–1574); French scholar, diplomat, and royal librarian Guillaume Budé (1467–1540); and French jurist and law professor François Duaren (1509–1559) were instrumental in reinterpreting Roman law such that money's intrinsic quality became secondary or irrelevant, and instead its value in exchange and liquidity was elevated to the fore. Their thinking was illustrative of the radical reinterpretations of both the Bible and Roman law characteristic of Renaissance humanism.

French jurist and leading humanist scholar François Hotman (1524–1590) likened money to a bond, valued not for its (nearly worthless) physical content but "from law and from its power."[30] Spanish theologian and philosopher Gregorio de Valencia (1549–1603) celebrated the role of public authority in designating items as money, to be used as the medium of exchange. In so doing the authority turned something virtually worthless into something valuable, much as an artisan could turn a useless piece of wood into a useful box.[31] Forcadel, Hotman, and others cited examples from antiquity to their own time, from Rome to China, where fiat money was used in practice.

But if Hotman was right and money was like a bond, then there had to be a mechanism by which the promise represented by the bond, to provide something of intrinsic value in the future, could be enforced. This is the Achilles' heel of fiat money. For as the Spanish canonist González

Téllez (died 1649) observed, the traditional canonist prohibition of excessive seigniorage could be practically justified in that it "necessarily increases the prices of goods and makes everything more expensive, as we have experienced more than once in our times."[32] That is, the ruler's power to create value from the valueless by designating it "money" was bound to lead to inflation. Subjects, therefore, were only likely to use such money under compulsion. Italian ecclesiastical jurist Sigismundus Scaccia (died 1620) thus observed that fiat money was only tenable in a closed economy, one which did not trade abroad. Italian mathematician and astronomer Geminiano Montanari (1633–1687) explained this as follows: "If a state had no commerce with the other states and lived solely on its own productions, as China and a few others have done for so long, the prince could set the value of money as he pleased, and make it of whatever content he wished. But if a prince wants his own coins of gold and silver to be accepted by foreigners, so that his subjects can trade with them, he cannot value them if he does not set the right content."[33] In other words, national fiat monies are incompatible with "globalization," as an effective legal compulsion to accept the valueless as valuable stops at the border.

Renaissance law liberated the secular authorities from the medieval doctrine that a creditor had the right to demand like for like—gold for gold, silver for silver—irrespective of the ruler's preferences. A debt incurred in gold could now be satisfied by returning copper pennies at the rate established by the ruler. In the formulation of French monetary authority Henri Poullain (years of birth and death unknown), pennies were like chips in a poker game, conveniently substituting for money: "Within the state," Poullain remarked, bad coins "stand in for, and serve just as well as, the good ones; no more or less than in a card game, where various individuals play, one avails oneself of tokens, to which a certain value is assigned, and they are used by the winners to receive, and by the losers to pay what they owe. Whether instead of coins one were to use dried beans and give them the same value, the game would be no less enjoyable or perfect."[34]

Yet this did not prove to be so. As in Dumoulin's France, creditors were angered by receiving "dried beans" for gold, and stopped providing credit on the ruler's terms. Specific denominations were required in repayment, or multiple prices were posted based on denomination. In response, authorities were obliged to place legal tender restrictions on small change all over Europe—Venice, Florence, Aragon, Germany, the United Provinces, France, and England—which set limits on its use in satisfying debts. In presaging our age of fiat money, in which central banks are charged with limiting money in circulation in order to prevent inflation, Montanari observed that token coins could only successfully substitute for precious metals where the ruler "does not strike more of them than is sufficient for the use of his people, sooner striking too few than striking too many."[35] Overissue, on the other hand, would result in the bad coins driving out the good, generalized inflation, and merchants having to pay a premium to acquire the good coins needed to pay foreigners. When dealing with foreigners, it has always been, and is certainly in our time, beyond the ability of the ruler to enforce his "dried beans" as money, for as Budé conceded, "without respect to the mark [of the ruler on the coin] they value our gold and silver as it is tried and weighed."[36] In other words, foreigners can always demand intrinsic value in payment.

Spanish Jesuit historian Juan de Mariana (1536–1624) was, in intellectual temperament, the prototypical economist—"two-handed" and dour—in his judgments on the world of fiat money. On the one hand, he saw the token Spanish vellón as a sensible way for the king to economize on silver. On the other, the incentive to issue lots of it could drive it to worthlessness and lead to large price increases, as debasements always had in the past. In the end, he predicted rightly, it would all end in tears: excessive debasement, inflation, and the king's subjects inventing their own rules of exchange. Indeed, after 80 years of disastrous monetary policy under Philip III (reigned 1598–1621), Philip IV (reigned 1621–1665), and Charles II (reigned 1665–1700), small coinage in Castile became in 1680, as elsewhere in Europe, full-bodied copper, with face value close to intrinsic value. Medieval money was reborn.

The Rise of the Gold Standard

> . . . neither a State nor a bank ever has had the unrestricted power of issuing
> paper money, without abusing that power; in all States, therefore, the issue
> of paper money ought to be under some check and control; and none seems
> so proper as that of subjecting the issuers of paper money to the obligation
> of paying their notes, either in gold coin or in bullion.
> —David Ricardo[37]

Today, every government which issues its own currency designates a specific unit of account, like the dollar in the United States, and guarantees convertibility of smaller denomination coins into the unit of account at a fixed rate: four quarters to a dollar, ten dimes to a dollar, and so forth. The total amount of currency in circulation is determined by the government, but people can decide for themselves in what denominations they would hold their currency.

Until the nineteenth century, however, normal practice was very different. Governments authorized coins of different denominations to be minted at set prices, in terms of weights of metal, and allowed subjects to decide for themselves whether to bring metal to the mints to be turned into coins at these prices. This practice routinely produced severe monetary problems, the causes of which were not generally understood. In particular, small denomination coins (usually silver) had a persistent tendency both to depreciate vis-à-vis large denomination coins (usually gold) *and* to fall into short supply. This apparently strange state of affairs has a logical explanation, although that logic is far from obvious.

Basically, it worked like this. There were sporadic periods in which the exchange rate of large coins in terms of small coins appreciated. As small coins depreciated as currency, they eventually became more valuable as metal than as coins. This encouraged people to melt them, and produced a shortage of the small coins. This was a problem, as small coins can be used to purchase anything, whereas large coins can only be used to purchase valuable things. Governments then debased the small coins—required less metal from their subjects in exchange for them—in order to encourage new minting, but debasement led to further appreciation of the large coins, increased counterfeiting of the small coins, and runaway inflation, as the small coins were generally the unit of account in which prices were quoted. These monetary systems were thus inherently unstable.

What was the solution to this problem which recurred over centuries, and why was it so hard to identify and implement?

In order to avoid depreciations and shortages of small denomination coins, governments needed to impose a single commodity anchor, such as gold coins or bills redeemable in gold, and to make smaller denominations into limited-supply tokens, convertible into the commodity anchor money at a fixed rate guaranteed by the government (such as four quarters to a gold dollar). This is now widely referred to as the "standard formula." The gold standard, which emerged in nineteenth-century Britain, was the first successful application of it.

Why did it take so long? Some have argued that "it took a long time before theorists recognized the superiority of tokens over full bodied coins."[38] Essentially, the monetary messiahs were just a long time in coming. We are skeptical of this Great Theorist theory, as it simply assumes the existence of a stable political structure capable of credibly guaranteeing the long-term integrity of the convertibility promise, something which has rarely existed in history. Without such a political structure, however, the "superiority of tokens over full bodied coins" is a chimera.

A second explanation is vastly more credible. Successful application of the standard formula depended on the existence of technologies which allowed the minting of token coins that were costly and difficult to counterfeit.[39]

Britain experimented with, and frequently stumbled into, a remarkable range of monetary systems over the seventeenth, eighteenth, and early nineteenth centuries. These regimes were based alternatingly on competitive markets, private monopoly, and government monopoly. They were based on silver as the unit of account and, later, gold as the unit of account. They were based on full-bodied commodity money and, at times, token subsidiary coins. They involved some of the nation's most storied thinkers, such as John Locke and Isaac Newton, in momentous debates over the merits of one system over another. And they were heavily influenced by technological advances, such as the installation of steam-driven minting presses at the Royal Mint in 1805. Indeed, Angela Redish has termed the supplanting of bimetallism by the much more successful gold standard a "side-effect of the Industrial Revolution," which saw the emergence of a minting process that dramatically reduced the scope for counterfeiting token coins and notes.[40] Finally, a monetary system could emerge which not only provided a useful medium of exchange but a stable price level.

The birth of the British gold standard can be dated to the passage of the Coinage Act in 1816, which established gold coin as the sole standard of value. In principle, it differed significantly from the standard formula in that free minting of silver was allowed and convertibility not guaranteed.

Neither of these "flaws" was consequential, however. Free minting was to begin at a future date to be announced, but the mint simply never announced that date, fearing that it would be swamped with silver, owing to silver's market price being below the mint's set legal price. As for convertibility, the Bank of England, then a private institution operating under government charter, voluntarily established the practice of accepting silver coins at face value in exchange for gold or its notes.[41]

The system was, by historical standards, a remarkable success, generating no small coin shortages or troublesome depreciations that had afflicted Europe for centuries. Neither did it undermine private commerce and destroy the people's wealth through inflation, which is hardly just a scourge of the distant past.

Germany adopted a gold standard in 1871, and the United States in 1873. The Latin Monetary Union—binding France, Belgium, Italy, and Switzerland to coordinate policies on subsidiary coinage—was founded in 1865 on a bimetallic standard, but the sharp drop in the market price of silver vis-à-vis gold in the 1870s led to a formal suspension of free silver coinage in 1878. By the end of the nineteenth century, then, Britain, France, Germany, and the United States were all approximating the standard formula under a gold-based regime.

Gold, it must be emphasized, was not a nirvana money. No such thing has ever existed, or will ever exist, outside the simplified world of textbooks. Gold is subject to supply shocks that, while leaving the barest of imprints on an inflation record extending a century or more, produced some significant disruptions throughout the second half of the nineteenth century. Gold discoveries between 1849 and 1851 yielded an upward trend in prices that reversed itself in the last quarter of the century, resulting in deflationary pressures. The periodic economic downturns of the late nineteenth century prompted a debate on monetary reform that culminated in the post–World War II Keynesian economic revolution, marked by ever more discretionary monetary and activist fiscal policy, only to collapse with the "stagflation"—rising inflation and unemployment—of the 1970s. Figure 4.1 illustrates the U.K. and U.S. inflation performance from 1800 to 1992.

The essential point to make about gold as the nineteenth-century global monetary anchor, however imperfect it was as a price stabilizer over short

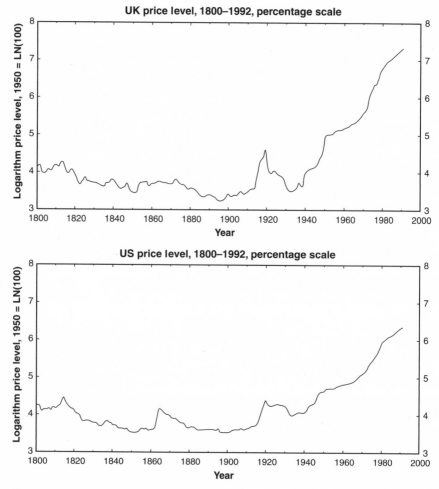

Figure 4.1. U.K. and U.S. price level histories.
Source: Flood and Mussa (1994).

periods, is that no alternative has ever proven remotely as successful in producing an integrated and stable international economy. Sargent and Velde believe the story of nineteenth-century money represents "The Triumph of the Standard Formula,"[42] but we see it differently. The formula itself was undoubtedly important for the critical insight into how subsidiary coinage should be managed. The triumph, however, was in eliminating the horrors of runaway inflation and unifying the world economy, as we shall see below, through governments forswearing discretion—

renouncing "sovereignty"—in monetary policy, in favor of an implied rule that served to maintain stable prices. The nineteenth-century rule was convertibility of paper money and token coinage into gold on demand, but its effect has been successfully mimicked since the 1980s, at least in some countries for some periods, by what is now known as inflation targeting. The major difference between the two is that under the gold standard *absolute price levels* tended to be stable over the long run (that is, inflation was followed by deflation), whereas under inflation targeting it is the *rate of price increases* that tends to stabilize (that is, above-target inflation is followed by a return to target inflation, not deflation).[43]

It is important to note that Britain in the nineteenth century did not ever actually commit to gold convertibility, commitment being fundamental to the standard formula (otherwise it wouldn't be called a formula), nor does the U.S. Federal Reserve today actually commit to maintaining a specific low rate of inflation. The success of the two regimes is based on public expectations, built up over time, of the behavior of the nineteenth-century Bank of England and the late twentieth-century Federal Reserve when faced with political pressures to debase, or inflate. As Cannan wrote of Britain in 1918, "In this country, there is little doubt that in case of a considerable falling off of demand the Government would be compelled to take back enough of the coin to keep up its value, and the obligation might just as well be acknowledged at once."[44]

The Beginning of the End of Commodity Money

> . . . merchants had to have faith in the stamp of the person who first sealed the coin—usually another merchant, a government official, or a banker. It was only one more step from this process to keep the gold coins in a safe place and circulate only the label.
> —Jack Weatherford[45]

Commodity monies have faced significant obstacles to their perpetuation throughout history. Some of these were largely outside the control of state authorities. Coins wore down over time, meaning that the ratio of their face value to intrinsic value in metal would, all else being equal, fall gradually. Coin "clippers," who illegally clipped small bits of metal from coins to be melted down, together with counterfeiters often had much more immediate and serious effects. But these factors were largely negated through technological developments such as coin "milling" in the sixteenth century, which foiled clippers, and steam-driven minting in the early nineteenth century, which significantly raised the cost of counterfeiting.

Far more important have been factors that have driven governments to undermine their own monies, factors which Redish classified as fiscal, monetary, and political.[46] Debasing coins, by producing greater minting profits, proved an effective short-term means for rulers to raise large sums of money without having to secure consent. This was particularly useful when fighting wars. Monetary pressures were inevitable in bimetallic systems, where large and small coins exchanged at a fixed rate while the market price of the different constituent metals fluctuated. This would lead to one type of coin trading above par and frequent coin shortages, which the authorities would try to counteract through a depreciation. Once bank notes became a monopoly of the state, as they did in England, France, and the United States by the end of the nineteenth century, depreciation became simple to achieve by merely suspending convertibility of notes into coins and forcing more notes into circulation. Like physical coin debasements of earlier ages, depreciation led to considerable political conflict, particularly in the eighteenth and nineteenth centuries. Finally, political pressures from exporters, who favored depreciation;[47]debtors, who favored inflation; and miners, who favored their metal as the monetary standard over others, frequently acted against a common public interest in monetary stability.

The international monetary regime which emerged, with no formal agreement, around 1880 and survived until 1914, known as the classical gold standard, proved to be the zenith of the earth's commodity money system. The physical constraints of coins and the confluence of fiscal and political pressures to maintain the system provided a fortuitous environment for extended monetary stability and the consequent expansion of global trade and capital flows. Yet it carried within it "the seeds of its own destruction."[48]

So-called fiduciary money, notes and coins convertible into gold, provide a critical advantage over fiat money, convertible only into other denominations of itself, in that it provides a nominal anchor for the price level. That anchor has been criticized for being somewhat arbitrary, in that the price level depends on factors such as success in finding and mining gold, and demand for gold in nonmonetary uses. Nonetheless, having a firm anchor for the price level provides the sort of long-term monetary stability that is conspicuously lacking in most fiat regimes. The unambiguous advantage of a fiat regime over a fiduciary one, however, is that it is far less wasteful. Gold set aside in a vault for future redemptions is unlikely ever to be called upon, the more so when people are confident that it will always be there for that purpose. But if the gold is never going to be redeemed, it could, in principle, be put to much more productive use for or by the people.

The temptation to use gold for purposes other than sitting in reserve eventually proved too great to resist. This is the fundamental conundrum facing a fiduciary money regime: the better it works, the more compelling the logic for letting it slide toward a fiat regime.

Over the course of the late nineteenth and early twentieth centuries, governments reduced their gold reserves in favor of holding notes and deposits of Britain, the United States, and others whose notes were, in principle, convertible into gold. This practice was attractive for the seigniorage revenue it brought in to the governments. But as the gold standard slipped into a gold-exchange standard, swapping the public credibility of inviolable government commitment to gold convertibility for the seeming benefits of flexibility in managing reserves, a pyramid of credit was built up on an ever-shrinking base of gold. Foreign currencies represented only 12% of reserves of fifteen central banks in 1913, but 27% in 1925 and 42% in 1928.[49] The credibility which underpinned the system disintegrated, leading to recurrent crises. It collapsed once and for all with the onset of global deflation in the 1930s, as Britain in 1931, precipitated by a run on its insufficient gold stock, followed by the United States in 1933 and France in 1936, chose to suspend convertibility rather than honor redemption pledges.

This deflation, the flip-side of a fall in the price of gold, which brought price levels in 1933 back roughly to where they had been in 1914 (and 1832, for that matter), was the mirror image of the price rises that occurred during World War I, and was almost certainly inevitable given that the price of gold had not been raised during the 1920s to offset the wartime inflation. This effect—inflation on leaving a gold standard and deflation on returning to it at the same parity—was logically and historically to be expected. Had gold been revalued (that is, sterling devalued) in the 1920s, the system could conceivably have survived quite a bit longer. Failure to do so left sterling roughly 5% to 15% overvalued,[50] but the British government accepted this fate believing that more lasting damage would be done through abandonment of the so-called restoration rule of the gold standard—a return to the original parity after any period of conversion suspension.[51]

Mundell has argued that revaluing gold would not only have salvaged the gold standard but ensured "no Great Depression, no Nazi revolution, and no World War II."[52] Evidence from France supports Mundell on the economics, if not necessarily the politics. At the recommendation of one of the twentieth-century's greatest economists, Jacques Rueff, the French government reentered the gold standard in 1926 at one-fifth the prewar parity. The economy picked up robustly, without significant inflation. Mundell, however, perhaps underplays the odds that British abandonment of the "restoration rule" of the gold standard would on its own have been enough to collapse confidence in the system (sterling and the dollar being the only currencies freely convertible into gold in the period 1925–1930), while imposing on history a greater degree of monetary determinism than we can accept. There is, in any case, clearly a compelling historical correlation between monetary collapse and political upheaval which suggests a powerful causal relationship, and therefore also suggests caution in dismissing Mundell's political speculation lightly.

Revived in the form of a dollar-based gold-exchange standard after World War II, under the so-called Bretton Woods system, with currencies convertible into dollars and only dollars convertible into gold, for which the United States was only required to keep a 25% gold cover behind its currency and deposit liabilities, the last remnant of 2,500 years of commodity money collapsed in 1971 when the United States chose to unbind its money supply from the shackles of a gold pledge.[53]

The system's disintegration had become inevitable by the early 1960s, by which time prices in the United States had more than doubled since the gold price had been fixed by President Roosevelt at $35 an ounce in 1934. The United States was generating perpetual balance-of-payments deficits, which under a pure gold standard would automatically correct as gold would flow out of the United States and into creditor countries. But the United States had insufficient gold to allow for redemptions in gold, the nominal value of which had deteriorated dramatically with inflation. Creditors therefore simply accumulated more and more dollars which, when deposited in U.S. banks, led to credit *expansion*, rather than the *contraction* necessary to reverse the balance of payments deficits. This fuelled inflation not just in the United States, but worldwide, owing to the fixed rate of exchange. This vicious spiral made it inevitable that foreigners would at some point balk at further dollar accumulation, and demand redemption in gold instead. Since any significant redemption was likely to bring about a collapse of the credit structure in the United States—built as it was on the same dollars being constantly reused to support more borrowing, it was a logical certainty that, without a massive revaluation of gold, the United States would be forced to end convertibility in order to prevent the loss of its entire gold supply.[54]

Mundell, provocatively, characterized the dollar's supplanting of gold as an example of Gresham's law in action, or bad money driving out good.[55] In destroying the remnants of commodity-based money, the Nixon Administration can be said to have played the role, ordained by John Maynard Keynes, of "madmen in authority, who hear voices in the air . . . distilling their frenzy from some academic scribbler of a few years back."[56] That scribbler is Keynes himself, who in the 1930s called for national autarky in macroeconomic management. The big difference was that Keynes had wanted autarky supplemented with generalized capital controls, which the United States rejected. The modern era of fiat money and currency crises was born.

The Unbearable Lightness of Fiat Money

Such a power [of issuing paper currency], in whomsoever vested, is an intolerable evil. All variations in the value of the circulating medium are mischievous: they disturb existing contracts and expectations, and the liability to such changes renders every pecuniary engagement of long date entirely precarious. . . . Not to add, that issuers may have, and in the case of a government paper, always have, a direct interest in lowering the value of the currency, because it is the medium in which their own debts are computed.
—John Stuart Mill[57]

> The trouble with paper money is that it rewards the minority that can ma-
> nipulate money and makes fools of the generation that has worked and
> saved.
> —George Goodman (a.k.a. TV's "Adam Smith")[58]

Most of us on this planet have no recollection of a time in which true
money was gold, and bills and coins were claims on gold. Our conception
of money is of bills and coins adorned with national symbols and religious
incantations, and we have not the slightest expectation that any government office would redeem them for anything other than a different combination of the same bills and coins. What is so unusual about this is that
hardly any of us think it unusual, given the fact that it is such a radical de-
parture from all human history through 1971.

The post-1971 international monetary "system," certainly a misnomer,
is comprised of about 150 currencies, primarily national, all circulating in
the form of irredeemable IOUs, or IOUs redeemable only in other
IOUs. Some trade freely against others, some trade freely but with governments buying and selling so as to maintain a desired price, and some
are subject to exchange restrictions by their government issuers. This
would appear a recipe for global chaos, but it functions with far more
stability than one might expect, given the complete absence of agreed
rules or an agreed international money. This is because one currency, the
U.S. dollar, is widely accepted voluntarily as money for the purposes of
international transactions.

The mass psychology which sustains such a system is not amenable to
any falsifiable explanation, and what connection it might have with rationality, as economists would define it, can only be loosely inferred. As the
U.S. government, issuer of the de facto international currency, does not
commit to redeeming its money in terms of anything bearing intrinsic
value, the dollar is accepted as a global store of value under the broadly
held premise that it will, with a high degree of certainty, always be accepted
by Americans, as a last resort, in exchange for American assets bearing intrinsic value. Such a premise is itself premised on expectations regarding
the preservation of property rights in the United States, the perpetuation
of a large and prosperous U.S. economy, and an enduring commitment
on the part of the U.S. government strictly to limit dollar issuance so as to
control price inflation and maintain the integrity of debt contracts. This

psychology mirrors that which Cannan, whom we quoted earlier, described in early twentieth-century Britain.

This psychology, however, as history has shown, is fragile. The dollar's glory years were the period from 1959 to 1967, beginning right after Western European countries made their currencies convertible for current account transactions. The United States pegged the dollar to a fixed weight of gold, $35 an ounce, and the rest of the world pegged to the dollar. The dollar emerged as the key international reserve currency, driven by both growing cross-border private sector demand and central bank use for intervention. However, by the late 1960s, growing capital mobility was straining the fixed exchange rates, and the United States, trying to finance the Vietnam War partly through monetary expansion, failed to play its anchor role by maintaining price stability. Exporting its inflation around the world through the exchange parities, the United States triggered the collapse of the system by undermining the willingness of the others to continue accumulating dollars. When France decided to cash in its dollars for gold in 1971, President Nixon closed the "gold window," ending convertibility.[59] The era of the Great Inflation,[60] America's only peacetime inflation,[61] had begun.

Over the period of what has become known as the classical gold standard, 1881–1913, inflation in the developed world was virtually nonexistent, averaging a mere 0.3% in the United States (and the United Kingdom as well). Over the course of the Bretton Woods fixed exchange-rate period, 1946–1970, U.S. inflation was a moderate, but considerably higher, 2.8% (both before and after convertibility in 1959). It is important to note that the formal stated commitment to convertibility was actually much greater during the Bretton Woods regime than it was under the classical gold standard. The gold standard was, in effect, a set of implied commitments from governments and central banks, the critical ones of which simply evolved, whereas the Bretton Woods system was a formal international agreement, with rules and obligations—"the first monetary order designed by experts."[62] The vastly better inflation record under the gold standard, which survived nearly three times longer than the convertible phase of Bretton Woods, however, indicates that it was not words that lent credibility to policy, but rather the public's perception of governments' willingness to foreswear exercising sovereignty over money in pursuit of other short-term agendas which could be aided through inflation, such as reducing debt burdens or stimulating employment.

By the end of the 1960s, it had become clear that the U.S. government was far more committed to a loose money supply policy than to fulfilling any stated commitment to back the dollar with gold sales. Indeed, the United States had over the course of the 1960s erected numerous barriers to prevent conversion of dollars into gold.[63] As Brad De Long characterized the period, "No one had a mandate to fight inflation by allowing the unemployment rate to rise. Indeed, there was close to a mandate to do the reverse—to throw overboard any institutional arrangements, like the Bretton Woods international monetary system, as soon as they showed any sign of requiring that internal economic management be subordinated to external balance."[64]

From the beginning of the modern period of floating exchange rates, 1974, until 1982, three years into Paul Volcker's tenure as the Federal Reserve (Fed) chairman, inflation averaged 7.8%. Inflation surpassed 10% in 1981, and the prime interest rate surged to 21.5%. It was only the Volcker Fed's painful disinflationary high interest rate policy that restored credibility to U.S. monetary policy and, in consequence, to the dollar as an international store of value. U.S. inflation from 1983 to 1987, and under Alan Greenspan's tenure as Fed chairman from 1987 to 2005, averaged 3.1%. This dramatic and sustained improvement was accomplished without the adoption of any commodity anchor or formal inflation target. Indeed, the "dual mandate" established for the Fed in the Keynesian-flavored Full Employment and Balanced Growth Act of 1978 (known widely as the Humphrey-Hawkins Act) actually gave the Fed a wholly confused remit, which paints price stability as an objective only insofar as it could not be construed to inhibit growth and employment. As Arthur Burns, Fed chairman from 1970 to 1978, characterized the act's guiding economic ethics, "[It] continues the old game of setting a target for the unemployment rate. You set one figure. I set another figure. If your figure is low, you are a friend of mankind; if mine is high, I am a servant of Wall Street."[65] Given the politics of monetary policy at the time the act was written, it is in no sense hyperbole to accord the lion's share of the credit for the eventual defeat of inflation, and for the establishment of global faith in the new fiat dollar as a store of value, to the transparent personal economic convictions of Paul Volcker. He probably did more to liberate money from politics than any human in history.

It is remarkable how this short recent history of floating exchange rates among fiat currencies has affected popular thinking about what is eternally normal and proper in the economic system. In 1937, a leading monetary thinker and practitioner, Feliks Mlynarski, wrote that "the automatic functioning of the gold standard and a system of free trade were the leading ideas of the nineteenth century."[66] The U.S. plan for reviving the world economy after World War II, laid out by Harry Dexter White at Bretton Woods, was likewise based on the principle of free trade and a gold monetary anchor.[67] Yet in 2006 Senators Charles Schumer and Lindsey Graham wrote matter of factly in the *Wall Street Journal* that "one of the fundamental tenets of free trade is that currencies should float."[68] Such a "tenet" would have been considered monstrous during the previous great period of globalization—a subject to which we now turn.

A Tale of Two Globalizations

By 1914, there was hardly a village or town anywhere on the globe whose prices were not influenced by distant foreign markets, whose infrastructure was not financed by foreign capital, whose engineering, manufacturing, and even business skills were not imported from abroad, or whose labor markets were not influenced by the absence of those who had emigrated or by the presence of strangers who had immigrated.
—Kevin O'Rourke and Jeffrey Williamson[69]

Gold had done what no conqueror or religion had managed to do: it had brought virtually all people on earth into one social system.
—Jack Weatherford[70]

Lovers and haters of globalization tend to unite on one belief: that the world economy has become integrated to a wholly unprecedented degree. During the late nineteenth and early twentieth centuries, however, the global economy was actually comparably integrated on the basis of trade metrics and better integrated by a number of important financial metrics.

The ratio of U.S. merchandise trade to gross domestic product (GDP) is roughly the same today as it was a century ago. It declined dramatically in the 1920s and only began a sustained recovery after the 1970s, as shown in Figure 4.2. What is very different about the rise of global goods market

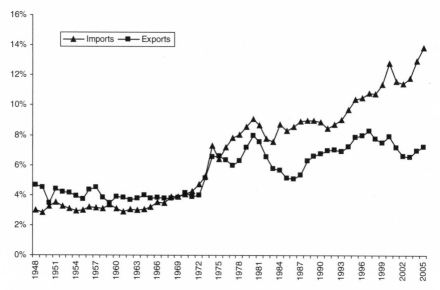

Figure 4.2. U.S. merchandise trade as a percent of GNP, 1948–2005.
Data source: U.S. Bureau of Economic Analysis.

integration in the late nineteenth century and the late twentieth century is that the former was overwhelmingly driven by a steep decline in transportation costs whereas the latter was driven far more by a decline in trade barriers. Between 1870 and 1913, the freight rate index on U.S. export routes fell by more than 40% in real terms. Tariffs, however, actually crept up in most European countries over this period. There is some debate about precisely how significant the decline in shipping costs has been in the post–World War II era,[71] but a strong consensus on the critical role of tariff cuts. In 1914, average tariffs were about 20%, and were still at that level in 1950. Today, however, they are under 5%.

These statistics do not, of course, take account of the rise of the service economy in the late twentieth century. U.S. tradable goods production is roughly half the proportion of total GDP that it was in 1900 (20% versus 40%). Figure 4.3 shows that U.S. merchandise exports as a percentage of production was about 2.5 times higher at the end of the twentieth century than it was at the beginning. This means that the segment of the economy devoted to merchandise production today, though smaller, is significantly more subject to the forces of international trade than it was a century ago.

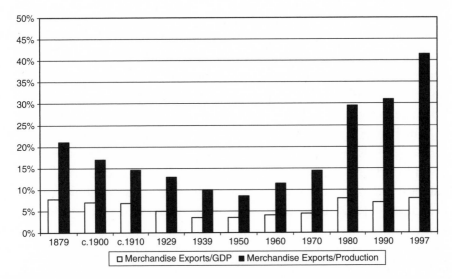

Figure 4.3. Trade in the U.S. economy.
Source: Bordo, Eichengreen, and Irwin (1999).

With the rapid growth of the service sector since the 1960s, U.S. service exports have risen from a mere 1% of GDP and 30% of merchandise exports to 3.2% of GDP and 41% of merchandise exports. Services were a miniscule portion of trade in the early 1900s. Finally, U.S. direct investment abroad was stable at about 6% of GDP in 1914 and 1960, but has since tripled. Similarly, foreign direct investment in the United States rose dramatically in the 1990s.[72]

In short, the world is indeed more integrated today in terms of trade than it had ever been previously, but the pace of integration in the late nineteenth century was certainly impressive by today's metrics. The more interesting findings come from the financial flows data.

Capital exports from Western Europe in the late nineteenth and early twentieth centuries were enormous by historical metrics, notwithstanding the hyperbole lavished on today's "global capital" by its fans and detractors. Mean current account surpluses and deficits as a percentage of GDP in 1880 were roughly twice as high as they are today. British net foreign investment reached 7.7% of GDP in 1872, and a high of 8.7% in 1911—nearly twice Japan and Germany's peaks in the late 1980s. Most of this was portfolio investment—stocks and bonds; 79% for Latin America, and 85% for

North America and Australia in 1913. And most of the debt held was government issued, as it is today for most of the developing world's foreign-held debt. Studies have also shown that domestic investment was less constrained by domestic savings, meaning that capital flows were doing more of the job of matching available capital to investment needs than they are today.[73]

Purchasing power parity, measured according to wholesale (that is, tradable goods) prices, and equalization of real interest rates across the world held to a degree not seen previously or since.[74] Commodity prices were aligned internationally about as well as they were across regions within countries.[75] Today, in contrast, we are so accustomed to a world of autarkic national currencies that we consider it right and normal not for commodity prices to align internationally, but for the *entire structure of prices* in each country to shift up and down, often dramatically, against the entire structure of other countries' prices. Thus a fall in the global (dollar) price of a commodity like coffee tends not to produce necessary diversification away from inefficient types of coffee production, but rather an engineered economy-wide inflation and devaluation in countries in which coffee exporters are politically powerful. The coffee price fails to perform its function of adapting coffee supply to demand; rather, the central bank distorts all other prices in the economy to prevent adaptation. This practice, virtually unique to the late twentieth century, is at the root of development stagnation for so many poorer countries.

There are many reasons why economies became dramatically more integrated after 1870, both within and across countries. Among these are tremendous technological advances in transportation and communication, particularly the railroad, steamship, telegraph, cable, and refrigeration. The spread of free-trade thinking from Britain to the European continent, underpinned by vested interests in Germany and France which saw greater export opportunities afforded through trade liberalization, also contributed to large declines in some import tariffs. But the disintegration of markets internationally, particularly capital markets, coincided strongly with the tribulations and eventual collapse of the classical gold standard after 1914. The heyday of globalization was an historical period in which monetary nationalism was widely seen as a sign of backwardness; adherence to a universally acknowledged standard of value a sign of abiding among the civilized nations. And those nations that adhered most reliably to the gold standard (such as Canada, Australia, and the United States) paid lower borrowing rates in the international capital markets than those which adhered less (such as Argentina, Brazil, and Chile).[76] The gold standard not only reduced exchange risk, but country default risk. The evidence suggests strongly that being on the gold standard represented the most credible form of commitment to pursuing prudent fiscal and monetary policies over time, given the ever-present temptation to inflate away the burden of debt and manufacture seigniorage revenues.

As notable an opponent of the gold standard as Karl Polanyi took it as obvious that monetary sovereignty was incompatible with globalization. Focusing on nineteenth-century Britain's interest in growing world trade, he stated that "nothing else but commodity money could serve this end for the obvious reason that token money, whether bank or fiat, cannot circulate on foreign soil. Hence the gold standard—the accepted name for a system of international commodity money—came to the fore."[77] Yet what Polanyi considered nonsensical—global trade in goods, services, and capital intermediated by national token monies—is exactly the way in which globalization is advancing today. And national token monies, we argue, have turned out to be the Achilles' heel of globalization. Were it not for the regular recurrence of devastating national financial crises, of which token monies in open economies are the root cause, resistance to globalization would be far less virulent and carry far less resonance.

To be sure, financial crises were not invented in the late twentieth century. They did occur under the nineteenth-century gold standard, but the credibility of the Bank of England's commitment to convertibility meant that short-term capital flows actually played a highly *stabilizing* role, allowing rapid adjustment to balance-of-payment disturbances through interest-rate arbitrage: trade deficits not offset by an inflow of long-term capital could be reliably financed by short-term inflows stimulated by a modest rise in short-term interest rates.[78] The cross-border flow of gold itself was peripheral to the adjustment mechanism. Given how commonplace is the perception today that short-term capital flows are *inherently* destabilizing, the lessons of the gold-based globalization era simply must be relearned. Just as the prodigious daily capital flows between New York and California are so uneventful that no one even comments on them, capital flows between countries sharing a single currency, such as the dollar or the euro, or using currencies which are merely claims on gold, as in the nineteenth century, attract not the slightest attention from even the most passionate anti-globalization activists.

That the destabilizing effects of today's short-term cross-border capital flows should be considered, even by economists who should know better, a manifestation of "market imperfection" or "irrationality" is, to us, astounding. The fundamental difference between capital flows under indelibly fixed and nonfixed exchange rates was well-known generations ago, decades before the modern era of globalization. Consider this excerpt from a lecture by Friedrich Hayek in 1937:

> Where the possible fluctuations of exchange rates are confined to narrow limits above and below a fixed point, as between the two gold points, the effect of short term capital movements will be on the whole to reduce the amplitude of the actual fluctuations, since every movement away from the fixed point will as a rule create the expectation that it will soon be reversed. That is, short term capital movements will on the whole tend to relieve the strain set up by the original cause of a temporarily adverse balance of payments. If exchanges, however, are variable, the capital movements will tend to work in the same direction as the original cause and thereby to intensify it.[79]

This was because "Every suspicion that exchange rates were likely to change in the near future would create an additional powerful motive for shifting funds from the country whose currency was likely to fall or to the country whose currency was likely to rise. I should have thought that the experience of the whole post-[first world] war period and particularly of the last few years had so amply confirmed what one might expect *a priori* that there could be no reasonable doubt about this."[80] Hayek's logic was mirrored precisely by the radical change in capital flow behavior that accompanied the crumbling of a credible international monetary anchor between the first and second world wars. In the words of Ragnar Nurkse,

> After the monetary upheavals of the [first world] war and early post-war years, private short-term capital movements tended

frequently to be disequilibrating rather than equilibrating: a depreciation of the exchange or a rise in discount rates, for example, instead of attracting short-term balances from abroad, tended sometimes to affect people's anticipation in such a way as to produce the opposite result. In these circumstances the provision of the equilibrating capital movements required for the maintenance of exchange stability devolved more largely on the central banks and necessitated a larger volume of official foreign exchange holdings.[81]

This is not simply a matter of whether exchange rates are "fixed" or floating. Exchange rates were fixed within the European Monetary System in the late twentieth century, but capital flows served to *destabilize* rather than stabilize it. Interest rate increases will not automatically attract capital flows where the credibility of the fixed parity is inherently weak. This goes to the heart of the difference between the gold standard and fixed exchange rates among fiat currencies: the former was based on a highly credible commodity standard in which the market, rather than government, determined the money stock, whereas the latter is based on an agreement between fiat money issuers, each of which faces incentives to manipulate the money stock in a way which undermines the exchange rate commitment.[82] The presence of active monetary policymakers will invariably undermine the stabilizing tendency of capital flows.

Yet, perversely as a matter of both monetary logic and history, the most notable economist critic of globalization, Joseph Stiglitz, has argued passionately for monetary nationalism as the *remedy* for the economic chaos of currency crises.[83] When millions of people, locals and foreigners, are selling a national currency in fear of impending default, the Stiglitz solution is for the issuing government simply to decouple from the world: lower interest rates, devalue, and stiff the lenders. It is precisely this thinking, a throwback to the disastrous 1930s, which is at the root of the cycle of crisis that has infected modern globalization. Again, Hayek foresaw it in 1937:

> The modern idea apparently is that never under any circumstance must an outflow of capital be allowed to raise interest rates at home, and the advocates of this view seem to be satisfied

that if the central banks are not committed to maintain a particular parity they will have no difficulty either in preventing an outflow of capital altogether or in offsetting its effect by substituting additional bank credit for the funds which have left the country.

It is not easy to see on what this confidence is founded. So long as the outward flow of capital is not effectively prevented by other means, a persistent effort to keep interest rates low can only have the effect of prolonging this tendency indefinitely and of bringing about a continuous and progressive fall of the exchanges. Whether the outward flow of capital starts with a withdrawal of balances held in the country by foreigners, or with an attempt on the parts of nationals of the country to acquire assets abroad, it will deprive banking institutions at home of funds which they were able to lend, and at the same time lower the exchanges. If the central bank succeeds in keeping interest rates low in the first instance by substituting new credits for the capital which has left the country, it will not only perpetuate the conditions under which the export of capital has been attractive; the effect of capital exports on the rates of exchange will, as we have seen, tend to become self-inflammatory and a "flight of capital" will set in. At the same time the rise of prices at home will increase the demand for loans because it means an increase in the "real" rate of profit. And the adverse balance of trade which must necessarily continue while part of the receipts from exports is used to repay loans or to make loans abroad, means that the supply of real capital and therefore the "natural" or "equilibrium" rate of interest in the country will rise. It is clear that under such conditions the central bank could not, merely by keeping its discount rate low, prevent a rise of interest rates without at the same time bringing about a major inflation.[84]

Hayek goes on to explain how the monetary nationalists must then inevitably argue for capital controls, as Stiglitz has of course done, in order to stop the people from disturbing the government's control of national credit conditions. But the government cannot stop there, as "exchange control designed to prevent effectively the outflow of capital would really have to involve a complete control of foreign trade, since of course any variation in the terms of credit on exports or imports means an international capital movement."[85]

Indeed, this is precisely what the Argentine government has been doing since 2002. Since writing off $80 billion worth, or 75% in nominal terms, of its debts, the government has been resorting to ever-more intrusive means in order to counteract the ability of its citizens to protect what remains of their savings and to buy or sell with foreigners.

In 2003, the Argentine government introduced capital controls and domestic price controls, targeting the energy sector. The goal was to keep the exchange rate from rising in order to "maintain export competitiveness" while simultaneously containing the inflation that policy was giving rise to.

In 2004, energy sector controls were extended to include export taxes on crude oil, in order to "insulate the domestic price from the full effect of international fluctuations,"[86] in the words of the economy minister, and partial export bans were imposed on natural gas and oil. President Kirchner excoriated gas and oil companies for "underinvestment," though investment was irrational given the price controls. The government founded a state energy company, Enarsa, which it was then able to order to undertake unprofitable investments. The government also began the first of its major attacks on foreign investors, repealing a 1997 airwave licensing contract with a French company, Thales Spectrum, declaring the precrisis privatizations to have been a failure.

In 2005, President Kirchner called for a nationwide boycott of Shell after it raised Argentine oil prices in line with global oil prices. French company Suez announced it was leaving the country, selling its controlling share in Aguas Argentina, the Buenos Aires water supplier, after years of losses following a 2001 freeze in utility prices. New currency rules were imposed, forcing companies to convert most foreign proceeds into pesos and limiting the amount of foreign currency that individuals could acquire to invest abroad. Government price controls were extended throughout the economy. President Kirchner attacked supermarkets for rising inflation, which had surpassed 12%, demanding that they accept "voluntary" price controls. Incoming economy minister

Felisa Miceli dismissed her predecessor's concerns about rising inflation as "an argument to maintain low wages." She announced that she would not resort to "orthodox methods" of inflation control, such as tightening money supply or raising interest rates.[87]

In 2006, President Kirchner expanded his price control campaign to foreign consumer goods companies, summoning executives from Procter & Gamble, Unilever, and Kimberly-Clark to demand that they stop raising prices. Targeted companies complied by reducing the size of their products, thus raising unit price without raising the shelf price. Local textile companies were next in line, being forced to sign an agreement with the government pledging a price freeze. In an effort to hold the official inflation rate at 1% per month, President Kirchner then called for "voluntary" price freezes on about 300 products, such as sugar, flour, noodles, bread, shampoo, and pencils, targeting particularly component products of the official consumer price index. Beef exports were also banned in an attempt to increase domestic supply, but this had the effect of exacerbating the trend of Argentine landowners converting cattle pastures to soya bean fields. "Voluntary" price control agreements were further extended to items as diverse as medicines and private school tuitions. In October, President Kirchner announced that price controls expiring at the end of 2006 would be extended until the end of 2007, just after the scheduled autumn presidential election. Kirchner's successor—his wife, Cristina Elizabet Fernández de Kirchner—further extended the price controls and export taxes.

What used to be the most cosmopolitan nation in Latin America is now following the Stiglitz path of monetary nationalism religiously. And the results, when crises spread yet again to the likes of Venezuela, Turkey, Indonesia, and other countries struggling to reconcile monetary nationalism with globalization, will almost certainly be as ordained by Hayek:

> . . . it is an illusion that it would be possible, while remaining a member of the international commercial community, to prevent disturbances from the national monetary policy such as would be indicated if the country were a closed community. It is for this reason that the ideology of Monetary Nationalism has proved, and if it remains influential will prove to an even greater extent in

the future, to be one of the main forces destroying what remnants of an international economic system we still have . . .

But even more serious seem to me the political effects of the intensification of the differences in the standard of life between different countries to which it [will] lead. It does not need much imagination to visualize the new sources of international friction which such a situation would create.[88]

Argentina could not be a more fitting fulfillment of Hayek's fears. Since the 2002 devaluation, the Argentine government has been in continuous conflict with its European counterparts over the expropriations imposed on the latter's bondholders and corporate direct investors, and the population has turned viscerally anti-American, anti-IMF, and anti-globalization.

The Dollar's Destiny

The dollar's role as a global currency is defined largely by the degree to which it dominates the foreign exchange reserves of the world's central banks as well as the invoicing of international trade, the two of which being related, as governments hold reserves partly to pay their import bills. Roughly 64% of global foreign exchange reserves are denominated in dollars, up about eight percentage points since 1995 but down twenty since 1973. About 60% of world trade is invoiced in dollars, the same as for the British pound sterling between 1860 and 1914.[89]

The logic behind the rise of the U.S. dollar as the foundation of international commerce and finance has been concisely captured by Filippo Cesarano of the Bank of Italy:

The special role of the United States arose spontaneously, driven by market forces behind the diffusion of a vehicle currency that, from a theoretical point of view, mirrors the origin of money. The information-producing mechanism inherent in the development of an exchange medium is replicated at the international level, leading all countries to converge on the use of a single currency internationally. The smoothness of this market-led process contrasts with the difficulty of designing reform schemes based on a supranational money, like the Keynes Plan, arising from the problem of sharing sovereignty.

The use of a currency as a vehicle itself reinforces that currency's usefulness. Hence, only a particularly disruptive shock can alter the equilibrium and usher in a new international money. Throughout history, the currencies of the dominant powers have succeeded one another as international monies: the Roman-Byzantine monetary order, which lasted twelve centuries; the Venetian ducat of the late Middle Ages; Spanish domination in the early Renaissance, later challenged by the Dutch; and sterling three centuries later.[90]

The dollar's fate as a global currency, however, is neither etched in the fabric of the cosmos nor threatened by policy abroad—at least not on its own. It is America's blessing and burden to be the master of the dollar's fate. Political stability, low inflation, fiscal rectitude, and sensible tax and regulatory policies will ensure a dollar that continues to function as a reliable store of value, giving foreigners little more incentive to abandon dollars for euros or some yet-to-be-created world money than they currently have to abandon English for French or Esperanto. Britain's fall from empirely grace is widely assumed to be the cause of the decline of sterling's international primacy, but cause and effect between power and economics worked in both directions, and the decline of the pound's international role was much more rapid than can be explained by politics alone. As Barry Eichengreen has concluded, "this is a lesson of British history in the sense that an inflation rate that ran over 3 times U.S. rates over the first three quarters of the 20th century, in conjunction with repeated devaluations against the dollar, played a major role in sterling's loss of reserve currency status."[91] Chinn and Frankel use regression analysis to illustrate plausible scenarios in which the dollar is overtaken by the euro as the leading international reserve currency by 2025, driven largely by a combination of new euro-area entrants and continued deficit-driven dollar depreciation.[92]

The weakness of the dollar's position today is, interestingly enough, captured vividly by Jacques Rueff, writing in 1965, a half-decade before the collapse of the Bretton Woods dollar-based gold-exchange standard:

. . . the gold-exchange standard attains such a degree of absurdity that no human brain having the power to reason can defend it. What is the essence of the regime, and what is its difference from the gold standard? It is that when a country with a key currency has a deficit in its balance of payments—that is to say, the United States, for example—it pays the creditor country dollars, which end up with its central bank. But the dollars are of no use in Bonn, or in Tokyo, or in Paris. The very same day, they are re-lent to the New York money market, so that they return to the place of origin. Thus the debtor country does not lose what the creditor country has gained. So the key-currency country never feels the effect of a deficit in its balance of payments. And the main consequence is that there is no reason whatever for the deficit to disappear, because it does not appear. Let me be more positive: if I had an agreement with my tailor that whatever money I pay him he returns to me the very same day as a loan, I would have no objection at all to ordering more suits from him.[93]

Today, with the U.S. current account deficit running at over 5% of GDP, necessitating the import of about $2 billion a day to sustain, the United States is in the fortunate position of the suit-buyer whose Chinese tailor instantaneously returns all his payments in the form of a loan—generally purchases of U.S. treasury bonds. The current account deficit is partially fuelled by the budget deficit, which will soar in the next decade in the absence of reforms to curtail federal "entitlement" spending on medical care and retirement benefits. At the time of writing, the Fed funds rate is well below inflation, which has also provoked the most explicit comments ever from Chinese and other creditor-country officials about loose U.S. monetary policy undermining the dollar's "status as the world currency."[94] The United States, as well as the Chinese tailor, must therefore be concerned with the sustainability of what Rueff called an "absurdity."[95] In the absence of renewed long-term fiscal and monetary prudence, the United States risks undermining the faith foreigners have placed in its management of the dollar—that it can continue to restrain inflation without having to resort to growth-crushing interest rate hikes as a means of ensuring continued high-capital inflows.

Mythology versus Psychology

Money speaks sense in a language all nations understand.
—Aphra Behn, Surinam-born dramatist (1677)[96]

So much of barbarism . . . still remains in the transactions of most civilized
nations, that almost all independent countries choose to assert their nation-
ality by having, to their own inconvenience and that of their neighbours, a
peculiar currency of their own.
—John Stuart Mill[97]

We contrast the mythology of money, which has metamorphosed over
history in tandem with religious and political thought, and the psychology of money, which is constant. Myths are shared popular beliefs over
ideals which need not be accepted as true in an empirical sense in order to
compel desires and behavior. A Latin American may oppose dollarization
and international capital flows as violations of state sovereignty while simultaneously demanding dollars in payment and sending them abroad for
safekeeping. Here, myth and psychology clash.

No one has illuminated the psychology of money more compellingly
than Georg Simmel. If we wish to make sense of the role of money in late
nineteenth-century globalization, Simmel or Polanyi's accounts will do
equally well. But if we wish to make sense of its role in late twentieth-
century globalization, only Simmel's account will do.

"The spread of trade relations," Simmel argued, "requires a valuable
currency, if only because the transportation of money over long distances
makes it desirable that the value should be concentrated in a small volume.
Thus, the historical empires and the trading states with extensive markets
were always driven toward money with high material value," such as gold.
"When the scope of trading expands," he continued, "the currency also
has to be made acceptable and tempting to foreigners and to trading partners," something which is missing in most of the world today—a world in
which only dollars and a handful of alternatives have achieved acceptabil-
ity. Simmel continued:

> The extension of the economic area leads, *ceteris paribus*, to a re-
> duction of direct contact; the reciprocal knowledge of conditions
> becomes less complete, confidence more limited, and the possibil-

ity of getting claims satisfied is less certain. Under such conditions, no one will supply commodities if the money given in exchange can be used only in the territory of the buyer and is of doubtful value elsewhere. The seller will demand money that is valuable in itself, that is to say accepted everywhere. The increase in the material value of money signifies the extension of the circle of subjects in which it is generally accepted, while in a smaller circle its negotiability may be secured by social, legal and personal guarantees and relationships.[98]

Polanyi would have agreed, and, equating gold with material value, concluded that gold was a necessary, albeit undesirable, foundation for widespread international trade. Here Simmel departs from Polanyi, presaging the emergence nearly a century later of a global fiat money, the U.S. dollar, which would engender widespread confidence even in the absence of any material value:

> If we suppose that the usefulness of money is the reason for its acceptance, its material value may be regarded as a pledge for that usefulness; it may have a zero value if negotiability is assured by other means, and it will be high when the risk is great. However, expanding economic relations eventually produce in the enlarged, and finally international, circle the same features that originally characterized only closed groups; economic and legal conditions overcome the spatial separation more and more, and they come to operate just as reliably, precisely and predictably over a great distance as they did previously in local communities. To the extent that this happens, the pledge, that is the intrinsic value of the money, can be reduced. . . . Even though we are still far from having a close and reliable relationship within or between nations, the trend is undoubtedly in that direction. The association and unification of constantly expanding social groups, supported by laws, customs and interests, is the basis for the diminishing intrinsic value of money and its replacement by functional value.[99]

Simmel correctly adjudged that ever closer interactions among people living in far-flung states would lead to a convergence of expectations and interests that would eventually pave the way for international money divorced from gold. This mass psychology is as much to be desired for its political benefits as for its economic benefits, for, as Simmel argues, money is a "reified social function," a physical representation of a voluntary bonding among individuals, and the exchange it facilitates is a *creator* of such bonds rather than a result of them: "The function of exchange, as a direct interaction between individuals, becomes crystallized in the form of money as an independent structure. The exchange of products of labour, or of any other possessions, is obviously one of the purest and most primitive forms of human socialization; not in the sense that 'society' already existed and then brought about acts of exchange but, on the contrary, that exchange is one of the functions that creates an inner bond between men—a society, in place of a mere collection of individuals."[100]

This is perhaps one of the most eloquent expressions of the desirability of globalization ever written. The ability of people to enter into freely sought exchanges is what makes of them a society—rather than a family, on the one hand, or a mere assortment of individuals on the other—and people who perceive themselves to be part of a common society are more likely to behave cooperatively and less likely to address differences through violence. Unfortunately, the myth of monetary sovereignty, which we who were raised in a world of national fiat currencies have all come to share to a greater or lesser degree, in spite of our deeper psychological impulses which contradict it, too often functions to bar the political way forward.

5

GLOBALIZATION AND MONETARY SOVEREIGNTY

Money and the Global Economy

In chapter 4, we contrasted the mythology and psychology of money. The powerful mythology surrounding money's status as a timeless manifestation of state sovereignty is in constant tension with the psychology of its users, who in their buying, selling, saving, and lending behavior treat it entirely as a private asset.

As a tool of state political and economic control, money needs to be mutable in value. In order for the state to use money to influence the way the national economy operates, central banks must be able to control the levers determining the rate of change of domestic prices (that is, the inflation rate) as well as the exchange rate against other currencies. This implies a natural difference between money's acquisitive power domestically and internationally. Central banks need to sever the connections between the domestic and international financial markets in order to conduct monetary policy—to exercise monetary sovereignty. Otherwise, international markets, not the central bank, dictate national monetary conditions such as interest rates. A currency of immutable value is not compatible with monetary policy because the very aim of such policy is to allow for directed change in the value of money—to reduce it by lowering the rate of interest (or increasing the rate of money creation), or to raise it by increasing the rate of interest (or reducing the rate of money creation).

Users of money, however, even those who hoe passionately to the mythology of monetary sovereignty, invariably behave consistent with the belief that money worth the name should maintain its value across both time and space. They take action, often in conflict with the central bank's aims, to ensure that its value does not disintegrate in storage or in future transactions with foreigners. Money which people value is inherently an integrating and globalizing vehicle. Its value lies not in its capacity to change and divide, but to endure and unify.

Historically, protectionism and monetary nationalism have tended to coincide. In the eighteenth century, when mercantilist economic policies were in vogue, governments were frequently devaluing their currencies relative to the precious metals that defined them. Seen from an international perspective, then, national monies fluctuated against one another, which was consistent with broader government efforts at the time to isolate their economies.

In the late nineteenth and early twentieth centuries, economic and monetary policies also coincided, but this time on the side of globalization. The trade liberalization that marked the period was accompanied by widespread international commitment to a universal monetary standard, gold, which excluded the possibility of governments exercising monetary sovereignty. The mythology of money thereby converged with the psychology of money internationally to a degree never seen before or since.

In the 1930s, in the midst of the Great Depression, countries returned to the ideas of economic and monetary nationalism, retreating from both free trade and a universal monetary standard. Protectionism went hand in hand with continuous competitive devaluation.

After World War II, the victorious powers began a conscious effort to return to the free trade of the past and to the well-ordered monetary organization that had prevailed under the gold standard, establishing the General Agreement on Tariffs and Trade (GATT) for the attainment of the first objective and the International Monetary Fund (IMF) for the second. The GATT was to preside over the dismantling of the complex structures of protection that had been put in place during the Depression era, while the IMF was to become the central institution in a modified gold-standard system known as a "gold-exchange standard": countries would define the value of their currencies in terms of the U.S. dollar, and the dollar would be defined in terms of gold (a dollar would be redeemable for 1/35th of an ounce of gold). The idea was that the value of the dollar in terms of gold would remain stable through time. In essence, the victors envisioned a return to globalization along the dimensions of both trade and money.

Yet, in the last third of the twentieth century, the two dimensions of economic policy veered apart. Trade was increasingly liberalized, whereas money was resubsumed under the umbrella of state economic sovereignty. Following President Nixon's severing of the dollar gold link in 1971—an inevitable result of deep flaws in the operation of the gold-exchange standard, masterfully laid bare by Jacques Rueff in *The Monetary Sin of the West* (1972)—all the world's national monies became irredeemable, allowing states to pursue independent activist monetary policies. As in the mercantilist eighteenth century, this meant that currencies continuously fluctuated in value against one another, although governments intervened in currency markets to varying degrees in order to influence or control their currency's value, generally against the dollar.

Thus, the traditional pairing of trade and monetary regimes was broken in the last third of the twentieth century. A trade regime consistent with globalization is coexisting with a monetary regime traditionally associated with ideas of unlimited state economic sovereignty. Moreover, financial globalization, the free movement of money across borders, is coexisting with monetary sovereignty, the right of states to determine what is money within their borders.

This decoupling poses some important questions. In particular, is there a contradiction between globalization in trade and finance, on the one hand, and monetary sovereignty on the other? If so, what are the consequences for the world economy? Will something give and, if so, which will it be—globalization or monetary sovereignty?

We began this book with an exploration of the historical, political, and philosophical aspects of sovereignty and globalization. Over the next three chapters, we focus on the hard economic issues raised by the tension between them. We will set out by juxtaposing the pressures that the emerging economic geography is imposing on the international monetary system with what the system can reasonably deliver. The landscape is a treacherous one—in the here and now for smaller and poorer countries, but, in the longer run, as we will argue in chapter 7, for all of us.

The New Economic Geography

Instantaneous global communications and, by historical standards, extremely low transportation costs have changed the economic geography of the world, producing the phenomenon we refer to today as globalization. But the same term has also been used to refer to an earlier era of economic integration—the one that began with the Industrial Revolution and ended with the Great Depression. In between the two great eras of globalization, from the Great Depression until the end of World War II, trade-limiting policies of national economic sovereignty prevailed. The key difference, for our purposes, between the two eras is the nature of what is being globalized.

In the nineteenth century, globalization was primarily a phenomenon of trade in commodities and finished goods. International trade carried raw materials from developing to developed countries. Finished goods were then distributed around the world. While globalization brought centers of industrial production nearer to their sources of supply and their foreign sales points, it did not significantly affect the way in which production was organized within firms and industries.

The new globalization is much broader. Modern connectivity has made it possible to coordinate complex tasks at a great distance. As a result, chains of production that were traditionally tightly organized within a single location are becoming more and more spread out internationally.[1] Product subcomponents can be assembled around the globe in accordance with the classical economic concept of "comparative advantage," whereby countries specialize in economic activities in which, relative to other activities they could focus on, they have a leg up on others. Thus while the old globalization extended trade to the ends of the earth, today the chain of production itself is being globalized.

Just a few decades ago, foreign investment in developing countries was driven by two main motivations: to extract raw materials for export, and to gain access to local markets heavily protected against import competition. Attracting the first kind of investment was simple for countries endowed with the right natural resources. Companies readily went into war zones to extract oil. Governments pulled in the second kind of investment by erecting tariff and other barriers to competition so as to compensate foreigners for an otherwise unappealing business climate. Foreign investors brought money and know-how in return for monopolies in the domestic market.

This cozy scenario was undermined by the advent of globalization. The trade liberalization of the past two decades opened most developing countries to imports in return for export access to developed countries, and huge declines in the cost of communication and transport have revolutionized the economics of global production and distribution. The reasons why foreign companies invest in developing countries have in consequence changed. The motivation to extract commodities remains, but the motivation to gain access to domestic markets has largely disappeared. With the exception of larger developing economies such as China and Brazil, it is generally no longer important to produce in a country in order to sell in it.

But globalization has produced a compelling new reason to invest in developing countries: taking advantage of lower production costs, and integrating local facilities into global chains of production and distribution. Now that the market is global rather than local, countries compete with others for investment, and the factors defining an attractive investment climate have changed dramatically. Offering foreign investors protection against local and import competition no longer motivates them. On the contrary, since protection increases the prices of goods that foreign investors need as inputs for production, it reduces their global competitiveness.

Globalization is extending a ladder of economic prosperity to the developing world, comprised of rungs with higher and higher value-added work, on which countries can climb by developing their skills base. The key is management capacity, which is concentrated in developed countries and, until recent decades, could largely be applied only locally. With modern communications and transport, however, production managers at a Swedish cell phone company can apply their skills globally, allowing them to produce far more phones with far less capital by allocating specialized tasks across far-flung locales. This is Adam Smith's famous pin factory example writ global. Just as division of labor in the manufacture of items as simple as pins can be shown to increase pin output per worker hundreds or even thousands of times, the global connectivity revolution is introducing startling productivity gains across a rapidly expanding array of goods and services—all driven by the same simple idea, specialization, that Smith showed to be the supply-side driver of the eighteenth-century Industrial Revolution.

What does this process mean for work and wages in the developed world? Most industrial processes involve activities with widely differing requirements in terms of skills and knowledge. For example, the production of an automobile requires the inputs of highly skilled engineers to design the product and the production line, and well-trained workers to control the machines producing delicate components. But it also requires much less sophisticated work to produce the simpler components. Before contemporary globalization, the limited ability of firms to coordinate complex tasks from afar meant that all of these components had to be produced in the same location, and often in the same building. This is why the production of certain products tended to concentrate in limited geographic areas, such as cars in Detroit and medicines in Zurich. The suppliers of parts tended to cluster around the main users of their wares.

The mix of complex and simple jobs had a positive impact on the wages of less skilled workers. High incomes earned by high-skill-level workers supported the prices of nontradable goods in their locale. These high nontradable prices, relative to places where high-skilled workers were not prevalent, in turn supported the wage level for unskilled workers. Thus unskilled workers in developed countries tended to have much higher incomes than workers with limited skills in developing countries. It is the main reason that companies now move their low value-added activities to developing countries, and why globalization is so strongly opposed in some quarters in developed countries.

The wages of the unskilled have deteriorated relative to those of the skilled. From 1972 to 1992, the income gap between college and high school graduates in the United States increased from 43% to 82%, while that of people with advanced degrees over high school graduates more than tripled, from 72% to 250%.[2] The burgeoning wage gap between highly and minimally educated workers is starkly illustrated in Figure 5.1. As seen

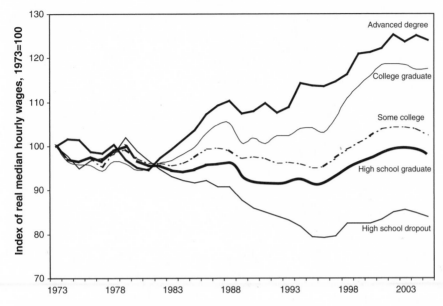

Figure 5.1. U.S. wages and education, 1973–2005.
Data source: Mishel, Bernstein, and Allegretto (2007).

in Figure 5.2, the real wages of the unskilled, which had been growing faster than gross domestic product (GDP) per capita until the late 1970s, began to fall thereafter. They recovered somewhat during the boom of the 1990s, but by 2006 they were at the same level as in 1968 — a period over which GDP per capita doubled.

Throughout much of the twentieth century, the U.S. educational system increased the supply of skilled workers faster than technology was driving up demand for them. A slowdown in the pace of educational advancement has, however, over the past three decades significantly increased the wage premium for each additional year of university education.[3]

It should be clear that any viable long-term policy solution to the problem of deteriorating wages among the unskilled in advanced countries cannot be focused on keeping them employed in low value-added jobs, but must instead help them move up the value-added ladder. Reducing the cost of labor, as with all other production inputs, through automation and "outsourcing" to cheaper locales is a process that has played out continuously, in myriad contexts, since the Industrial Revolution. Technological

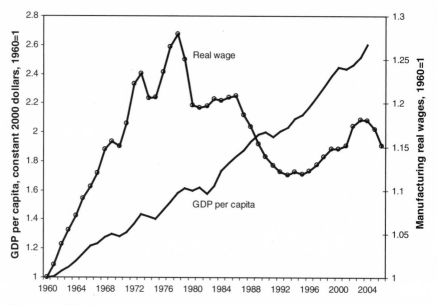

Figure 5.2. U.S. GDP per capita and manufacturing real wages, 1960–2006.
Data source: World Bank World Development Indicators and IMF International Financial Statistics.

advance, for example, led to the migration of rural workers to urban areas, where they generally became industrial workers with much higher incomes. Seventeen percent of the U.S. labor force was employed in agriculture in 1940 compared with only 1.5% today,[4] and the United States is a vastly richer country now because of it. Cities themselves have undergone similar transformations. The leather industry, for example, migrated out of New York City to make room for much higher value-added industries, such as financial services. These transitions clearly did not benefit everyone at the time. Had policies been enacted to stop them occurring, however, the economic effects would have been overwhelmingly negative for many millions more in successor generations.

Higher value-added jobs, of course, do not simply appear instantaneously whenever lower value-added jobs disappear. Policies supporting the supply side of the labor market (in particular, education and training) and the demand side (in particular, reducing unnecessary costs of business start-up and expansion) are vital. One of the problems that Europe is facing in adapting to globalization is that it is not generating sufficient new employment in higher value-added activities, largely because of policies that inflate the cost to businesses of hiring and firing, and thereby discourage the former.

Developing countries need policy change as well. In order to take advantage of work opportunities that, prior to globalization, used to be available only to rich country workers, developing countries need to dismantle the trade protections they built up over decades to promote "import substitution"—that is, blocking imports in order to encourage locally produced substitutes.

Clearly, those that benefit from trade protection (not least of which politicians) have an interest in opposing change and supporting policies which isolate the country from the rest of the world. Yet it is clear from Figure 5.3 that the developing countries that have embraced globalization, mainly in Asia and Eastern Europe, have been closing their per capita income gap with the rich world, whereas those that are actively resisting it, found mostly in Latin America, Africa, and the Middle East, are lagging behind—so badly, in most cases, that their per capita income gap with the rich world has actually been widening.

The closed national economy is a dead-end street. No country has succeeded in developing on that model, even with massive amounts of foreign aid. Romain Wacziarg and Karen Horn Welch examined the fifty developing national economies that converged on the rich ones in the 1990s, and found that only five could be classified as "closed"—and two of these five were China and India, whose convergence only began with their dramatic openings over recent decades.[5]

Development requires helping the poor find their way from farm to factory, and from factory to office, classroom, and laboratory. This requires massive investment, which in turn requires sophisticated financial intermediation. It is for this reason that the trade and financial dimensions of globalization are complementary.

Money Matters

Monetary stability and access to sophisticated financial services have emerged as essential local components of today's investment climate. Today's globalized trade is not limited to physical goods. It includes services,

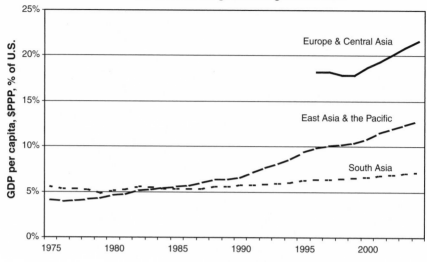

The winners, integrated into globalization...

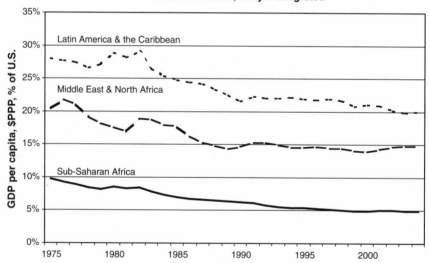

...and the losers, not yet integrated

Figure 5.3. Globalization: Winners and losers.
Data source: World Bank World Development Indicators.

particularly financial services, as it did in the nineteenth century, when Britain and, to a smaller extent, France, financed the economic development of the United States,[6] Canada, Australia, New Zealand, and large parts of Asia, Africa, and Latin America. In those years, as today, international lending and investment were major sources of international financial flows. During the interwar interregnum of economic sovereignty, in contrast, governments disdained and discouraged capital flows. They slapped strict controls on them. Trade, though highly restricted itself, drove international economic relations, and capital flows occurred almost exclusively for the purpose of settling trade imbalances. Today, in contrast, autonomous capital flows actually *cause* the changes in trade (and other current account transactions) necessary to bring the balance of payments into equilibrium. We discuss this phenomenon in greater detail in chapter 7.

Developing countries are poorly positioned in today's global financial system. Figure 5.4 shows how much higher inflation and lending rates are in Latin American countries with national currencies than in those which simply use the U.S. dollar as their currency: Ecuador, El Salvador, and Panama. (We exclude Brazilian lending rates which, at 44.3% in January 2008, are so high as to distort the figure massively.)

Traditionally, governments in developing countries established the most important borrowing and lending interest rates, the maturities of loans, and even the beneficiaries of credit. This required severing financial and monetary links with the rest of the world, and was accomplished by tightly controlling, or prohibiting, international capital flows. As a result, the supply of investment funds was restricted to the generation of domestic resources, which was discouraged by artificially low interest rates and high rates of inflation. People preferred to deposit their savings in strong currencies, which they did by exporting their resources to developed countries in what was called "capital flight." Starved of the resources of local savers and isolated from the international markets, local financial systems remained weak and underdeveloped.

But as production and distribution globalizes, economic growth in different countries and regions is more and more determined by investment decisions funded and funneled through the global financial system. (Borrowing in low-cost yen to finance investments in Europe, while hedging against the yen's rise on a U.S. futures exchange, is no longer exotic.) It is

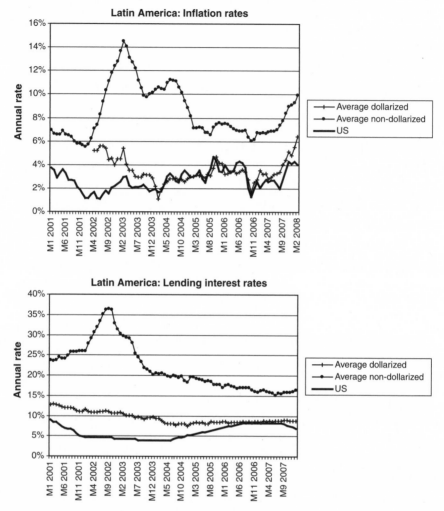

Figure 5.4. Latin America: Inflation and interest rates.
Data source: IMF International Financial Statistics.
Note: We exclude Brazil, whose lending rates were a massive 44.3% in January 2008.

increasingly difficult to differentiate the domestic financial systems of the developed countries from the wider international one. (The highly successful German securities exchange, Deutsche Börse, is today itself a large listed multinational company with over 90% of its share capital owned by non-Germans.) Thus, unrestricted and efficient access to the global capital market, rather than the ability of governments to manipulate parochial monetary policies, is becoming increasingly important for development.

Yet owing to the unwillingness of foreigners to hold their currencies, developing countries find their local financial systems largely isolated from the global system. Their interest rates tend to be much higher than those in the international markets, and their financial operations extremely short, not longer than a few months in most cases. In consequence, they remain dependent on dollars for any long-term credit available to them, which forces them to run foreign exchange risks in those operations. Their un-wanted currencies make the capital flows they so badly need dangerous: Both locals and foreigners will sell them en masse at the earliest whiff of a devaluation, since devaluation makes it more difficult for a country to ser-vice its foreign debts. These problems are grave obstacles to development in an environment of advancing globalization. Monetary nationalism in developing countries operates against the grain of the process, and thus makes future financial problems even more likely.

Spontaneous Dollarization

The transformation of developing economies to developed ones, driven by the climb to higher and higher value-added work in the global workshop, requires significant investments. These can easily be financed by the rapidly growing international financial system—witness the remarkable recent expansion of U.S. and European private equity capital restlessly seek-ing investment opportunities. Yet the presence of extreme foreign exchange risk—the risk of periodic national currency collapse, in which investments can suddenly lose half or more of their value—creates a serious obstacle for the flow of finance from international financial markets. There is therefore a huge chasm between the opportunities afforded by globalization and the monetary systems in place across most of the developing world, which are based firmly on the isolating principles of monetary nationalism.

This situation is not stable. Financial globalization is eroding the power of national central banks to sever the connections between the domestic and international financial markets. Transferring financial resources across the world has become fast, cheap, and easy, and people in the developing countries are taking ample advantage of this.

As we noted earlier, capital flight is not a modern phenomenon. Even during the heyday of economic sovereignty in the middle decades of the twentieth century, people could move money abroad in many ways. Argentines have long been masters of this process. Roughly 90% of Uruguayan bank deposits are in dollars, with Argentines accounting for the lion's share. All sorts of schemes have long been used to move money to the United States, including buying expensive jewelry for pesos in Buenos Aires and returning it for dollars in New York. Venezuelans are using credit cards to exploit the difference between the official and black market dollar price of the bolivar; for example, flying to Aruba, buying $5,000 worth of gambling chips on credit (the maximum allowed by the Venezuelan government), and cashing in the chips for dollars, which they can then sell at a hefty profit back home on the black market. Others use bolivars to buy Venezuelan securities on foreign exchanges, which they then redeem for U.S. treasury notes deposited in offshore accounts. Yet others borrow bolivars, buy Venezuelan government dollar bonds at the official exchange rate, and then sell them at black-market rates, effectively taking free dollars from the Venezuelan reserves.[7]

Today, people in developing countries are increasingly bringing international currencies into their local markets and, in most cases, are doing so with the connivance of their own central banks. As international money transfer has become increasingly easy, the ability of developing country central banks to isolate their countries monetarily has become highly limited. They face an uncomfortable choice: either to allow people to operate in an international currency in their domestic markets, or accept that their country's already scarce financial resources will fly abroad. The choice is not an easy one. Allowing domestic banks to receive deposits and grant loans in foreign currency dramatically reduces the grasp of the central banks over the supply of money, interest rates, and other financial levers they use to implement monetary policies. If, for example, the central bank tries to lower interest rates relative to those prevailing in the domestic dollar markets, depositors will immediately shift their deposits from the local currency to dollars. This limits the central bank's ability to manipulate interest rates.

In the early part of this decade, dollar and euro deposits in developing countries represented at least 25% of total deposits in each of the developing regions of the world, and in some of them their share was above 50%.[8] When these deposits are deducted from total deposits, the fragility of the local currencies becomes evident. While a ratio of deposits to GDP of 60% is generally considered healthy in a developing country, the ratio of *domestic currency* deposits to GDP is only about 15% in South America, 19% in the formerly communist countries of Eastern Europe and Central Asia, 37% in South and Southeast Asia, and 39% in the Middle East.

Table 5.1 compares local and foreign deposits in thirty-three developing countries. Notice that the ratio of deposits (which are themselves a form of money) to GDP is on average 34%, but falls to 22% when the foreign currency deposits are deducted. This is so despite the fact that many of these countries actually impose major restrictions on foreign currency deposits. For example, in Turkey, where they represent 35% of total deposits, they can be held only by Turks living abroad. The table understates the degree of spontaneous dollarization in many countries along at least two additional dimensions. First, in many countries there is a parallel financial system, located offshore, which operates in foreign currencies. This parallel financial system is frequently controlled by the owners of local banks and is therefore part of the local financial system, even if it is effectively beyond the regulatory power of the local authorities. The volume of their operations is usually not reported to anyone, so that the total extent of the participation of foreign currencies in the domestic market is not known. These offshore facilities played a crucial role in the Venezuelan financial crisis of 1994 and the Dominican one a decade later. Second, in many of these countries long-term contracts are denominated in a foreign currency, so that their value in domestic currency is adjusted continuously to devaluations.

Of course, deposits in foreign currency put their holders out of the reach of the local central bank, even if the funds are deposited locally. The funds are not just immune to inflation and devaluation, but they actually gain in local currency terms whenever there is a real devaluation. This neuters the central bank in its efforts to use tools such as devaluation for the purpose of controlling domestic demand.

Spontaneous dollarization is also dangerous because it embeds foreign exchange risk in the accounts of the banking system. The risk can take

Table 5.1 Foreign and local currency deposits, 2006

	Total deposits (percent of GDP)	Share of foreign currency in local deposits	Percent of GDP	
			Deposits in foreign currency	Deposits in local currency
Uruguay	43%	92%	39%	4%
Croatia	54%	53%	28%	25%
Nicaragua*	34%	68%	23%	11%
Egypt*	78%	29%	23%	56%
Bolivia	35%	62%	22%	13%
Mauritius	81%	22%	17%	63%
Cambodia	18%	96%	17%	1%
Mongolia*	39%	44%	17%	22%
Costa Rica	35%	47%	16%	19%
Jamaica*	41%	40%	16%	25%
Bulgaria	35%	45%	16%	19%
Turkey	44%	35%	15%	29%
Honduras*	40%	38%	15%	25%
Vietnam*	49%	30%	15%	34%
Bosnia and Herzegovina	28%	47%	13%	15%
Philippines	44%	27%	12%	32%
Romania	27%	41%	11%	16%
Peru	17%	60%	10%	7%
Moldova*	23%	42%	10%	13%
Ukraine	25%	38%	10%	16%
Kazakhstan	24%	35%	8%	15%
Trinidad & Tobago	28%	23%	7%	22%
Azerbaijan	9%	74%	6%	2%
Paraguay	11%	50%	6%	6%
Indonesia	31%	14%	4%	27%
Armenia	7%	53%	4%	3%
Guatemala*	23%	13%	3%	20%
Russia*	9%	23%	2%	7%
Argentina	19%	10%	2%	17%
Tunisia	36%	4%	2%	34%
Thailand	93%	2%	1%	92%
Pakistan	12%	7%	1%	11%
Morocco	24%	1%	0%	23%
Average	34%	38%	12%	22%

*Data are from 2005.

Data source: Moody's Investors Service (2007) and IMF International Financial Statistics.

many shapes, depending on the specific nature of the currency mismatch. Even where the regulatory authorities oblige banks to match assets and liabilities in different currencies, the banks are not immune to exchange risk. If a bank taking local dollar deposits lends out dollars to, say, real estate developers, the bank is exposed to the risk that devaluation will reduce the ability of the developers to repay. Some authorities go further, therefore, and try to enforce a matching not only of the currency denomination of bank assets and liabilities, but the currency denomination of borrowers' loans and their incomes. But squeezing a balloon just makes the air move elsewhere. In this case, the efforts to further reduce loans in dollars reduces the amount of dollar deposits that local banks can take, therefore encouraging deposits to go abroad—exactly what the authorities were trying to discourage in the first place. Rightly, the IMF is extremely concerned about spontaneous dollarization, and has been advising countries to eliminate it. Yet they have identified no means of achieving this that addresses the reasons why locals are demanding dollars in the first place.

Furthermore, even if it were feasible to ban foreign currency deposits the dangers of economy-wide currency mismatch would still exist through capital flows. This is why so many prominent commentators, including rich-country economists who would be up in arms if their government tried to stop them from investing their book royalties abroad, have for some time now been advising banning all but "long-term" capital flows (to finance factories and other fixed assets) into developing countries. "Think of capital flows as a medicine with occasionally horrible side effects," says Harvard economist Dani Rodrik. "The evidence suggests that we have no good way of controlling the side effects. Can it be good regulatory policy to remove controls on the sale and use of such a medicine?"[9] These "side effects" are indeed evident in Iceland, one of the richest countries per capita in the world, which has been repeatedly buffeted by wild swings in capital flows into and out of its currency, the krona. But where are these side effects in Ecuador, in El Salvador, in Panama, in Greece, or in Portugal? Nowhere to be found. These are countries that have abandoned monetary sovereignty in favor of adopting the dollar or the euro, the two major internationally accepted currencies. The problem Rodrik identifies is therefore clearly in the currency, and not the flows. This suggests that the medicine should be directed at the currency, and not the flows.

Isolating a country's private sector from access to international financial markets in order to protect a political ideology, monetary nationalism, that produces a scarcity of local resources is hardly sound economics. Imagine what Microsoft and Amazon.com would be today if their small home state of Washington banned "short-term" capital flows. They would be capital-starved corporate pygmies. Now imagine such a capital-flow policy writ large, state by state, across the American continent. The damage to the development of the U.S. economy would be massive.

The theoretical case for capital flows is compelling to the point of being obvious. When capital can flow freely from where it is overabundant to where it is scarce, the return on savers' capital is maximized and its cost to growing companies is minimized. Free capital flows also allow financial risks to be pooled, and therefore lessened through diversification, and better allocated among those with different abilities to bear and manage them.

Norway was a huge importer of capital, as high as 14% of GDP, in the 1970s, allowing it to develop its oil reserves far more cheaply than it could have relying on domestic savings. Singapore, on the other hand, was a mirror-image exporter of capital in the 1990s, allowing its citizens to achieve much higher returns on their savings than they could ever have achieved at home.[10] When capital flows function in this manner, they are a major stimulant to economic growth and higher living standards.

Are high levels of capital inflows inherently dangerous? Not on their own. Between 1870 and 1890, Argentina imported capital equivalent to 18.7% of GDP, compared with barely over 2% from 1990 to 1996, in the years prior to a major currency crisis. Indeed, international capital flows for twelve major trading nations were roughly 60% higher as a percentage of GDP from 1870 to 1890 than they were in the 1990s (3.7% versus 2.3%).[11] There is proportionately less capital crossing borders today than there was a century ago.[12]

Consider too that capital today flows freely, instantaneously, and often massively within countries. During the 1990s tech boom, billions of dollars were raised in New York and invested in California. When the tech bubble finally burst with the dawning of the new millennium, both the

California and New York economies were hit hard, as companies and their investors suffered the grim aftermath of irrational exuberance. Yet through the highs and the lows, there were no current account crises, no speculative currency attacks, no cessations of credit, no interest rate spikes, no bank runs, no IMF missions, no violent protests, and no political upheavals.

We know of no economist who questions the wisdom of free capital flows between the continental United States and the commonwealth of Puerto Rico; or Panama, Ecuador, and El Salvador—which all use the U.S. dollar as their currency—for that matter. While the evils of "hot money" rushing into and out of emerging markets are widely proclaimed, the condemnation is reserved exclusively for dollars sweeping through states whose governments restrict their use, or refuse to use them in dealings with their citizens. In other words, it is not the movement of money between the rich and poor parts of the world that is damned, but the movement of *dollars* in and out of countries whose governments don't want their citizens to use them. The political presumption on the part of capital-flow critics is in favor of the governments, and therefore the solution is always to stop citizens from importing or exporting capital.

Commodities to the Rescue?

For some of the countries in Table 5.1, the ratio of foreign to local currency deposits has declined in recent years. For example, Russia witnessed a decline in foreign currency deposits from 35% of total deposits in 2003 to 23% in 2005.[13] This is consistent with the positive empirical correlation between commodity prices and the exchange rates of commodity-export–dependent developing countries, and the negative correlation between exchange rates and the foreign currency component of deposits.[14] The latter is illustrated in Figure 5.5 for the case of Chile.

The clash between the mythology and psychology of money, between its role as an emblem of sovereignty and a fundamental tool of individual choice, is not always visible. It can lay dormant for years. Years of high and rising commodity prices have improved fiscal and current account balances in many developing countries, and supported solid economic growth. Many developing country currencies have appreciated in consequence,

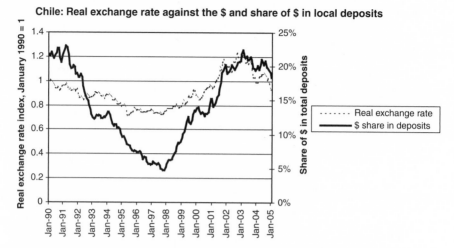

Figure 5.5. The effect of exchange rates on Chilean dollar deposits.
Data source: IMF International Financial Statistics and Central Bank of Chile.
Note: A fall in the real exchange rate index represents a rise in the Chilean peso.

spreading optimism and willingness to run currency exposure risks in such countries—in particular, on the part of rich-country institutional investors. Yet, as has happened repeatedly in the past, storm clouds will return once commodity prices start falling again. Currencies will depreciate, fiscal and current account deficits deteriorate, capital inflows turn to outflows, and foreign exchange exposures turn into big losses. Currency crises will return as locals and foreigners alike scramble for dollars, and the mythology and psychology of money will diverge once again.

This history has repeated itself many times. The rise and fall of commodity prices was the basis of the 1890 London panic, in which the storied merchant bank Barings faced near-collapse over failed loans to Argentina during the decade prior. It was the basis of the 1980s currency and debt crises that followed the reversal of the commodity price boom of the 1970s. We saw it yet again in the late 1990s.

At the time of writing in spring 2008, investor exuberance for developing countries is in full bloom once more. The usual arguments for trusting the long-term viability of developing country currencies are being advanced. Whole developing regions like Latin America are accumulating current account and fiscal surpluses, repaying their debt, and building their net international reserves.

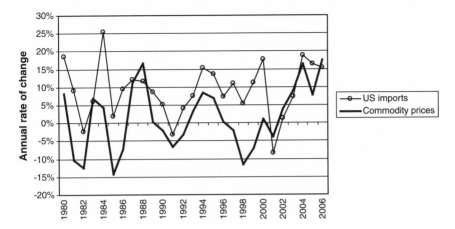

Figure 5.6. U.S. imports and real commodity prices.
Data source: World Bank World Development Indicators and IMF International
Financial Statistics.
Note: Commodity price changes are the average of the rates of change of the prices of
fifty-two commodities published in IMF International Financial Statistics. Real prices
are estimated by dividing nominal prices by the consumer price index.

But what would happen if commodity prices were to weaken? There
are, after all, precious few signs of structural change in these economies
that would allow them to buffer the blow.

Figure 5.6 suggests what would happen. It shows how closely the prices
of commodities have been associated with the volume of U.S. imports
over the past three decades. This positive correlation should not be a sur-
prise, given the size of the U.S. economy. More than one in every three
dollars (or euros) spent in the world is spent in the United States, and the
United States exerts enormous influence on commodities prices—not just
because U.S. commodity imports are so huge, but because the United
States imports so much production from countries that themselves import commodities to process into export manufactures.

There are many ways for the current massive global imbalances to be resolved, but they all involve a reduction, or at least a very considerable
slowdown in growth, of U.S. imports. This clearly spells bad news for
commodity prices.

Figure 5.7 now shows what happens when commodity prices go down,
focusing on one of the main commodity producing areas and current

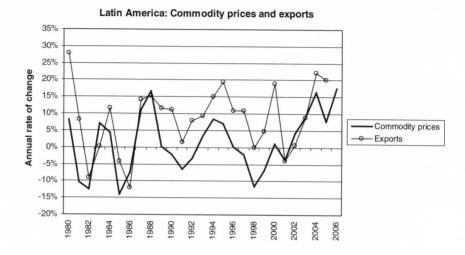

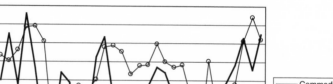

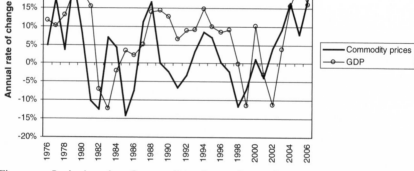

Figure 5.7. Latin America: Commodity prices and growth.
Data source: World Bank World Development Indicators and IMF International
Financial Statistics.
Note: Commodity price changes are the average of the rates of change of the prices of
fifty-two commodities published in IMF International Financial Statistics.

beneficiaries of positive investor sentiment: Latin America. The figure
shows the enormous impact of commodity prices on the region's rate of
export and GDP growth. A decline in commodity prices can therefore be
expected to hit such growth hard, which would in turn transform current
account and fiscal surpluses into deficits and drive down local currencies.

Slicing the dollar value of local currencies in half, not at all uncommon when commodity prices tumble, would double their debt to GDP ratios. Large depreciations would as well lead, once again, to soaring holdings of dollars in the local banking systems.

Looking Local

A number of developing country governments have in recent years undertaken some successful efforts to stimulate the growth of local currency bond markets—in particular, the Czech Republic and Hungary in central Europe, Turkey in central Asia, Indonesia and Malaysia in southeast Asia, and Brazil and Mexico in Latin America. To the extent that such markets can facilitate capital raising without generating currency mismatch, they are much to be welcomed. They have, however, been riddled with shortcomings.

First, developing country local currency bond issuance has been largely limited to governments. There has been little private sector activity. Second, in many countries, the domestic holders of such bonds are concentrated in the banking sector, and these holdings are frequently concentrated in short-term securities issued by the central bank to sterilize official foreign exchange assets. In short, such local currency bonds represent little more than effluence of the conduct of local monetary policy. Third, direct foreign participation in such markets has generally been very low, with the exception of central Europe, Mexico, and Turkey, although anecdotal evidence from investors and local authorities suggests that indirect participation through derivatives is significant in countries like Brazil and Korea. Hedge funds appear to dominate the foreign investor base in local currency markets. But hedge funds using levered derivatives positions to speculate on developing country currency moves is hardly a recipe for ending currency instability. A steep fall in the Turkish markets in 2006 has been widely attributed to the rapid unwinding of precisely such positions.[15]

Much more fundamentally, issuing bonds in local currency does not eliminate the fundamental problem that governments sought to address by issuing dollar bonds in the first place—that is, foreign investors' fears of local currency depreciation. Foreign investors ultimately care about the return on their investments measured in "tradables"—that is, dollars or euros or other things that are accepted worldwide as wealth. Issuing bonds in dollars was a way, however faulty, for governments to insure foreign investors against depreciation. If investors are lending in local currency instead, then, in the words of Jean Tirole, their "overall interest lies in a strong domestic currency, [and] the market underincentivizes the government to take precautions that decrease the likelihood of a depreciation of the currency. Adopting policies—or forcing the country to adopt policies—that encourage borrowing in domestic currency only aggravates moral hazard in this environment."[16] It is not surprising, therefore, that foreign participation in local currency markets should occur largely in the form of speculative derivatives positions designed to facilitate quick exit at the earliest whiff of currency vulnerability.

Going Global

The most sensible, but clearly also the most politically radical, option for developing countries looking to integrate their economies globally is simply to retire the local currency in favor of one in which the local population actually prefers to save and borrow, such as dollars or euros. Dollarization eliminates the financial crisis dangers of currency mismatch, reduces local interest rates, simulates local saving and investment, and safely opens the economy to capital flows. Globalization is transformed almost overnight from threat to opportunity. Iceland, for example, which has been wildly buffeted by currency speculation, has more than enough foreign exchange reserves to "euroize" the country unilaterally, quickly and painlessly, just by swapping, at the current exchange rate, euros for the krona its people currently hold. From then on, Iceland's current account deficit would be of no more interest to speculators than Florida's deficit.

Yet surrendering monetary sovereignty is unthinkable for most governments and many macroeconomists who still believe that the road to progress is paved with national monetary and exchange rate policies. Such policies become meaningless in countries without their own currency.

While people around the globe persist in seeing timelessness and universal value as the main characteristics of any money worth the name, many simultaneously attach great importance to the maintenance of their country's monetary sovereignty without noticing the inherent contradiction in their beliefs. This clash between the psychology and the mythology of money is poignantly illustrated in this e-mail message received by one of us regarding an article he had published in *Foreign Affairs*, arguing that the world had too many monies:[17]

> Just the mere mention in an article of your remarks on the obsolescence of many nations' currencies brought my heart into my throat. I've been fighting for years to garner acceptance for Gold Coins, The Liberty Dollar and just about every other alternative currency I could find in America that hasn't been outlawed by the Federal Government. I'm abhorred by the thought that you would want to dissolve individual, sovereign nations' currencies based on the fact that they are unstable or obsolete. . . . I will fight to my death for the continuance of the dollar, but on the terms that it is backed by an un-manipulatable physical source of value.

Our impassioned correspondent did not seem to realize that while he believed himself a defender of a sovereign U.S. dollar, he was in fact arguing for a return to nonsovereign gold money—money for which sovereignty was limited to patriotic symbols imprinted on bills and coins. He was in reality pining for the days of the global gold standard, when the value of each currency, including the dollar, was defined in terms of gold. In those days, money was not actually the dollar, or the pound sterling, or any other national currency, but a commodity. Dollars and pounds were vouchers exchangeable for the commodity at a fixed price.

This contradiction in beliefs is very common in developing countries, where people typically think it normal for themselves and their neighbors to hold their savings in dollars, but simultaneously think it inconceivable that the "country" as whole could do so—which would naturally imply no need for a national money.

Since the days of the ancient Lydian tyrants, governments have issued currencies, and, for most of this time, they have insisted on a formal monopoly of issuance. Through their control of the supply of money, they have defined what thing would be used as money as well as the rate at which it would be created. This, at least, is how things have been on the surface. Reality has been more complex than this, since the acquiescence of the people has always been essential for the workings of the system.

When individuals have not agreed that what governments called "money" was actually money, because it failed to sustain its purchasing power through time, they have developed, legally or illegally, alternative monies and mechanisms of valuation. In our times, technological advance is tipping the scale increasingly toward individuals and away from governments. That is, it is becoming ever easier for people to transform the denomination of their savings from one money to another.

Minds and Money

The most important feature marking out a legitimately useful currency is that it succeeds in becoming a standard of value in the minds of its users. Such a currency establishes credibility that it will keep its value through time. Its users willingly use it in large transactions and long-term contracts. More abstractly, its users "think" in that currency. They measure value in it. They keep their accounts in it. They plan their futures in it.

Few of the world's currencies actually make the grade on this basis.

The monetary world can usefully be divided into three groups of currencies. The first, elite group is comprised of a handful of currencies that are widely accepted by foreigners. The U.S. dollar is clearly first among these. In Asia, as seen in Table 5.2, over two-thirds of exports and imports are invoiced in dollars. In Europe, the figure is roughly a third. The euro is also in this first category of currencies, but its attraction outside the eurozone is much more geographically limited, concentrated around its perimeter. There has been no general uptrend in noneurozone use of the euro, in trade invoicing or debt issuance, in recent years. The euro share of global central bank foreign exchange reserves has also been stable at around 25%, compared with 65% for the U.S. dollar. Ten to 15% of euros in circulation are held abroad, compared with 60% of U.S. dollars.[18] The Japanese yen, the U.K. pound sterling, and the Swiss franc also have limited roles as international currencies.

The second group is comprised of currencies of other wealthy countries such as Canada, Sweden, and Australia. They are not widely used outside their national borders, but have established themselves as a standard of value within them.

Table 5.2 U.S. dollar use in trade invoicing

	Date of observation[1]	U.S. dollar share in export invoicing	U.S. dollar share in import invoicing
United States	2003	95.0%	85.0%
Asia			
Japan	2001	52.4%	70.7%
Korea	2001	84.9%	82.2%
Malaysia[2]	1996	66.0%	66.0%
Thailand[2]	1996	83.9%	83.9%
Australia	2002	67.9%	50.1%
European Union			
Belgium[3]	2002	31.9%	33.5%
France[3]	2002	34.2%	43.2%
Germany[3]	2002	32.3%	37.9%
Greece[3]	2002	71.0%	62.0%
Italy[3]	2002	20.5%	30.8%
Luxembourg[3]	2002	35.7%	38.0%
Portugal[3]	2002	33.4%	34.5%
Spain[3]	2002	32.8%	39.5%
United Kingdom[4]	2002	26.0%	37.0%
EU-Accession			
Bulgaria	2002	44.5%	37.1%
Cyprus	2002	44.7%	34.9%
Czech	2002	14.7%	19.5%
Estonia	2003	8.5%	22.0%
Hungary	2002	12.2%	18.5%
Latvia	2002	36.2%	29.8%
Poland	2002	29.9%	28.6%
Slovakia	2002	11.6%	21.2%
Slovenia	2002	9.6%	13.3%

[1]Data are annual except for Japan (January 2001), Germany (third quarter, 2003), Estonia (January–August 2003), and the United States (first quarter, 2003).
[2]Data are for overall trade and not broken down by exports and imports.
[3]Invoicing data are for extra-euro-area trade.
[4]Invoicing data are for extra-EU-14 trade.
Source: Goldberg and Tille (2005).

The third group is the largest. It consists of the currencies of virtually the entire developing world, as well as quite a few developed countries (like Iceland). People in these countries generally adopt a foreign currency as the standard of value for all things monetary. The dollar plays that role widely, particularly in Latin America. Latin Americans tend to measure worth in dollars, plan in dollars, save in dollars, and, where feasible, conduct large transactions and write contracts in dollars.

People in this third group react to changes in the external value of their national currency very differently than Americans do. This is clear in Figure 5.8. The top panel shows that when developing country currencies depreciate against the dollar, interest rates in those currencies go up. This is because people in such countries demand higher interest rates on local money holdings as compensation for the loss of value relative to their standard of value, which is the dollar. The bottom panel shows that this effect is absent in the United States, where the relationship between the dollar exchange rate (in this case, against the euro) and dollar interest rates is the reverse. Lower interest rates in the United States encourage investors, American and foreign, to shift money into other currencies, whose interest rates now become more attractive. This leads the dollar to depreciate. But unlike in the developing world, depreciation does not lead Americans to demand higher interest rates for the loss of their currency's value against euros or other foreign currencies. This is because the dollar is firmly entrenched as the standard of value in the United States.

Currency is the central instrument of economic integration. By its nature, money's role is to connect people and markets, trade and financial flows, and, most importantly, the present and the future. A currency can do all these things because it provides a standard of value that is accepted by different people across time within its area of domain. A credible currency that provides a standard of value conveys, in economics lingo, enormous "positive externalities"—that is, the more people who come to accept it, the more services it can provide, and the more benefit the existing users get from holding it. This creates a virtuous cycle, reducing transaction costs and promoting economic integration as the currency area organically widens.

The border between two currency areas interrupts this integration. The

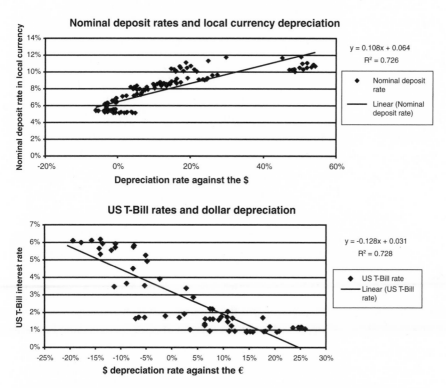

Figure 5.8. Currency depreciation and interest rates: III developing countries, January 1997–December 2007; and the United States, January 2000–December 2004.
Source: Hinds (2006), updated with data from IMF International Financial Statistics.

automatic connection between trade and financial magnitudes, and between past, present, and future flows, breaks down, increasing transaction costs. An exchange rate is needed to measure the value of things on the other side of the border, and people operating across it face exchange risk that cannot always be cost-effectively hedged. If the costs inflicted by the multiplicity of currencies are significant in trade terms, they tend to be considerably higher when financial flows are involved.

Yet there are important reasons why the idea of "one nation, one currency" has always been attractive to governments. The first is that issuing an exclusive territorial money is an assertion of political sovereignty, a statement of "who's in charge," aimed at both locals and foreigners, going back over 2,500 years. The second is narrowly economic: a government-issued currency can generate revenue for the government. There are two sources of such revenue: seigniorage and inflation.

Seigniorage and the inflation tax are frequently confused with each other. Seigniorage is the net revenue that a currency issuer derives from providing the stock of currency that people use. It is the rental price of the resources that people lend the issuer in exchange for the currency, after deducting the costs of producing it. When a country has its own currency, its government earns interest on the foreign reserves it receives from those who buy the local currency, yet pays no interest to holders of the currency. Seigniorage represents the profit the government earns from issuing noninterest-bearing local currency in return for interest-bearing foreign assets, like U.S. Treasury bills. It naturally grows as demand for currency increases—as people demand more money, they give more resources to the issuer in exchange for the currency they want.

Governments also profit from inflation. But unlike seigniorage, the inflation tax takes away resources from the currency users by debasing the stock of money. Governments collect it by forcing the use of currency beyond what people demand at the existing price of the currency, which they do by using newly created money to cover government expenditures. In the process, the inflation tax lowers the price of the currency in terms of other currencies, or things of intrinsic value (like gold). Naturally, demand for the currency falls. Thus, seigniorage and the inflation tax work at cross-purposes, because inflation lowers the real demand for money and this, in turn, diminishes the real resources captured by seigniorage. For this reason, currency issuers must tailor their policies to collect one or the other.

This choice has a crucial bearing on the political decision to separate from the global monetary and financial markets. Seigniorage can be collected in a competitive monetary market because people are willing to pay for the services provided by the currency generating it. Thus, the issuers of currency in high demand, which are the ones that can collect seigniorage, do not gain by fragmenting the monetary markets. On the contrary, the possibility of earning seigniorage increases with the size of the market. This has been the experience with all international currencies, like the U.S. dollar. In contrast, people will not pay the inflation tax in a competitive monetary market. They have to be forced to use an inflationary currency. Thus, the desire to collect the inflation tax provides a strong reason for governments to separate their monetary markets from those of the rest of the world.

Moreover, even governments responsibly looking to extract seigniorage and not the inflation tax may find it useful to separate their monetary and financial markets from the global ones if their currency competes with a currency that has higher demand. The government cannot collect any seigniorage if people use the other currency. Since an internationally accepted currency would always have more demand than one that is accepted only locally, it is natural that governments have typically preferred to close their markets and force people to use national money.

Governments' desire to acquire seigniorage or inflation tax revenue has been a powerful political cause of currency fragmentation since time immemorial. In the case of seigniorage, the separation was necessary to appropriate resources that would otherwise go to another government in an open market. In the case of the inflation tax, the separation was indispensable to force people to pay it. Since the separation of markets can work only if governments force it, the markets that have emerged around local currencies have been highly restricted. Imposing significant limitations on what can be imported or exported, or at what price (particularly the case with financial resources), has come to be seen as a responsible exercise of sovereign rights. Today's post-crisis Argentina is a perfect case in point. This separation is the cost people must bear to permit governments to exercise such rights.

Monetary Nationalism as Science

The monetary regime that emerged in the early 1970s is unprecedented in two important dimensions.

First, it is not linked to any commodity. Up to the time of the demonetization of gold in the early 1970s, money had been either a commodity, usually gold, or, particularly since the nineteenth century, a claim on gold. Paper money was effectively just a voucher exchangeable for a fixed amount of gold.

Under the gold standard system of the late nineteenth and early twentieth centuries, the most trusted currency in the world was the U.K. pound sterling. It derived its strength from the credibility of the Bank of England's commitment to redeem a pound into a specified quantity of gold.

During the short life of the post–World War II Bretton Woods system, national currencies were all claims on the single international currency, the U.S. dollar, which in turn was a claim on gold at a fixed price. That is, the commodity, gold, was the ultimate repository of value, not the paper dollar. The commodity link, however, disappeared altogether when the United States abandoned its conversion commitment in 1971. Since then, a dollar is just a claim on the things that others are willing to exchange for a dollar at any given point in time. All other currencies define themselves in terms of the dollar.

Second, for the first time in history, the international monetary regime is based on a very large number of currencies fluctuating in value continuously against one another by design. Exchange rates had, of course, fluctuated widely in previous centuries. But it has been only since the 1970s that such behavior has been widely viewed as connatural with an international monetary system. Before that, it was taken for granted that the promotion of cross-border trade and financial transactions required a system of fixed exchange rates relative to a widely accepted international standard of value.

The innovation of continuously fluctuating exchange rates among national currencies was not introduced by conscious redesign, but rather imposed by political reality: in particular, the determination of the United States to loosen its monetary policy in the 1960s, while still foreswearing devaluation against gold, irrespective of the effect on the credibility of its commitment to redeem dollars with gold. Yet a new body of economic theory emerged to provide an intellectual foundation for the new system: the theory of Optimum Currency Areas (OCAs).

Much in the way that medieval scholastics reconciled Aristotle and Jesus, economists of the 1960s and 1970s reconciled money and nationhood through the development of OCA theory. Fathered in 1961 by a Nobel Prize–winning economist who has, paradoxically, emerged as the most prolific advocate of shrinking the number of national currencies, the theory evolved over the subsequent decades into a quasi-scientific foundation for sustaining them.

Robert Mundell, like most mainstream macroeconomists in the early 1960s, shared a postwar Keynesian mindset that manifested great faith in the ability of national monetary and fiscal policymakers to fine tune aggregate national demand in the face of natural business cycles and what economists call "shocks" to supply and demand.[19] His seminal article "A Theory of Optimum Currency Areas" asks the question "What is the appropriate domain of the currency area?"

"It might seem at first that the question is purely academic," he observes, "since it hardly appears within the realm of political feasibility that national currencies would ever be abandoned in favor of any other arrangement."[20] He then goes on to build an economic argument in favor of flexible exchange rates between regions, rather than nations, and to develop criteria that would define the contours of such regions such that they would be optimal areas for the exercise of independent monetary policy.

It is important to note that, since Mundell's original OCA theory focused on an abstract notion of "regions" rather than actual countries, applying the theory to the real world could result in prescribing the use of more than one currency in one country, or the use of one common currency among countries appearing to share the same business cycle, or even the creation of currencies that would be common to parts of two or more countries but not to the whole of any of them. The economics profession, however, subsequently latched on to Mundell's analysis of the merits of flexible exchange rates in dealing with economic shocks affecting different regions or countries differently to provide a rationale for existing nation-states as natural currency areas.[21] The arguments were grounded in the observation that with barriers to trade and labor mobility across borders, activist national governments were needed to offset shocks—such as a shift in demand from the goods of country A to those of country B—through the control of national monetary policy. These were bolstered by later econometric analyses of potential regional currency areas, such as the pre-euro eurozone, which, particularly when using the United States as a benchmark, tended to conclude that they were far from Optimum.[22] Monetary nationalism thereby acquired a rational scientific mooring. Much of the mainstream economics profession came typically thenceforth to see deviations from "one nation, one currency" as misguided in the absence of prior political integration.

Decades after the publication of OCA theory, the number of currencies in the world can, not surprisingly, be predicted much more accurately by counting the number of countries than by trying to apply the theory to the economic geography of the globe. "In 1947, there were 76 countries in the world, today there are 193, and, with few exceptions, each country has its own currency," noted economists Albert Alesina and Robert Barro. "Unless one believes that a country is, by definition, an 'optimal currency area,' either there were too few currencies in 1947 or there are too many today."[23]

Nonetheless, governments have learned to love the theory for its utility as a scientific basis for countering those who deny the natural harmony of money and nationhood. Ironically, Mundell has emerged as the most prominent of the deniers. In the 1990s, he became a passionate supporter of European Monetary Union, and is today widely referred to as "the father of the euro." In 2000, he did a lecture tour in Brazil expounding a regional currency link to the dollar as means of bringing down interest rates to U.S. levels and paving the way for an eventual Mercosur regional currency. A former Brazilian central banker cited Mundell against Mundell to defend an independently managed Brazilian national currency, observing that "there is virtually no labor mobility between the Mercosur countries. As a result, the region does not constitute an optimal currency area—one of Mr. Mundell's insights." As for the possibility of simply adopting the U.S. dollar, as Panama, Ecuador, and El Salvador have done, the response was more emphatic. "It assumes," said the central bank's head of international affairs, clearly offended, "that we are incapable of implementing a prudent and sustainable policy ourselves."[24]

There has never been any serious political attempt at reforming the current international financial architecture since its emergence in the 1970s. The alarm bells that sounded during the 1998 Russian and Asian currency collapses, clear manifestations of the system's dangerous vulnerability, prompted a boom in academic currency crisis literature, but otherwise no more than a shuffling of the deck chairs aboard the global monetary ship.

Strange Science

The rationale that OCA theory provided for separating regions from the global monetary and financial markets was based on the proposition that macroeconomists had become so skilful that they could systematically outsmart the market, making it dance to their tune. Through their manipulations of monetary variables, such as the rate of monetary creation, the nominal interest rate, and the exchange rate, they could durably improve the performance of the real economy—increasing its rate of growth when depressed, reducing it when overheating, increasing exports or imports at will, adapting to external shocks, and so on.

But macroeconomists needed economies that met certain conditions in order to accomplish these feats. First, since the monetary tools that the macroeconomists can use have only one dimension—expanding and contracting the money supply to expand and contract overall domestic demand—they need an economy structured in such a way that all its sectors expand or contract in a synchronized fashion. Otherwise, any monetary policy would be excessively expansionary for some sectors, excessively contractionary for others, and maybe optimal for only a few of them. To ensure synchronicity in all possible circumstances, OCA theory specifies that all or most sectors in the region in question should have a common business cycle and react in the same way to external shocks. This would allow the authorities to design a monetary policy that would fit the needs of all sectors; it would be expansionary when all sectors needed to expand and contractionary when all sectors needed to cool off. Second, openness to the rest of the world can spoil even the best, most synchronous Optimum Currency Area. To avoid this, the economy must be relatively closed to the rest of the world.

There are big theoretical problems with the concept of Optimum Currency Areas, as it has developed, which have big practical implications.

First, OCA theory actually conflicts with some of the most basic assumptions of economic theory. For example, standard economics says that a decline in banana prices signals the need to divert scarce resources away from banana production. Not so OCA theory, which implies that a banana republic—highly reliant on banana exports for income—should, in the face of a decline in the international price of bananas, devalue its money, making everything the country needs to import more expensive, in order to support banana production at the same level. This thinking is at the very root of development stagnation in so many poor countries around the world.

Second, OCA theory also conflicts with the standard economics of risk, which prescribes diversification as the means to reduce it. OCA theory establishes the homogeneity of economic structure as the primary condition for a region to qualify as an Optimum Currency Area. This is so because regions with homogeneous economies—such as countries dependent on the export of a single commodity, like bananas—will tend to move in identical ways through the business cycle and react in identical ways both to external shocks and to the monetary policies devised by the central bank to counterbalance them. In contrast, macroeconomists would have problems devising monetary policies for nonhomogeneous economies with sectors or regions moving in nonsynchronous ways. In such a case, the monetary policy that would be optimal for one sector or region would be suboptimal for, or even damaging to, other sectors or regions. Said in another way, a financial and monetary environment in which all risks are highly correlated would be safer, according to OCA theory, than one in which the risks were uncorrelated. OCA theory thus clashes with the basic mathematics of risk, on the assumption that central bank macroeconomists can correct for the undesirable correlation of economic risks more efficiently than a diversification of the economy.

Third, OCA theory assumes that the uniformity of business cycles and reactions to external shocks are a geographical, rather than a sectoral, feature. This is far from apparent in reality. It is very common, for instance, to see countries that produce a commodity which follows one business cycle and at the same time other products which follow very different ones. The United Kingdom, being an oil producer, an industrial country, and an international financial services center, is a clear example. A fall in oil prices would not necessarily reduce activity in London's financial sector, or that of the country's various industrial activities. Seen logically from the perspective of OCA theory, the city blocks in London where the buildings of BP and Shell are located should have one currency, while the blocks where Citigroup and Goldman Sachs are headquartered should have another. This would doubtless create jobs on the corners of these blocks, as exchange houses would emerge to serve the neighborhood cafeterias. A buoyant derivatives market might also develop to hedge against exchange rate divergences between salaries, on the one hand, and housing costs and the like on the other. The question of what currency should be used in residential neighborhoods would be an interesting one, as next-door neighbors could work in different currency areas. In short, logically dividing economies by region, as OCA theory does, may have made some sense in the days when California mined gold, Chicago made sausages, Georgia spun cotton, and Boston wove textiles, but in today's modern diversified economy it makes little sense.

Finally, OCA theory assumes a static economy. Yet the introduction of new economic activities, which follow different business cycle paths, will logically erode the optimality of a currency area. For example, it would, from a monetary perspective, be detrimental for a country dependent on coffee production to develop industrial activities with business cycles uncorrelated with that of coffee, even though the experience of the last several decades demonstrates the importance to economic development of diversifying the economy away from dependence on coffee—as dollarized El Salvador has done. But this would interfere with the ability of macroeconomists to optimize monetary policy for a coffee-dependent country, and is therefore frequently cited by them as a reason for having a national currency and a floating exchange rate, rather than as a reason for ending the deadly dependence on coffee exports. To remain Optimum, a coffee-producing country should produce more coffee, but never drift into producing machinery or software. Economic progress would create tremendous inconvenience for the central bank.

The OCA vision of a currency operating over a static, homogeneous, closed economy is of great practical importance in the workings of the current international monetary system, founded as it is on national fiat currencies. Politicians, central banks, and the IMF have frequently aligned in opposition to opening local money and financial markets to globalization precisely for fear that capital flows will play havoc with the task of the local macroeconomists, whose jobs depend on the existence of local currency and barriers to financial transactions with foreigners.

OCA theory is mute on the phenomenon of currencies voluntarily used internationally. By definition, a currency used widely internationally, like the U.S. dollar, cuts across different regions and sectors and business cycles. People using it are subject to widely asymmetric economic shocks. Any monetary policy applied to this currency can be, at best, Optimum for one economy but sub-Optimum and even damaging for the rest. If the monetary policy is set at the average of what is needed, it may be sub-Optimum for everyone involved. According to OCA theory, therefore, international currencies should not exist. They are sub-Optimum by definition.

This is a big problem for OCA reasoning, as international currencies do exist. People around the globe demand dollars and euros even if they live outside the United States and Europe, and they do it not just for international but for domestic transactions, in direct competition with the supposedly Optimum local currencies. They do so to escape from their local, Optimum currencies through the process of "spontaneous dollarization" we described earlier. This suggests that the meaning of Optimum is different for OCA theory and human beings.

OCA theory stands out from the entire body of microeconomic theory in presuming that consumer preferences are irrelevant. Even if every one of a country's citizens chooses to save in dollars and demands them in payment, OCA theory is no less likely to be invoked to conclude that dollarization is against the country's economic interests. This obviously divorces the concept of a country from its citizens entirely, and elevates it to a transparently absurd level of abstraction.

In the late 1980s, a common joke in Poland ran: "What do America and Poland have in common? In America, you can buy everything in dollars and nothing in zlotys. In Poland, it is exactly the same." If there were a macroeconomist's retort, it would probably be: "Stupid Poles. Do they really think America and Poland are an Optimum Currency Area?" Currencies issued by governments in relatively closed national economies with homogeneous economic structures, subject to highly correlated risks, may be Optimum playgrounds for macroeconomists in charge of manipulating the monetary variables, but not for the people who are supposed to use them.

We have heard countless times in our conversations with fellow economists that the option of retiring a national currency, and unilaterally adopting an internationally accepted one in its stead, is only feasible for the smallest developing countries. This is consistent with the observation that only the smallest have actually done so—such as Panama, Ecuador, and El Salvador, which have dollarized; and Bosnia, Montenegro, and Kosovo, which have euroized. But large countries with allegedly indispensable currencies frequently have economies smaller than small regions within the richest countries. Brazil's economy is less than half the size of California's. Even China's economy is only the size of California's and Florida's combined. The U.S. economy is 50% larger than that of all developing countries combined. Two-thirds of the world's economy operates under just three currencies: the dollar, the euro, and the yen. The other one-third operates under well over a hundred currencies. Many of these countries have a GDP equivalent to that of a few blocks in the City of London. Thus the notion that countries are somehow "too big" to do without a unique currency is difficult to rationalize.

A Perfect Union?

OCA theory has been invoked not merely to defend monetary nationalism. It has, in fact, at times been invoked to support currency unions. The problem is that these are precisely the wrong sort of currency unions.

An example is the planned, though highly uncertain, 2010 union of the currencies of the Gulf Cooperation Council (GCC) countries: Bahrain, Kuwait, Oman, Qatar, Saudi Arabia, and the United Arab Emirates. This grouping is particularly interesting economically. GCC member states are very powerful in terms of their impact on the global energy market: They control 40% of the world's known oil reserves and 20% of its known gas reserves.[25]

The economic logic of a GCC monetary union is powerful, according to conventional OCA theory, as explained in a recent Chatham House economics paper:

> Oil and gas dominate all the national economies. Although recent efforts to diversify, notably by Bahrain and the UAE, have made some impact . . . oil remains central to the economic outlook. Overall, it accounts for a third of the GCC's GDP, three quarters of GCC government revenues and three-quarters of exports. This dominance naturally makes the economies of the GCC relatively synchronized. Given the lack of other significant sources of revenue, with no general tax framework in place in the GCC, fiscal trends are subject to similar pressures. . . . The relatively high level of homogeneity between the GCC economies and their growing integration underlines the suitability of the GCC for monetary union.[26]

The fact that all the GCC countries currently depend on oil for their economic survival ensures the homogeneity of the region as a whole, which

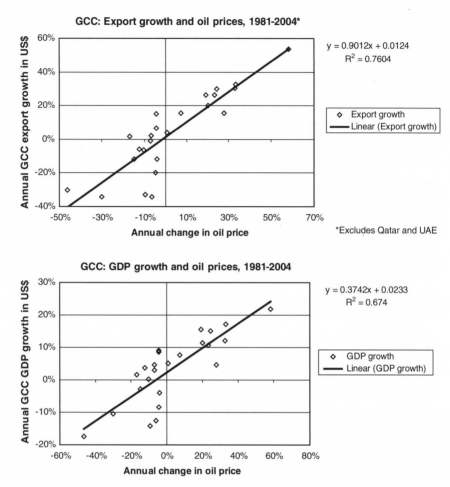

Figure 5.9. The impact of oil prices on GCC export and GDP growth.
Data source: IMF International Financial Statistics.

moves in unison with changes in oil prices. This is evident in Figure 5.9, which shows the rates of growth of exports and GDP of the GCC area as functions of changes in oil prices from 1980 to 2004.

It is difficult to find anywhere on the globe a more perfect example of an international Optimum Currency Area. The GCC national economies move closely in sync with one another because all of them depend highly on the export of a single commodity. According to OCA theory, the uniformity of GCC economic structure should allow a multinational GCC

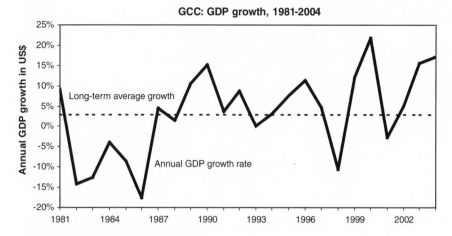

Figure 5.10. GCC economic volatility.
Data source: IMF International Financial Statistics.

central bank to manipulate monetary variables in such a way as to smooth out business cycles and accommodate external economic shocks optimally.

But have the region's national central banks been able to approximate this to date, which would herald even greater success by combining them? Unfortunately, the answer is no.

The economic volatility of the GCC is evident in Figure 5.10. Whereas the average annual rate of GDP growth from 1980 to 2004 was 2.89%, the rate has been as high as 20% and as low as −17%—clearly not the kind of behavior one should want from an Optimum Currency Area, whose main advantage is supposedly its ability to smooth out volatility. A GCC monetary union would also face serious fiscal instability. Because of the uniform economic structure, the fiscal situation across the GCC improves dramatically when oil prices rise and worsens equally when they fall.

The EU's Maastricht Treaty established two criteria to define fiscal sustainability in the European Monetary Union (EMU). The first is that the fiscal deficit should not be larger than the long-term rate of growth of the economy. This would ensure that the debt would not be growing over time. In the case of EMU, this prescribed maximum deficit level was 3% of GDP. The second criterion is that the ratio of public debt to GDP should not exceed 60%. As shown in Figure 5.11, the GCC countries have over the past thirty years had trouble keeping their deficits within the EMU-

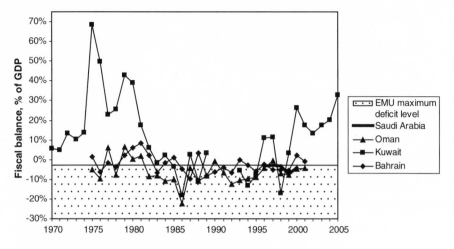

Figure 5.11. Selected GCC country fiscal balances, 1970–2005.
Data source: IMF International Financial Statistics.

prescribed range when oil prices fall. These deficits have not to date caused an economic crisis, as the countries started with relatively low levels of debt and the deficits were offset by periodic large surpluses, yet this could change if and when the GCC countries begin to exhaust their oil reserves.

These problems would be less worrisome if monetary policies could actually resolve fiscal problems. Yet it is well known that this is not the case. Not even the proper direction of monetary intervention is clear. OCA theory is grounded in the assumption that negative external economic shocks will be met with expansionary monetary policies. In the case of the GCC, this means that falling oil prices would be met by the central banks with interest rate cuts and currency devaluations. The hope would be that oil exports would rise, imports would decline, and growth would increase. Meanwhile, interest rates would stay low, where the central bank wants them.

Reality, however, is not so simple or benign. Oil production depends on imported capital goods, which become more expensive with a devaluation. So oil exports would not necessarily increase, at least not on a sustainable basis. Moreover, interest rates would not remain low. As experience shows (see Figure 5.8), they are likely to *increase* at least proportionally with the level of devaluation.

Yet this was precisely the strategy that many countries followed in the 1970s and 1980s in the face of economic shocks. The result was not renewed growth, but stagflation—low growth and high inflation. This is why the IMF typically prescribes a *restrictive* monetary policy in these circumstances—an increase in interest rates to quell domestic demand while the fiscal deficit is brought down.

To understand why interest rates in a GCC monetary union will not work the way OCA-weaned central bankers would hope, consider this question: "Who would want to hold a currency that rises and falls with oil prices?" Within the oil-rich GCC, people will naturally want to hedge against falling oil prices by denominating their savings in a diversified currency like the dollar. They will certainly not want to compound the negative effects of an oil price fall on their income by denominating their financial assets in a currency that *falls* in line with oil prices. Potential foreign users of a GCC currency will be even more skeptical. They will certainly not want to hold a currency for which the only product with stable prices is oil. Therefore both GCC residents and foreigners will demand an interest rate premium to denominate their financial assets in GCC money. A devaluation of such money will only push up the premium they demand.

Diversification of the GCC economies is the only effective means of addressing the fiscal challenges posed by volatile oil prices. Yet GCC monetary union is not merely irrelevant to this question, but is being supported on OCA grounds precisely *because* diversification is not foreseen.

Up to this point we have been assuming that the GCC monetary union would manage its currency as OCA theory would suggest: let it float against other currencies, so that the authorities can freely move interest rates up and down. After all, why retain the ability to make monetary policy if you are not going to use it? Yet precisely because of the problems we have been discussing, it is easy to make the case for a fixed exchange rate against an international currency like the U.S. dollar. A fixed exchange rate would protect the population against compounding the losses they suffer when oil prices decline. And, of course, a GCC central bank would need large dollar reserves to withstand large external economic shocks without risking a currency crisis.

Not surprisingly, most of the GCC countries have thus far chosen precisely this strategy to manage their individual currencies: fixed exchange rates and high international reserves. The exchange rates of five of the six GCC countries have not changed in twenty years, in spite of very considerable volatility in the oil prices. Only Kuwait's exchange rate has fluctuated, by very modest amounts, over this time period.

Thus if a future GCC central bank would logically follow the same strategy as the constituent countries do at present, one must ask why it is they need a monetary policy at all. If the GCC's aim is to have a currency that behaves like the dollar, creating a new currency tied to oil prices can hardly be the way to go. Instead, the GCC states can simply use their foreign exchange reserves to buy up the existing national money stocks and replace them with the money they actually want. Dollars.

This is not to say that the dollar is the Optimum Currency, for the GCC or anyone else. As we argue in chapter 7, there are good reasons to be concerned about the dollar's future as the dominant international money. The euro, for example, could, under plausible circumstances, provide a superior alternative at some point in the distant future. (Approximately one-third of the GCC's imports come from the EU.) The world may also move to some new monetary standard, no longer based on government fiat monies such as the dollar and the euro. The essential point is that the GCC's economic development is intimately tied up with the process of globalization; that globalization is evolving, as in the late nineteenth century, around an international transactions vehicle and standard of value; and that imposing a floating petrocurrency for local transactions can only hinder people living in the region from durably securing the global purchasing power of their savings.

6

MONETARY SOVEREIGNTY AND GOLD

Do countries need monetary sovereignty? Does ensuring national economic welfare require that governments have the unfettered power to produce money at will? In contrast to the ideas that prevailed before the 1970s, the mainstream of contemporary thought now says yes. In particular, the belief is widespread that when governments lack the power to produce money, either because countries are using a foreign-produced currency, like the dollar or the euro, or because money production is constrained by the need to acquire stocks of gold, as it was during the days of the international gold standard, the inevitable result is periodic deflation and depression.

In this chapter we take a critical look at this perspective in the context of the previous great age of globalization, from the early 1870s until World War I, and then the interwar period that followed. During the pre–World War I period, governments around the world foreswore monetary sovereignty in favor of a set of rules that strictly tied the supply of money to the supply of gold. National interest rates were largely dictated by inflows and outflows of gold, and exchange rates were fixed, as national currencies were just claims on gold at a fixed price. Deflation was a consistent feature of this period, and indeed a necessary feature of the mechanism by which the changes in the balance of payments[1] created changes in the supply of money.

During the interwar period, governments struggled to reestablish the gold standard, making some fatal errors along the way. There were two in particular, both related to how countries chose to deal with the inflation outburst caused by suspension of the gold standard during World War I. The first was Britain's decision to restore convertibility at the prewar parity, without adjusting for accumulated inflation in the interim, which deliberately imposed a severe deflation that hampered its economic recovery. The second was a deeply flawed attempt to make the gold standard compatible with the application of monetary sovereignty. The most significant element of this was a 1922 international agreement that misleadingly characterized the pre-1920 rise in prices as a "shortage of gold," and encouraged central banks to economize on it by holding foreign paper money in its stead. This wreaked havoc with the gold standard's automatic mechanism for controlling the money supply. The error was repeated after World War II under the so-called Bretton Woods system. Both times the result was deep international friction, policy errors, collapse of public confidence, and significant economic damage.

Contrary to popular perception, the evidence suggests that depressions cannot be explained by episodes of deflation brought about by the natural operation of the classical gold standard. Declines in real income frequently accompanied inflation, and rises in real income frequently accompanied deflation. Instead, factors linked to government assertions of economic sovereignty, frequently related to deviations from the gold standard and interventions meant to support nominal wages and generate current account surpluses, are far more logically related to the devastating episodes of high unemployment, collapsing trade, and falling real income.

Exchange Rates and Economic Sovereignty

Economic sovereignty requires that the state be able to wall itself off from the outside world in such a way that the population living within the walls is left with no choice but to operate within the economic framework established by the government. On the so-called real side of the economy, the instruments that can be used to enclose the economic space are the well-known mechanisms of trade protection: import tariffs, import quotas, and outright prohibitions on trade. The corresponding instruments on the monetary side are those associated with the ability to create money at will, to set interest rates, and to control the exchange rate against other currencies.

Yet all states at all times face a classic macroeconomic "trilemma": it is logically and empirically impossible simultaneously to drive local interest rates away from the world rate, to fix the exchange rate, and to have capital flowing freely into and out of the country. Only two of these objectives can be mutually consistent at any point in time.

What did this mean in the world of the eighteenth century? Like today, each small piece of sovereign territory issued its own currency. Unlike today, there was no international monetary system to speak of. Certainly, there was a common element—each of these countries defined the value of its currency in terms of precious metals, silver and/or gold, which have had universal purchasing power since time immemorial. In this sense, these currencies could be thought of as carriers of international value— and, indeed, they did routinely move across borders. But the price of the currencies still shifted broadly, not only across countries but also through time, as governments tended to debase them using worthless alloys and other devices, thus raising the price of pure gold or silver, or both, in terms of the currencies.

Economic activities were mostly oriented inward. Trade beyond neighboring territories was limited to a small number of highly risky and adventurous companies, many of which operated under government charters that gave them monopolies over certain territories. These companies usually engaged in barter, and frequently fought against the people they traded with and against each other. The most important examples were the British East India Company, which created the British Empire in India, and the Dutch East India Company, which created the Dutch Indonesian Empire.

Two of the main barriers constraining the growth of trade and finance were the exchange rate risks and the difficulties involved in the settlement of international transactions—transportation of the international means of payment, gold, was both risky and cumbersome. Like today, financial engineering developed instruments that ameliorated these problems. Bills of exchange were introduced at the end of the Middle Ages, and a multilateral clearing system was created to deal with the settlements problem in the fourteenth century. Forward exchange markets to manage exchange rate risks were operating by the eighteenth century. The largest and most efficient of these markets operated in Amsterdam and London.[2] Thus, there was a certain similarity between currency markets then and now. In both epochs, currencies fluctuated in value against each other, and the market developed instruments (interbank and exchange-traded derivatives are modern counterparts to the seventeenth- and eighteenth-century forward markets) to ameliorate the problems that fluctuating currency values posed for trade and finance.[3]

These problems were solved in the nineteenth century through the global adoption of a common monetary standard. Trade and finance began to grow rapidly after the Napoleonic wars, driven by the nascent Industrial Revolution. Naturally, these two activities developed fastest in the country that led industrialization, Great Britain. The industrial scale of production exceeded the size of the British markets and demanded enormous flows of imported inputs. By the 1820s, British foreign trade was booming, and British companies were already investing in mining activities in Europe and Latin America. By 1830, manufactured goods accounted for 91% of the country's exports.[4] Along with industrialization, Britain introduced a monetary innovation that facilitated its growing trade: the gold standard. Gold had been the prime universal standard of value throughout history: there was nothing new in this respect. What was new was that the British committed themselves to a set of rules that linked the British pound sterling with gold in a credible way. As other countries came to adopt the same rules over the course of the nineteenth century, they evolved into the foundation of the first true international monetary system.

The standard was underpinned by four main principles. First, the currency had to be valued in terms of a certain amount of gold, underpinned by the commitment of the monetary authorities to buy or sell any amount of gold at a fixed price. Second, the money in domestic circulation could consist only of gold coins with the appropriate weight, or of tokens or banknotes fully convertible into gold. Third, people had to be free to melt gold coins into bullion. Fourth, the government would not impede the exportation of coins and bullion. These rules created a system that assured people in a transparent way that the government would not tamper with the value of the currency—because if it did, people were free to convert their banknotes into gold and, if they wished, export it. The system gave government what it wanted most, a monopoly on the issuance of money, but it also gave people the right and the means to protect their financial interests, by melting down and exporting their gold, if government failed to maintain the value of the currency against gold—a standard of value for people across the globe.

The advantage of the gold standard was that it set in motion a mechanism that automatically regulated the rate of monetary creation or contraction, based on natural market forces. When the price of gold in the private markets fell below the price fixed by the government, indicating that a contraction of the money supply had taken place, people would sell their gold to the government in return for currency. This would cause an expansion of the money supply, which in turn would generate inflation, which in turn would increase the price of gold until it reached the redemption price set by the government. When the market price of gold moved above the government's price, people would buy gold from the government with currency, thereby reducing the supply of money, inducing deflation, and pushing the market price of gold back down toward the government's price.

The system also had mechanisms to ensure international equilibrium. David Hume's model of the price-specie-flow mechanism described the theoretical functioning of the gold standard. Suppose that a country has a deficit in the trade balance. The deficit would be settled with gold, meaning that the supply of money would be reduced. This would create deflation. The lower domestic prices would encourage exports and discourage imports, thus acting to restore the trade balance.

Hume's model looked only at the trade-generated monetary flows between countries. This was justifiable because Hume wrote during the middle years of the eighteenth century, when capital flows took place as a result of the need to settle trade imbalances. This was not true, however, in the increasingly globalized world of the nineteenth century, when substantial amounts of capital flowed autonomously—that is, not just to settle trade accounts, but as a result of investments in the financial markets of foreign countries. John Stuart Mill highlighted this phenomenon, arguing in 1871 that "it is a fact now beginning to be recognized, that the passage of the precious metals from country to country is determined much more than was formerly supposed, by the state of the loan market in different countries, and much less by the state of prices."[5] That is, gold did not have to move out of a country running a current account deficit if the trading counterparts with the corresponding surpluses decided to invest in the deficit country's loan markets. It was only when there was an imbalance in the overall balance of payments that gold had to flow. This blunted the mechanism of trade adjustment, but was consistent with globalized capital markets and gave short-term capital flows a stabilizing role.

The Gold Standard in Britain

Britain moved gradually onto a gold standard during the eighteenth century. Silver's role declined over the course of the eighteenth century: By 1774, silver was recognized as legal tender only for transactions up to 25 pounds sterling; twenty years later, it was recognized only for transactions of less than two pounds. The Napoleonic Wars delayed Britain's full conversion to a gold standard. The government suspended its obligation to redeem monetary commitments with gold (the first of three British suspensions over the next 174 years). Cessation of hostilities in 1815, however, accelerated the transition. The Coinage Act of 1816 established gold as the sole standard of value, and the Resumption Act of 1819 restored redemptions at the same gold price that had prevailed throughout the eighteenth century.[6] Resuming payments at the preconflict price was widely seen as the foundation of the worldwide trust that propelled Britain to become the financial center of the world until 1913. It revealed a commitment to maintain the currency's value, a commitment that met the expectations of traders, savers, and borrowers around the globe. British trade and finance was built on that confidence.

Britain also embraced free trade during the first half of the nineteenth century, first dismantling the trade restrictions that had been imposed during the Napoleonic Wars and then eliminating other tariff and nontariff trading barriers. The repeal of the Corn Laws in 1846 is widely regarded as the act through which Britain committed itself to the principle of freedom of trade.

Almost at the same time, the Bank Charter Act of 1844, otherwise known as Peel's Act, perfected the gold standard, creating the legal basis for the modern British banking system. Before the Act, commercial banks had been able to print their own currency bills, provided that they followed the rules of the gold standard. The Act gave the Bank of England a monopoly on issuing new banknotes, but also mandated that such bills be backed with gold.[7] Banks were authorized to receive deposits and grant credit with the proceeds of such deposits.

The gold standard created by Britain is widely seen as the epitome of monetary rigidity. "My argument," writes Barry Eichengreen, in a book suggestively titled *Golden Fetters*, "is that the gold standard fundamentally constrained economic policies, and that it was largely responsible for creating the unstable economic environment on which they acted."[8]

The gold standard was certainly based on the strict application of rules. In fact, the standard could function automatically, without any intervention of the central bank. It worked in this way in the United States from its inception in 1834 to 1913, when the Federal Reserve was created. Canada adopted the gold standard in 1853, and only created a central bank in 1934. Eventually, however, all the countries on the gold standard created central banks under the model of the British gold standard.

The British system was not fully automatic, however. It allowed for a certain measure of monetary policy. Central banks could intervene using several tools in order to affect the functioning of the system in the very short term. They did so for several reasons, including smoothing out the operation of the system (as actual international transfers were lumpy), as well as operating as a lender of last resort in times of crisis. Central banks could use several instruments to separate the supply of reserve money (currency bills in circulation and deposits of the commercial banks in the central bank) from movements in their stock of gold.

Two of these instruments related to the manipulation of interest rates. In the absence of a central bank, interest rates would increase when gold flowed out of the country and decline when it flowed in. This would automatically equilibrate the market, as higher rates would attract capital inflows when gold flowed out and lower rates would encourage capital outflows when gold flowed in. Countries with central banks, however, had the power to manipulate rates independently of gold flows. They did so in two primary ways.

The first was fixing the rate of interest at which they were willing to lend money to commercial banks. This effectively established rates in the market. In Britain, the central bank lending rate was called "the Bank

Rate," or simply "the Rate." It had other names in other countries, most commonly "the discount rate." Central banks also engaged in so-called open market operations. Selling government securities into the market reduced the amount of money in circulation, increasing interest rates, and buying government securities increased the amount of money in circulation, reducing interest rates.[9] The use of these instruments empowered central banks to increase rates even as gold was flowing into the country, or reduce them even as it was flowing out. They could, however, only go against the natural tendency of the gold standard in the very short term. If a country was losing gold and market rates were rising, for example, a central bank pushing down rates would accelerate the speed at which the country was losing gold, further encouraging the trend of market rates to increase.

The system also allowed for monetary creation by the various commercial banks. The broadest measure of money, commercial bank deposit money, could move up and down almost independently from gold movements. Peel's Act established no constraints on the creation of deposits by commercial banks and the granting of credit with the proceeds of the deposits, so that banks could multiply the money issued by the Bank of England.[10] Thus, commercial bank deposits and transactions could grow at rates different from that of the supply of gold because of the influence of the multiplication of deposits carried out by the banking system. For example, reserve money could be contracting along with gold exports, yet the amount of deposit money could be growing if the multiplier of the banking system was increasing. When this happened, the ratio of reserves to deposits naturally declined because more deposit money was created out of the same amount of gold.

"The traditional representation of the gold standard takes it to be automatic, nondiscretionary adjustment," write Rudi Dornbusch and Jacob Frenkel. "Bullion flows are matched one-for-one by changes in the amount of currency outstanding. [But] this is, of course, not the case once the reactions of the [central bank] are taken into account. Changes in the reserve-deposit ratio of the [central bank] affect the money stock independently of the existing stock of bullion."[11] Dornbusch and Frenkel examined the accounts of the Bank of England during a financial crisis in 1847, and found that the Bank sterilized substantially the effects of the gold outflows that were taking place as a result, first, of trade deficits and, then, of capital flight. This resulted in a substantial reduction in the ratio of gold reserves at the central bank to bank deposits—from 46% in January to 19.6% in April, and then from 32% in June to 11.6% in October. Reducing this ratio allowed the Bank to create more money than allowed by the gold reserves it kept. Thus, the Bank was able to carry out monetary policy by allowing the ratio of reserves to deposits to vary over time, at least during crises. Students of a longer period, from the 1870s to the start of World War I in 1914, have also found that the Bank engaged in some countercyclical monetary policy, although within the context of maintaining currency convertibility (that is, people could convert currency into gold and export it).[12]

The discretionary power of the central banks was, however, very limited in the longer term. The creation of discretionary money could result in one of two outcomes. If the economy needed the additional liquidity, it would absorb the newly created money with little or no inflation. If it was not needed, however, there would emerge an outburst of inflation, and the price of gold would rise in the market relative to its official price (that is, the price the central bank was committed to for redemptions). People would then exchange currency for gold, melt it, and sell it in the domestic market or export it.[13] The falling stocks of gold in the central bank would contract the money supply, which in turn would lead to higher interest rates. The higher rates would encourage deposits and discourage credits, which would then result in a decline in demand for goods, including gold. This would result in deflation, which would continue until the market price of gold went down to the official level.

While it was therefore possible to carry out monetary policies, the system automatically compensated for any excess in their implementation, leading prices back to their initial equilibrium. It guaranteed the long-term stability of prices and established incentives for central banks not to tamper with the supply of money, because any excess in one direction meant a subsequent adjustment in the other direction.

Such adjustment, however, could be upset by either of two problems. First, the supply of gold available for minting could vary because of shifts in the overall supply of gold (that is, increases or decreases in the rate of gold mining) or in the overall demand for gold—for example, if countries not on the gold standard decided to adopt it, increasing worldwide gold demand. Second, central banks were not always as disciplined in practice as they were supposed to be in theory, and could expand the money supply beyond sustainable levels. In fact, many of the problems of the gold standard arose because countries carried out monetary policies within a system that did not allow for them outside narrow limits, and which automatically punished deviations that went beyond those limits.

Globalization of the Gold Standard

As we have seen, the gold standard allowed for some monetary sovereignty in the short run, as central banks could fix the interest rates at which they would lend to commercial banks and vary the ratio of reserves to deposits in the central bank. Yet the principles of the gold standard guaranteed that in the long run the market would fix the interest rates and that the ratio of reserves to deposits would have to be restored. Thus, in the long run, the gold standard allowed no room for monetary sovereignty in any meaningful sense, although it did accommodate the stamping of national symbols on the bills and coins. Governments could set the price level—that is, they could set the price of gold in terms of their currency—but this merely fixed a factor of conversion. Once this factor was fixed in terms of gold, all other prices were automatically determined. Critically, the rate of change of the price level was determined too—not just for one country, but simultaneously for all countries on the gold standard.[14]

That Britain formalized the gold standard and adopted free trade almost at the same time was no coincidence. The gold standard was the natural complement to the globalization of trade. It was not just that the gold standard created a standardized means of payment and settlement of debts, and thereby established the foundation for the first-ever globalization of finance. The gold standard was an extension of free-trade principles to currency markets. It was based on the freedom to trade gold, domestically and abroad. The two policies consciously aimed at creating a globalized economy.

The certainty of value provided by the gold standard set the stage for trade to grow and attain a global reach. London's banks and stock exchange financed trade and investment all over the world, and all of it was denominated in the same way—in terms of gold. The pound sterling

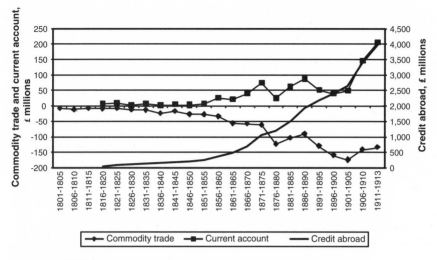

Figure 6.1. U.K. balance of payments, 1801–1913.
Data source: Imlah (1958).

became the first global currency in history because its value was fixed in terms of a commodity with worldwide value. All this began to happen decades before other countries adopted the gold standard. Being the only country under the gold standard gave Britain a powerful competitive advantage, not only for trade but also for the provision of trade services and the development of finance. Once the credibility of the British gold standard was established, companies and governments all over the world realized that they did not need to demand payment in physical gold. They had only to open accounts in London banks and use them to make and receive payments. These annotations in their accounts were equivalent to, but much cheaper than, transferring physical gold.

Britain became the financial center of the world and obtained enormous income from playing that role. As seen in Figure 6.1, the country had trade deficits that, when netted out with services and financial income, resulted in current account surpluses. Britain then used its surplus funds to finance the rest of the world. The new overseas investments then increased financial income further still, allowing the country to run larger trade deficits while maintaining current account surpluses. As is visible in the figure, Britain was playing the role of the world's banker well before most other countries began to adopt the gold standard in the 1870s.

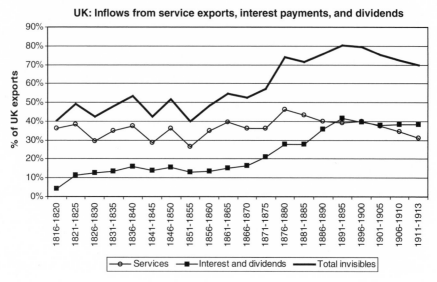

Figure 6.2. U.K. international inflows, 1816–1913.
Data source: Imlah (1958).

The stable value of the pound sterling in terms of the world's most widely accepted standard of value extended the country's competitive advantage to the provision of insurance and all other services that accompanied trade, investment, and production. Figure 6.2 shows the importance of these services, as well as the importance of income from interest and dividends, in the country's balance of payments. From 1816 to 1913, services exports averaged 40% of total physical product exports, while income from interest and dividends rose from 5% to 40% of those exports.[15] By the end of the nineteenth century and up to World War I, these two categories of income represented between 70% and 80% of British goods exports.

With the exception of Britain and the Low Countries, mercantilist restrictions on internal and foreign trade remained in place in most of Europe until the 1850s. But the last remains of the feudal guilds were mostly abolished in that decade, along with price controls and other instruments of the old economic order. Free domestic trade was followed by a liberalization of international trade, ushering in the first globalization of trade in modern times.

The Cobden-Chevalier Treaty of 1860 greatly liberalized trade between Britain and the longtime protectionist stronghold of France.[16] The trade liberalization process advanced rapidly through other bilateral agreements. France, for example, signed trade treaties with Belgium and the Zollverein (1862);[17] Italy (1863); Switzerland (1864); Sweden, Norway, the Hanse towns, Spain, and Holland (1865); Austria (1866); and Portugal (1867). The rest of the world, particularly Latin America, also moved toward free trade. One exception was the United States, which had gradually moved toward free trade since the early 1830s, but reversed course in 1861, with the outbreak of the Civil War, and moved back toward protectionism.

The general movement toward free trade involved the preparation of the physical and financial infrastructure needed to support it. Conventions were signed to standardize communication and transportation facilities such as the telegraph and railways. The Rhine was declared an international freeway in 1868. Navigation on the Scheldt, Elbe, Po, and Danube was also liberalized.[18] And the monetary infrastructure was built around gold.

Beginning in the early 1870s, countries one after another around the world moved toward the gold standard. No conferences were held, no treaties signed. Each state made the transition in independent contemplation of the national interest.

The popularity of the standard would seem to be curious from a modern point of view, as states adopting it voluntarily imposed a straightjacket on national monetary policy. They were abdicating monetary sovereignty. From today's perspective, it may seem as if they simply did not know of the advantages of free-floating currencies, combined with financial instruments aimed at mitigating exchange rate risks, that we associate with modernity. Yet it was *away from* such a system that they were choosing to move, and leaving little documentary evidence that they saw it as a radical political innovation.

Why did they do it? Just as few of us today would panic at the thought of having only dollars in our wallets when travelling around the globe, because we know we will find more than enough willing takers, people in the nineteenth century knew that others around the globe accepted gold as money. There was throughout Europe, for example, in the words of Mathias Morys, "an unsubstantiated feeling that ever more countries would be joining gold in the medium and long term—i.e. some kind of self-fulfilling prophecy."[19] This self-fulfilling prophecy is the essence of money; it is what establishes it as the standard of value. People adopt a currency when they believe that everybody else will accept it.

Moreover, this self-fulfilling prophecy offered tremendous new trading opportunities that states were eager to seize. States with a higher share of trade with gold standard countries, relative to gross domestic product (GDP), adopted the gold standard sooner.[20] And countries on the gold standard traded 60% more with each other than with countries on a different monetary standard.[21] States adopted the gold standard to gain access to the emerging global industrial economy. Trade and a single universal standard of monetary value went hand in hand. This flies in the face of the modern orthodoxy holding that a market in state-controlled fiat currencies is a natural complement to free trade, rather than a hindrance contrived by the modern political doctrine of monetary sovereignty.

How Depressing Is Deflation?

It was during this first period of globalization, from the early 1870s to the onset of World War I in 1914, that what is perceived as the main problem of the gold standard became manifest: its tendency to produce deflations. There was never a controversy regarding the connection between the gold standard and deflation. The theory of the gold standard recognized deflation as one of the mechanisms for correcting balance of payments imbalances. If a country ran a balance of payments deficit, it would export gold; this would lead to a contraction in its money supply and an increase in the interest rate. The increased interest rate would, in turn, result in deflation. With prices falling, the country's exports would be demanded abroad, which would lead the country to a balance of payments surplus and gold imports. This would again increase the supply of money, leading to inflation, which in turn would lead to a balance of payments deficit. The cycle would continue.

But deflation could happen in another way, affecting all countries at the same time, irrespective of their balance of payments situation. It would happen whenever the rate of growth of the worldwide supply of monetary gold fell behind the rate of growth of gold demand at the existing price. Equilibrium in these circumstances could be attained only

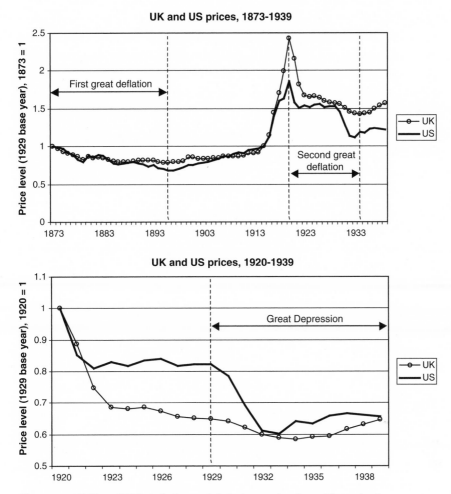

Figure 6.3. U.K. and U.S. inflation and deflation under the gold standard.
Data source: Friedman and Schwartz (1982: 122–137).

through a general deflation. Of course, in the context of that general deflation the tendency of prices to fall would be more pronounced in countries with balance of payments deficits than in countries with surpluses.

The deflations during this period were not insignificant. Their magnitude is visible in Figure 6.3, which shows price levels in Britain and the United States from the early 1870s to 1938, the year before World War II erupted in Europe.[22]

Between 1873 and 1896, prices fell in both Britain and the United States, by 20% in the former and by an astonishing 32% in the latter. As a result, even though prices increased in both countries from 1897 on, they were still lower in 1913 than they were forty years earlier. After a period of rapid inflation that coincided with the temporary abandonment of the gold standard during World War I (1914–1918), the two countries went into two more periods of sharp deflation: during the early 1920s and again in the early 1930s. Although the United States had a spell of slow inflation during the 1920s, Britain experienced deflation throughout the 1920s and most of the 1930s. The lower panel shows how, if U.S. and British prices are normalized (set equal to one) in 1920, their prices converged again at the end of the 1930s, suggesting that the 1920s and 1930s were part of one single deflationary period, with prices falling more steeply during the 1920s in Britain and falling more steeply in the 1930s in the United States. Thus, we can differentiate between two long periods of deflation during the life of the gold standard: from 1873 to 1896, and from 1919 to the early 1930s. During these two periods, prices tended to move in the same downward direction in the two most important countries on the gold standard, Britain and the United States.

Deflation is today widely believed to be a cause of economic depression. There are two main arguments linking deflation and depression. The first, summarized by Peter Temin, is known as the dynamic effect, or the Mundell effect, and operates through people's expectations: "If people expect the deflation to continue, they anticipate that prices will be even lower in the future than they are now. They hold off on purchases to take advantage of the expected lower prices. They are reluctant to borrow at any nominal interest rate because they will have to pay back the loan in dollars that are worth more when prices are lower than they are now. The deflation *causes* depression."[23]

The second argument is rooted in the assumption that the ability of prices to move in line with changes in supply and demand is not symmetrical: prices increase easily, yet are resistant to decreases. There are two prices that tend to show this resistance and introduce rigidity in the price system as a whole. One is the price of debts and the other is wages.

Deflation is worse than inflation in terms of the cost of repaying debts. During times of inflation, debts denominated in the inflating currency become cheaper to repay, in real terms. However, the decrease in the real price of debt can be offset by higher nominal interest rates. With deflation, the real price of debt increases, and interest rates would have to decrease to offset that increase. But there is a lower limit to interest rates: zero. If the deflation rate is high enough, fewer debts can be repaid, and defaults become more common. This is what Keynes called a "liquidity trap." This effect is also implicit in the Mundell effect.

The second rigid price is that of labor. It was not, in fact, rigid during most of the nineteenth century. But from the time of the development of trade unions in the early twentieth century, it became rigid. Workers became better able to resist reductions in nominal wages. This means that a broad deflation in prices, resulting in downward pressure on labor costs to restore equilibrium, would result in lower production and unemployment rather than lower wages.

Together, rigidity in debt and labor prices could, in the face of general price deflation, lead to bank failures, production collapse, and widespread unemployment. Thus, because the gold standard naturally produced episodes of deflation as well as inflation, it is widely believed that gold money must inevitably produce depression by way of deflation.

It is not possible to determine the relationship between deflation and depression in the abstract, as the arguments linking the two are based only on logical inferences about expectations or the behavior of two particular prices: debt and labor. Thus we need to examine whether deflations were actually accompanied by episodes of falling real income, and, where so, what third factors may have been at work.

Deflation before World War I

The period between the early 1870s and 1896 certainly confounds the notion that deflation causes depression. This period witnessed an enormous expansion of production, trade, and finance. It was during these years that the second phase of the Industrial Revolution—the emergence of the chemical, electrical, and telecommunications industries—took place, resulting not just in economic growth, but a thorough transformation of the industrial societies. All this happened as prices fell almost continuously. As shown in Figure 6.4, by 1896, the price level in

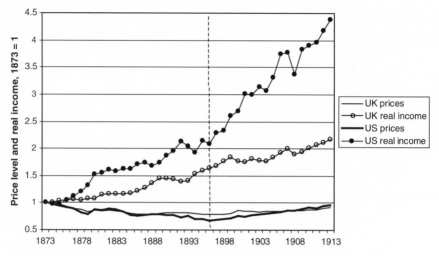

Figure 6.4. U.K. and U.S. prices and real income, 1873–1913.
Data source: Friedman and Schwartz (1982).
Note: Prices are measured through the implicit deflator of the national income.

Britain was less than 80% of what it had been in 1873—a 20% deflation. And yet real income was 65% higher. In the case of the United States, prices fell by 32% during the period, while real income jumped by 110%. After the long deflation ended, the economies kept on growing while prices increased. Thus, there was no relationship between deflation and real income growth during this period.

Speaking of this first long period of deflation, Milton Friedman argued that "Deflation did not prevent rapid economic growth in the United States. On the contrary, rapid growth was the active force that produced the deflation after the Civil War. . . . Prices came down as rapidly as they did only because output was rising so much faster than the quantity of money was."[24] Friedman did not deny that there was a relationship between deflation and the rate of growth of real income, but instead challenged the direction of causality typically presumed. The production gains he highlighted combined with purely monetary factors to generate the worldwide deflation. This was the period that witnessed the adoption of the gold standard virtually around the globe. As many large countries—including the United States, Germany, and France—built up their gold stocks, they dramatically increased the demand for gold while its supply could not keep pace. Since the price of gold could not increase, being fixed by the central banks, the price level had to decline instead.[25] Yet while the origin of the deflation may have been monetary, the productivity gains of the epoch contributed downward pressure.

Consider the case of steel. In 1875, the price of steel rails was $160 per ton. By 1898, Andrew Carnegie's U.S. Steel had brought the price down to $17 per ton through the use of new metallurgical and managerial techniques. By the late 1890s, the 4,000 workers at Carnegie's Homestead works in Pittsburgh produced three times as much steel as the 15,000 workers laboring at the Krupp works in Essen, Germany.[26] The lower price of steel worked its way through the U.S. economy, lowering the prices of myriad goods, as well as of those of the services that used those goods in their production.

Another example is the introduction of the assembly line in the Ford automobile factories in the early 1900s, which caused the price of cars, and eventually of all manufactured goods, to fall dramatically. The same story unfurled with electricity, and with many of the other powerful inventions that characterized the period. One example in our days is the rapidly declining price of computer power and telecommunications. When, as in the late nineteenth century, these productivity gains are taking place in all or most of the sectors in the economy, the natural result is broad downward pressure on prices.

Other economists have noted that deflation may be a positive sign where linked to productivity increases. Bordo and Redish extended the period of analysis to the entire time span of the international gold standard, and have classified the episodes of declining prices as "good" and "bad" deflations. "In the former case," they argue, "falling prices may be caused by aggregate supply (possibly driven by technology advances) increasing more rapidly than aggregate demand. In the latter case, declines in aggregate demand outpace any expansion in aggregate supply. This was the experience in the Great Depression (1929–33), the recession of 1919–21, and may be the case in Japan today."[27]

Deflation in the 1920s

Britain, the cornerstone of the international gold standard system, printed enormous amounts of money to finance its World War I efforts,

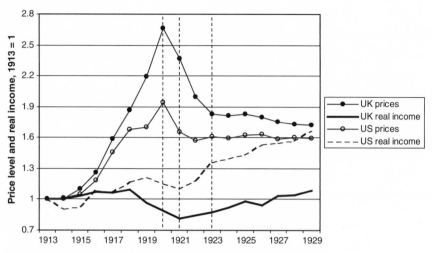

Figure 6.5. U.K. and U.S. prices and real income, 1913–1929.
Data source: Friedman and Schwartz (1982: 130–137).

far beyond what could be supported by its gold reserves. The country was forced, therefore, to choose between devaluing the pound in terms of gold or suspending convertibility into gold, ultimately opting for the latter in the belief that it would inflict less damage on the international monetary system. All other countries also suspended convertibility during the war.

All the warring countries imposed price controls during the war in an effort to dampen the inflationary impact of rapid monetary creation. Inflation naturally rose in the immediate postwar years as price controls were removed. As seen in Figure 6.5, prices in Britain rose over 2.5 times, and prices in the United States nearly two times, from 1914 to 1920. Most of the rest of the world suffered similar inflationary outbursts. Since the stock of gold had not increased commensurately, it was too small to back the money circulating in Britain, the United States, and elsewhere at the prewar price. This problem was frequently referred to as a "shortage of gold," whereas it was actually a surfeit of printed money. This problem had to be resolved for countries to return to the gold standard, and only two solutions were possible. The first was for governments to impose deflationary policies in order to reduce the price level to the point where gold stocks would once again be sufficient to back the money supply at the prewar price. The second was for gold to be revalued to offset the inflation of the war years.

The United States and Britain chose the first route. The United States restored full convertibility in 1919 at the prewar gold price despite cumulative price rises of 94% since 1913. At the same time, Britain began to apply contractionary monetary policies in preparation for an eventual return at the prewar price. This it accomplished in 1925. Figure 6.5 shows the significant deflation this policy choice naturally gave rise to in the United States and Britain in the early years of the 1920s. And since British prices started the decade at a considerably higher price level than the United States, they deflated twice as much, 36% to 18%, through 1929.

The association of the deflationary processes with GDP growth was different in the two countries. As seen in Figure 6.5, the United States suffered a recession from 1919 to 1920 and then grew without interruption until 1929, accompanied by stable prices after 1922. Britain, on the other hand, suffered a longer and deeper recession, from 1918 to 1921, as prices were rising sharply, and then growth resumed (except in 1925) through 1929 while prices fell.

The British economy grew much less than that of the United States, however, during the 1920s. By the end of the decade, the British economy was barely 12% larger than in 1919 while the U.S. economy had grown 38%. The poorer performance was evident along two dimensions: the initial downturn at the end of the war was much more pronounced, and the average rate of growth in the ensuing years was much lower.

Other countries decided against the deflationary route back to the gold standard. France, for example, let its currency float until 1926, and then went back on the gold standard after devaluing the currency by 80% in order to offset accumulated inflation. Figure 6.6 shows how French prices rose steadily after 1921, with growth outperforming both the United States and the United Kingdom. French unemployment also averaged only 1.2% during the 1920s, compared with 4.8% in the United States and 7.5% in Britain.

Because of its underperformance, Britain's decision to deflate its way back on to the gold standard was widely criticized at the time, even by

UK, France, and US prices, 1920-1929

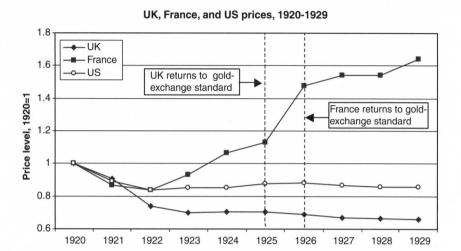

UK, France, and US GDP, 1919-1929

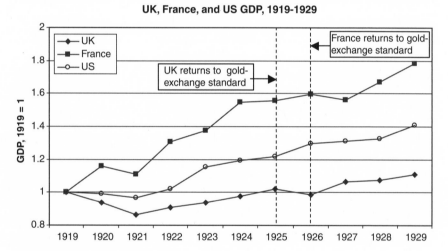

Figure 6.6. Prices and GDP growth.
Data source: Maddison (1991: 212).

economists who often seemed to agree on little else, such as Keynes and Hayek. In Hayek's words,

> The actual problems in whose solution these ideas were to play something of a fateful role began with Britain's return to the gold standard in 1925. Whether it was wise to return to the prewar parity with the aid of a difficult process of deflation is extremely

questionable. The events which have since occurred make it seem likely that Britain would have done better to have remembered Ricardo's advice. More than a hundred years previously, he wrote that he would never recommend a government to ease back to par a currency whose value had declined by 30 per cent. . . . Given the existence of falling prices, increasing unemployment and the persistently unfavorable position of the most important industries, even the years before 1929 looked like depression years in Britain.[28]

The choice confronting Britain, however, was not an easy one. Being the cornerstone of the international gold standard, the credibility of London as the monetary and financial center of the globe was at stake. The pound sterling held its special status by being the most credible voucher for gold. Thus, devaluing the pound against gold was tantamount to Britain defaulting on its debt to all those who were holding pounds as reserves, as well as to those who had made loans denominated in pounds. Seen from today's perspective, devaluing the pound relative to gold would be equivalent to New York banks defaulting on part of their dollar debts and still expecting New York to be the global financial capital. Losing competitive advantage as a financial center by defaulting was not without cost. British financial income was equivalent to 38% of goods exports. And, as discussed earlier, the positive externalities of being the world's financial center added significantly to the benefits.

The problem with this perspective was that Britain had already lost its dominant position in the world financial system. The country had during the war spent most of its financial assets abroad and liquidated most of its gold reserves. The United States, in contrast, shifted from a net-debtor to net-creditor position, having acquired substantial gold reserves. The changed situation marked a shift in the relative monetary power of the dollar and the pound sterling: the share of dollars in international transactions and international reserves rose substantially in the 1920s, while the pound share declined. This shift was important because of a trend that became manifest in those years: the use of foreign currencies as reserves in the central banks. The share of dollars in those reserves increased after the war, reflecting the rising economic power of the United States. Britain's attempt to recover the financial power it had held before the war was unrealistic, and the resumption of the gold standard at the prewar price did not prevent the country's economic decline. It actually accelerated it.

The substitution of currency for gold in central bank reserves was perhaps the key factor which destroyed, rather than preserved, the gold standard in the 1920s. As the world was never actually on a true gold standard for any significant part of the 1920s, the wild volatility of the period can only be linked to gold through the latter's disappearance as a monetary anchor. An International Monetary Conference in Genoa in April and May 1922 produced a fateful Resolution 9 urging "the conclusion of an international convention for savings in the use of gold by maintaining reserves in the form of foreign balances." The gold standard thus morphed into what became known as a gold-exchange standard (or bullion standard), eliminating the very mechanism by which gold regulated the money supply. Under the new gold-exchange standard, if France chose to deposit dollars in a U.S. bank, rather than redeeming them for gold, it could count the dollars themselves as part of its "gold" reserves. The gold was thus double-counted, first by the United States and then by France, allowing both to expand credit.

"I am inclined to the belief that this development has reached a point where instead of serving to fortify the maintenance of a gold standard it may, in fact, be undermining the gold standard because of the duplication of the credit structures in different parts of the world sustained by a few accumulations of gold in the hands of a few countries whose currencies are well established upon gold, such as England and the United States,"[29] wrote Federal Reserve Bank of New York Governor Benjamin Strong to his Bank of England counterpart in 1927. Strong died the following year, his warnings unheeded.

This problem of credit pyramiding was exacerbated by the infusion of politics into the process of managing gold flows. While the gold standard automatically settled international imbalances, under the gold-exchange standard these could be settled only through haggling among the central banks. Gold would always be "scarce" as long as countries pursued expansionary policies regardless of the flows of claims on gold. Being able to refuse to surrender gold, governments were monetary sovereigns, free to pursue whatever monetary policy they chose. This created immediate problems in international payments, as domestic prices could move independently from international ones while exchange rates remained fixed. If monetary policy in country A was inflationary relative to that of country B, gold would naturally tend to flow from A to B. But if A refused to surrender gold, B was obliged to bargain. Politics thus entered international monetary relations.

France, for example, in 1926 announced its intention to redeem its stock of pounds sterling from gold-starved Britain, thereby triggering negotiations which led to the Federal Reserve Bank of New York lending gold to Britain, facilitating partial satisfaction of French demands, and France changing its support prices (the rates at which it changed francs for dollars and pounds) in such a way that it encouraged the French to buy dollars rather than pounds.[30] This proved only a short-term fix. In May 1927, the governors of the British, French, and German central banks met with Strong at the Long Island home of Treasury Secretary Ogden Mills. In that meeting, the United States agreed to lower interest rates so that Britain and Germany, which were losing gold, did not have to increase rates to attract it back. The United States also agreed to buy pounds held by the French, paying in dollars. These and other more complicated negotiations became necessary to substitute for the automatic workings of the gold standard. Such scenarios would repeat themselves in the 1960s in the run-up to the collapse of the Bretton Woods gold-exchange system, to which we will return later in the chapter.

The Great Depression

The 1929 stock market crash marked the starting point for a deflation and terrible depression that raged across the globe for over a decade. In the years that followed, one of the predictions of the analysis of downwardly rigid prices, that the nominal rigidity of the price of debt would result in bank failures, became a nasty reality. Banks failed all over the world in several waves of panic. The episode is typically taken as living proof that deflations lead to depressions.

Some authors link the Depression with the deflations that had started with the return to the gold standard in the 1920s. "In fact, it was the attempt to preserve the gold standard that produced the Great Depression," writes Peter Temin. "These attempts imposed deflationary forces on the

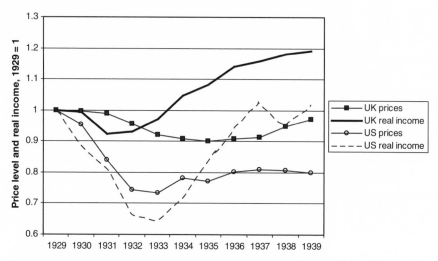

Figure 6.7. U.K. and U.S. prices and real income, 1929–1939.
Data source: Friedman and Schwartz (1982: 130–137).

world economy that were unprecedented in their strength and worldwide consistency. These deflationary forces were maintained long enough to cause an unprecedented interruption in economic activity."[31]

As depicted in Figure 6.7, the evidence shows that in the United States the deflation was closely associated with a sharp depression, and that the economy did not grow until prices began to increase. Yet in Britain, which had abandoned the gold-exchange standard in 1931, prices fell 9% from 1931 to 1935 while real income increased by 17%, which implies a healthy average annual growth rate of 4.1%. Certainly, as in the 1920s, the country with the worst deflation was the one that suffered the most in terms of real income growth. Yet the British performance further muddies the simple causal chain from gold to deflation to depression.

The French experience during the Great Depression was also different from that of the 1920s. Deflation was as severe, and GDP performance as bad, as that in the United States.[32] The star performer of the Great Depression years was Germany, which grew by 50% during the decade, even if, as is visible in Figure 6.8, its prices followed a path that was almost identical to that of U.S. prices. German GDP began to recover at a rapid rate in 1933, while prices were still falling. The data therefore suggest that

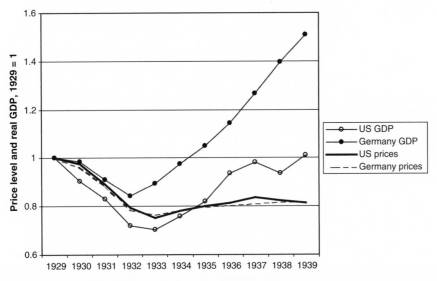

Figure 6.8. U.S. and German prices and real GDP, 1929–1939.
Data source: Maddison (1991: 212–215, 300–302).

there were must have been factors other than deflation depressing income during the 1930s.

Many economists, even those who believe in deflation as a cause of the Great Depression, have indeed pointed to other culpable factors. Structural misalignment in the economy is certainly the most compelling one: ". . . lower production may be the result of not only the traditional culprit, lack of aggregate demand, but also of shifts in the composition of demand," argues Peter Temin. "If demand shifts between industries, those losing demand will lay off workers. Industries with increasing demand will attempt to hire workers, but it takes time to reallocate workers. Unemployment is the result."[33] Temin believes such a structural misalignment resulted from the huge reallocation of demand following World War I, although he also believes it was largely resolved by the early 1920s. As we will discuss shortly, however, governments enacted trade, employment, and agricultural policies in the 1920s precisely to prevent the reallocation from playing out.

Structural misalignment can also occur when inefficient producers are able to conceal their inefficiencies as a result of abnormally favorable conditions, such as a credit boom. When the boom ends, they are no longer able to finance their operations and are forced into bankruptcy, generating unemployment and the need to reshuffle resources to more efficient parts of the economy. In such cases, expanding credit will not reactivate the economy. A shift in the structure of production is needed. In fact, expanding aggregate demand by increasing credit in such circumstances may worsen the problem by extending the life of inefficient enterprises, thus delaying the moment of the final adjustment and increasing the losses ultimately imposed upon the economy.

Some prominent economists have argued that the Great Depression started as a moderate recession, but snowballed into a depression because of misguided government interventions to expand credit. "Although there can be no doubt that the fall in prices since 1929 has been extremely harmful," wrote Hayek in 1932, "this nevertheless does not mean that the attempts made since then to combat it by a systematic expansion of credit have not done more harm than good":

> It is a fact that the present crisis is marked by the first attempt on a large scale to revive the economy immediately after the sudden reversal of the upswing [of the business cycle] by a systematic policy of lowering the interest rate accompanied by all other possible measures for preventing the normal process of liquidation, and that as a result the depression has assumed more devastating forms and lasted longer than before . . . it is quite probable that we would have been over the worst long ago, and that the fall in prices would never have assumed such disastrous proportions, if the process of liquidation had been allowed to take its course after the crisis of 1929. Only a rather superficial explanation of the crisis, like that advanced by most stabilization theorists, could have led to the assumption that it was possible to avoid a thorough reorganization of the whole production apparatus. . . . But if, as can scarcely be doubted, the immediate cause of the crisis lies precisely in this real misdirection of production caused by this, an element in the process by which production is necessarily forced to readjust, then the measures which the stabilization theorists advocate for preventing the process of liquidations can only have the effect of significantly prolonging the depression and the fall in prices.[34]

Other authors, including some writing in the latter half of the twentieth century, have also argued that the Great Depression could not have been resolved without a process to realign production.[35] Charles Kindleberger, one of the foremost scholars of financial crises, has argued that it is impossible to establish whether the cause of the Great Depression was a structural maladjustment of the world economy or a monetary problem caused by the central banks' failure to create enough money.[36] Yet it is possible to see the signs of structural misalignments in the world economy as it moved toward the depression, and to see how some of these misalignments were worsened during the depression—not because of the gold standard, but because of measures arising from the emerging doctrine of economic sovereignty, which was inconsistent with the gold standard.

The post-1929 deflation was, in Hayek's words, "a secondary phenomenon" caused by "the real misdirection of production" resulting from the credit expansion instigated by the collapse of the gold standard in the years preceding it.[37] It was neither a result of the gold standard nor a direct cause of the depression:

> The history of the gold standard over the last decade bears great similarity to the most recent history of capitalism. Every effort has been made to obviate its functioning at any point at which there was dissatisfaction with tendencies which were being revealed by it. As a result, it could finally be assumed, with some semblance of authority, to have become completely ineffective. The leading role in this process was initially played by motives relating to social policy, but the recent period has seen the appearance of increasingly overt nationalistic aspects, which have already become more dangerous in the area of monetary policy even than in that of trade policy.[38]

Yet the blame having been placed on the gold standard, the hopes were put on economic sovereignty.

The Rise of Economic Sovereignty

After World War I, the idea that the market had failed and that Adam Smith's "invisible hand" would have to be replaced by the visible hand of government took hold throughout the world in varying degrees, from its extreme fascist and communist expressions to its more moderate social democratic versions of state economic intervention. Proponents of government control over the economy portrayed it as an assertion of rationality over the chaotic disorder of free markets. According to this vision, the new rationality would be put to work to improve the lot of the majority, displacing the old chaos that had favored the rich in their exploitation of the weak. Those good intentions, more than the real consequences of their actions, shaped the perceptions that we still have of the Great Depression and the resurgence of economic sovereignty.

Monetary sovereignty was a central feature of this new thinking. "The theory of monetary sovereignty, which Irving Fisher in this country and J. M. Keynes in England developed in reaction against the international gold standard, served the purpose for which it was intended; namely, that of providing a theoretical basis for national monetary measures to avoid or minimize the impact of depressions in other countries," wrote economist Kenneth Kurihara in a journal article published a few years after the end of World War II. *"Monetary sovereignty is an attempt to insulate the domestic economy from adverse repercussions of a depression elsewhere."*[39]

Isolation was the logical prescription, given that the advocates of economic sovereignty saw imports and exports as the mechanisms that transmitted depression.

> Let us begin with the assumption that a major depression has occurred in one country. This depression will be transmitted to other countries having trade relations with that country through a resulting decrease in the latter's *imports*. From the standpoint of other countries this means that their income and employment will contract sharply via the backward or reverse operation of the foreign-trade multiplier. . . . The extent to which a depression in one country will affect the level of activity in another depends on the former's marginal propensity to import. . . . On the other hand, a depression abroad is transmitted to the domestic economy through a decline of *exports* and the resulting multiple contractions of domestic money income. . . .
>
> Overall import control is considered the most appropriate supplement to monetary and exchange control. It does not matter

whether import control is brought about by import quotas, exchange controls, or tariffs, as far as its effects on the balance of
payments are concerned.[40]

Economic sovereignty did not mean a complete separation from the rest of
the world, however. The aim was certainly to separate the domestic economy with regard to imports and capital flows, but it was also to accumulate
current account surpluses. This would allow countries to service their debts
or to amass international reserves. The overall objective, in short, was to increase exports while reducing imports as much as possible—very much like
the mercantilist policies of the past.

In practice, the programs aimed at introducing and enforcing economic sovereignty included the following measures. For the real, nonfinancial, side of the economy, the prescription was import tariffs, quotas,
and prohibitions, combined with export subsidies. For the financial system, the prescription was prohibiting capital export, foreign borrowing,
receiving foreign deposits, and operating in foreign currencies without
government approval. For the monetary markets, the prescription had a
number of important components. First, citizens would be prohibited
from holding foreign currency, and obliged to sell any such currency obtained in, for example, foreign trade, to the central bank at a set price. In
many cases, central banks established different exchange rates depending
on the source of foreign exchange, as a means to encourage some activities and discourage others. Acquiring foreign exchange would also require purchase from the central bank, at a set price, after the central bank
could determine that the funds were to be used for acceptable purposes.
Second, different interest rates would be established internally for different activities. Third, devaluations would be used to build current account surpluses.

Measures like these were supposed to create the machinery to promote
exports and discourage imports. As they expanded across the world during the 1930s, however, they came to be known as "beggar-thy-neighbor"
policies. With all countries doing the same, the results were quite different from those intended. The Great Depression witnessed the most severe peacetime contraction of international trade and finance in modern
history. It also produced some of the greatest economic losses. To a large

extent, the trade contraction and the financial losses that characterized the Great Depression were direct consequences of these policy innovations.

TRADE SOVEREIGNTY One of the most damaging manifestations of government intervention was the rise of trade protection. While trade barriers had not disappeared before World War I, they were never high enough to stem the tide of globalization. The protectionist measures that emerged in the war's aftermath were much more restrictive. As international trade collapsed during the war, countries were obliged to produce domestically many of the goods that they had previously imported. When the war ended, these newly created industries could not compete with those of countries that had a comparative advantage. But rather than make the difficult decision to allow foreign competition to these vestigial industries, countries raised protective tariffs to keep them alive. Even Britain, long the champion of free trade, adopted the McKenna duties in 1916. The United States quickly followed suit with the Fordney-McCumber tariffs in 1922. Their trading partners reacted by introducing tariffs of their own. Agriculture received import protection and export subsidies all over the world. Protection was perceived as the best means to keep people employed. It crept forward throughout the 1920s. In a turn of the tide that will be familiar to readers today, globalization came to be seen as something to be defended against. People saw international trade as a root cause of depression, so economic sovereignty became an essential defense. This created a huge lobby for protection that governments found difficult to resist.

Yet governments were quite aware of the negative externalities of trade restrictions. This is why the World Economic Conference, held by the League of Nations in Geneva in 1927, agreed on a tariff truce: tariffs would not be reduced, but neither would they be increased. Unfortunately, the political pressures to raise protection further did not diminish. In his 1928 presidential campaign, Herbert Hoover promised to propose legislation to increase protection in the United States. This promise was fulfilled in June 1930 with passage of the infamous Smoot-Hawley Tariff Act. It triggered retaliatory measures around the globe, as trading partners increased their own tariffs in response.

The proponents of economic sovereignty were extremely successful in their efforts at isolation in the early years of the Great Depression. They

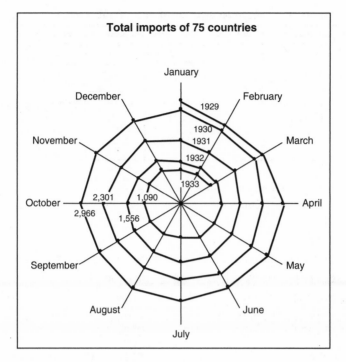

Figure 6.9. The contraction of world trade, 1929–1933.
Source: Adapted from Kindleberger (1986).
Data source: League of Nations (1934: 51).
Note: Imports are measured in millions of old U.S. gold dollars—dollars with the
$20.67 parity, prior to devaluation in 1934.

were actually too successful. As all of them tried to reduce their imports, they all succeeded in reducing their exports. The results were catastrophic. Figure 6.9 shows how by the end of 1932 the total imports of seventy-five countries had fallen to 30% of their value in 1929. This contraction was one of the most important reasons why the recession that had started in 1929 became the worst depression in history.

The negative effects of the protectionism that metastasized in the 1920s and 1930s were long lasting. Protective barriers that can be erected in no time can take decades of effort and political capital to dismantle. The new protectionism became entrenched for most of the subsequent two decades, and then only dismantled gradually over the three decades that followed.

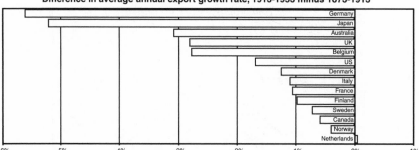

Figure 6.10. Export growth, 1913–1953 versus 1873–1913.
Data source: Maddison (1991: 312).

Figure 6.10 compares the rates of export growth of sixteen industrial countries in two forty-year periods, 1873–1913 and 1913–1953. As seen in the figure, only one of them, the Netherlands, had a (trivially) greater rate of growth in the second period than in the first one. All other countries experienced a decline in export growth. Thus, the result of the trade policies enacted in accordance with the new doctrine of economic sovereignty was an unmitigated disaster. It created economic havoc during the Great Depression and then slowed the recovery for many years after. Rather than helping countries to overcome the slowdown in economic growth, economic sovereignty helped them to sink into the gravest depression in history.

WAGES AND UNEMPLOYMENT   Another area in which government intervention appeared to have backfired is that of unemployment. According to the modern analysis of deflations discussed earlier, sustained falls in prices should lead to unemployment because wages tend to be sticky downwards. The evidence from the Great Depression on this score, however, is ambiguous.

The U.S. economy seemed to conform to the prediction of a very tight relationship between deflation and unemployment. This is visible in Figure 6.11. Unemployment clearly tended to increase when prices fell and to decrease when prices went up. The British economy, however, did not behave in this way. As shown in the lower panel, unemployment increased sharply in Britain as prices fell between 1929 and 1932. Yet unemployment declined rapidly while prices were still going down until 1935. Then it kept

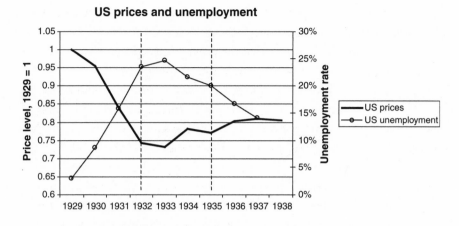

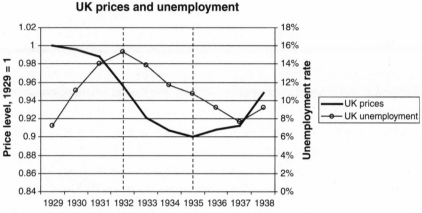

Figure 6.11. U.S. and U.K. prices and unemployment, 1929–1938.
Data source: Friedman and Schwartz (1982: 130–137) for price data, Maddison (1991: 260) for unemployment data.

on going down as prices increased, and increased again while prices kept on increasing as well. That is, the relationship between the two variables shifted sign several times during the decade. As a result, the statistical correlation between the two variables in Britain was zero.

The difference in the behavior of unemployment in the United States and Britain is all the more puzzling because of the common perception that British trade unionism was more pervasive and more combative than the American version. Thus it would have been expected that both countries would show a negative relationship between the direction of price movements and unemployment, and that the relationship would be tighter in Britain. The evidence contradicts these two expectations.

It is quite difficult to believe that the downward rigidity of wages could have played a major role in the escalation of unemployment during the Great Depression. It is reasonable to surmise that people would refuse to see their salaries reduced (in the same job or through a change in jobs) if the probability of getting another job with the same salary was high. Yet such refusal sounds unrealistic when, as was the case in the United States in the 1930s, the unemployment rate was on the order of 15% to 25%, and when the unemployed had to stand in line with their families just to get some charity soup. The testimonies of people living through these times do not talk of people refusing to work at the prevailing wage. On the contrary, people talk about their desire to work for any wage.

In fact, the real wage increased rapidly between 1929 and 1932 because wages remained constant in nominal terms while prices were going down. As prices declined by 25%, the real wage increased by 35%. With such a whopping real-wage increase, an increase in the unemployment rate from 3.5% to 23.5% should not be all that surprising. Yet the evidence suggests that the rigidity of nominal wages was not the result of workers' resistance to nominal wage reduction. Instead, it was business leaders, under great personal pressure from President Hoover, who refrained from lowering wages even as stock prices, profits, and employment fell.[41] This policy so delighted Keynes that he wrote a memo to the British prime minister supporting Hoover's action.[42] The fact that unemployment fell in Britain while deflation was raging supports the case that political meddling in the United States had more to do with the rise in unemployment than workers opting for near-starvation in preference to lower nominal wages.

AGRICULTURAL POLICY Kindleberger noted that the deflation that accompanied the Great Depression started in agriculture before it affected the rest of the economy: "From 1925 to 1929 a process of . . . structural deflation occurred in the world primary-product economy . . . there was excess supply. A few countries tried to meet the situation by absorbing the excess supply in stock piles. Without an adjustment in production, this only stored up trouble."[43] The international price of commodities fell by 30% between the end of 1925 and October 1929. At the same time, producers had been stockpiling inventories that they could not sell even at those depressed prices. Worldwide, these inventories grew by 75% between 1925 and 1929. And stocks are a better index of oversupply than prices because of government attempts to maintain prices by purchases.[44]

Such attempts at price manipulation, another manifestation of the new doctrine of economic sovereignty, backfired as well, and became yet another of the factors that detonated the Great Depression. The very fact that worldwide inventories of unsold commodities could have risen by 75% in four years, from 1925 to 1929, while their prices were falling is a clear sign of economic policy gone badly wrong.

The "valorization" program set up by the Brazilian government in 1917 to promote the planting of coffee through price guarantees was representative of the schemes that sprung up all over the world. Coffee plantations expanded throughout the southern part of the country, particularly in the state of Sao Paulo. The government abandoned the effort in 1924, but the state of Sao Paulo took over. By 1929, the stocks of unsold coffee had grown to 10 million pounds, while a normal annual crop was only about 7 million pounds. In that year alone, a bumper crop raised the inventories by another 10 million pounds. The state of Sao Paulo borrowed £100,000,000 in London to keep on financing the stocks. By the end of the year, the price had fallen by half.[45]

By the time the stock market crashed in October 1929, governments had accumulated huge hidden losses in stockpiles of coffee, rubber, wool, sheep, wheat, and sugar. The imagination spent in the design of these schemes was astounding. In Australia, for example, a Labour government elected in the autumn of 1929, right at the time of the crash, responded to the relentless downward pressure on wheat prices with a campaign called "Grow More Wheat," which succeeded in increasing wheat acreage by 22%. Because Australia did not have enough storage capacity for the additional wheat, it had to export the artificial bumper crop immediately, further depressing the international wheat price. Still, the lack of storage capacity was fortunate for Australia. Had the country stored it, it would have suffered even greater losses.[46]

The losses accumulated in the valorization schemes were realized when they could no longer be sustained for lack of financing. The selling of the inventories that had been kept off the market further depressed prices, which in turn dried up the financing of other valorization schemes.

Eventually the entire house of cards collapsed, as the old inventories swamped the markets and depressed prices to unprecedentedly low levels. The losses spread all over the world through the financial fallout, and then again through the unprecedented fall in agricultural commodity prices that took place after the stock market collapse in October 1929. From 1929 to 1932, U.S. agricultural prices fell by 35%. It was not until 1936 that agricultural prices returned to their 1929 levels.[47] Once again, unless it can be shown that gold makes governments stupid, the collapse of agricultural prices and its deadly ripple effects cannot be blamed on the metal's role as money.

BANKING CRISES   The most critical aspect of the Great Depression is the series of banking crises that followed the stock market collapse, particularly in 1931 and 1933, in the United States and elsewhere. Many commentators, prominently among them Milton Friedman and Anna Schwartz, have argued persuasively that these crises were instrumental in turning a recession into a Great Depression. But were these crises a result of monetary policy dictated by the gold standard?

It is important first to note that the depth of the depression was much worse in the United States than in other countries, particularly Britain, as reflected in the real-income and employment figures shown in figures 6.7 and 6.11. The evidence strongly suggests that the main factor that made the depression so much worse in the United States than in Britain was not the paucity of reserve money supply, but instead the broad collapse in confidence brought about by the bank failures. As shown in Figure 6.12, the supply of reserve money behaved very differently in the United States and Britain. In the United States, it fell sharply in 1930, and then rose very rapidly for the rest of the decade. In Britain, it declined steadily throughout the 1920s and then headed moderately upwards after 1931. Based on this evidence, and the idea that the rigid supply of gold was at the core of the Great Depression, it would be natural to expect that deflation and the depression would be worse in Britain than in the United States. We know, however, that it was precisely the other way around.

Furthermore, Figure 6.13 shows how the United States experienced an enormous contraction of money even as its reserve money was increasing. The problem was that people lost confidence in the banking system. The

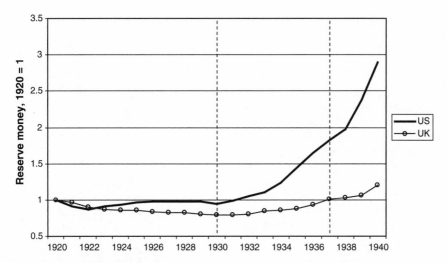

Figure 6.12. U.S. and U.K. reserve money, 1920–1940.
Data source: Friedman and Schwartz (1982: 130–137).
Note: Britain abandoned the gold-exchange standard in September 1931 and the United States in April 1933.

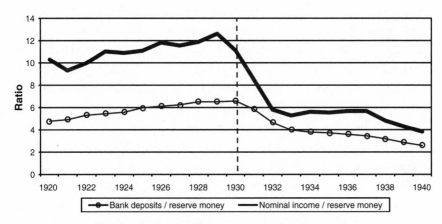

Figure 6.13. U.S. money multipliers, 1920–1940.
Data source: Friedman and Schwartz (1982: 130–137).
Note: Britain abandoned the gold-exchange standard in September 1931 and the United States in April 1933.

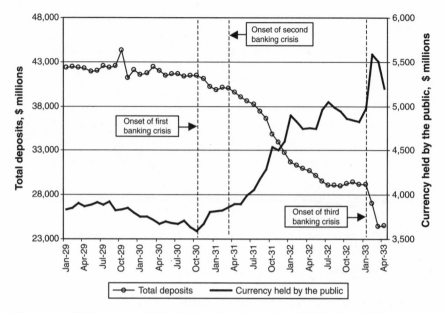

Figure 6.14. U.S. commercial bank deposits and currency held by the public, 1929–1933.
Data source: Friedman and Schwartz (1963: 712–713).

bottom curve shows how the capacity of banks to create deposits out of reserve money was increasing through 1929, until they created $6.60 for every dollar of reserve money in 1930, one year after the market crash. Then this ratio began to fall sharply, so that by 1932, they created only $4 in deposits out of each dollar of reserve money. This is a contraction of 40% in the supply of deposit money, the largest component of money. Almost at the same time, the ratio of nominal income to reserve money, which measures the ability of reserve money to generate income, fell from $12 to $5.20 of income per dollar of reserve money. The two ratios kept falling throughout the decade.

The ability of banks to create deposits out of reserve money collapsed because people were afraid of bank failures after the crises of 1930, 1931, and 1933, of which the third one was particularly vicious. Figure 6.14 shows how deposits fell while currency with the public was increasing fast.[48] The ratio of bank deposits to currency in the hands of the public dropped from 11 in 1929 to 4.7 by April 1933, the month the gold-exchange

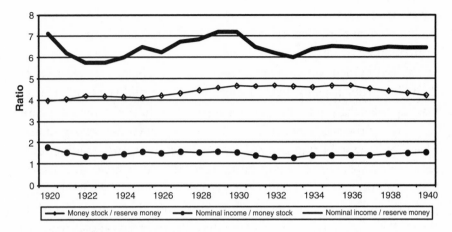

Figure 6.15. U.K. money multipliers, 1920–1940.
Data source: Friedman and Schwartz (1982: 130–137).
Note: Britain abandoned the gold-exchange standard in September 1931 and the
United States in April 1933.

standard was officially abandoned. It is apparent that people preferred to
keep their money under the mattress.

This stands in contrast with what happened in Britain, where the banking system was relatively unscathed. Figure 6.15 shows that the ratios
moved much less dramatically there. The difference with the United
States was that the ratio of money to reserve money actually *increased* during the initial, and worst, years of the depression. This allowed nominal
income to increase while reserve money was declining.

These data suggest strongly that the collapse in confidence brought about
by the bank failures was a crucial factor in worsening the Great Depression
in the United States. Importantly, monetary sovereignty played a part in
worsening, rather than alleviating, the fall in the money-multiplying power
of the banking system. After the initial crises, the Federal Reserve methodi-
cally increased the legal reserve requirements of the banks; that is, the Fed
lowered the portion of deposits that banks were permitted to lend out. The
tightening of reserve requirements is just one example of the contractionary
stance taken by the Fed took during those years. For instance, in early 1933,
as panic raged during the interregnum between the Hoover and Roosevelt
presidencies, the Fed decided to contract the money supply by selling off

government bonds. The money used to pay for the bonds moved from the banking system to the Federal Reserve, reducing the banks' capacity to generate credit and multiply reserve money.

The Fed's Open Market Committee could have helped to alleviate the illiquidity problem of the banks by just remaining idle. The United States was experiencing gold inflows from abroad which, under the automatic workings of the gold standard, would have expanded the money supply. Moreover, the gold standard did not rule out emergency lending, even when this implied a reduction in the ratio of gold reserves to currency. This we illustrated earlier with reference to the actions of the Bank of England during the 1847 financial crisis. Moreover, the famous dictum of Walter Bagehot, "lend freely at high interest rates based on collateral that would normally be considered good," had become the accepted doctrine to deal with banking crises within the gold standard since the publication of his *Lombard Street* in 1873.[49]

Hoover invited the Fed board of governors to make suggestions on halting the banking crisis, such as guaranteeing bank deposits, but they offered none. On March 4, 1933, the day after his inauguration, President Roosevelt confronted the crisis by invoking the 1917 Trading with the Enemy Act simply to close all the banks.[50]

The key question is thus why the Fed pursued a contractionary policy, and left the banks to fail, when it should have pursued an expansionary one. This remains to this day a matter of considerable debate. Some authors believe the answer is that Fed functionaries, like central bankers all over the world at that time, persisted in thinking within the constraints of the gold standard even after they had effectively abandoned it. Eichengreen holds that Fed economists believed that an expansion of credit to save the banks would have been self-defeating because it would have prompted gold losses, which in turn would have led to a contraction of the money supply. This effect could have been avoided if all countries had expanded the money supply at the same time, he argues, though it would have required a degree of cooperation and coordination that could not be achieved.[51] The problem with this argument is that the Fed was not applying the gold standard; it was contracting the money supply when the automatic workings of the gold standard would have expanded it.

Other authors blame the Fed's contractionary stance on technical mistakes. Temin argues that a misreading of a technical indicator fooled the Fed: during the early 1930s, they focused on the level of the borrowed reserves (the amount of money that banks borrowed to remain liquid) in order to assess the health of the banks. The level of borrowed reserves remained low throughout these years, leading the Fed to infer, wrongly, that monetary conditions were loose, and that no action was needed. The Fed should, however, have been watching the level of *total* reserves rather than borrowed reserves. Borrowed reserves were low only because deposits were low, and were therefore a symptom of the depression rather than monetary health. In any case, the principles of the gold standard cannot be detected in the Fed's decision making.

The application of independent sovereign monetary policies to sever the link between growth of the money supply and movements of gold was hailed at the time as a triumph of rationality over the primitive automaticity of the gold standard. The shift toward the gold-exchange standard in the early 1920s was the first fatal step on this path, blunting the mechanism through which the gold standard regulated the creation of credit across countries—allowing it to grow excessively when central banks did not intervene, and allowing central banks purposely to contract it when it should have been expanding. Misguided government interventions in trade, employment, and agriculture also contributed enormously to the contraction of economic activity worldwide. All together, the Great Depression must be seen as the result of the protracted inconsistencies that emerged between an international economic system that required countries to abide by an international discipline and the emerging doctrine of economic sovereignty, which rejected such discipline.

The Stubborn Power of Gold: The Bretton Woods System

One of the most fascinating aspects of the Great Depression period is that, in spite of the rise of economic sovereignty and the abandonment of the gold standard, gold remained the world's standard of value. As French economist Charles Rist wrote in 1934, "A wider and wider gap is opening every day between this deep-rooted conviction on the part of the public and the disquisitions of those theoretical economists who are representing gold as an outworn standard . . . the public in all countries is busily hoarding all the national currencies which are supposed to be convertible into gold."[52]

The International Conference on Monetary and Economic Questions convened in 1933 to discuss how to reverse deflation and stabilize currencies. Both objectives were defined in terms of gold—that is, the desired increase in prices was defined as a fall in the price of gold, and currency stabilization was defined in terms of a resumption of the gold standard. This was precisely because gold was not an invention of governments. It was the standard of value of the world's population, and, by their behavior, people showed that any solution to the world's monetary problems had to include gold.

Gold made its return as the foundation of the global monetary system at the end of World War II. Delegates from forty-four Allied nations convened a conference in Bretton Woods, New Hampshire, in 1944 to address three major problems they had inherited from the resurgence of economic nationalism triggered by the Great Depression.

The first was the disruption of trade. The conference created the General Agreement on Tariffs and Trade (GATT), which committed the signatory countries to reducing global trade barriers. The conference recommended the creation of an institution that would implement this mandate, but the signatories failed to ratify it. Still, GATT countries organized multiple rounds of trade talks which reduced protection over the next several decades, and ultimately created the World Trade Organization in 1995.

The second problem was the parlous state of international financial flows. The conference foresaw the need for enormous financial flows to aid the reconstruction of Europe and the economic development of the Third World. Believing that the collapsed private financial and capital markets would not be able to provide such flows, it created the International Bank for Reconstruction and Development, otherwise known as the World Bank. Initially, the World Bank concentrated its efforts on the reconstruction of areas ravaged by the war. However, finding that its help was not really needed there, it refocused its efforts on financing development projects in poor countries.

The third problem was the disorder in the international monetary system, which severely inhibited trade. The new "Bretton Woods system" established a gold-exchange standard built around the U.S. dollar, which would continue to be convertible into gold at $35 an ounce. A new International Monetary Fund was created to coordinate the smooth operation of this system.

The gold-exchange standard began fraying in the late 1950s. International monetary developments during the years 1958–1961 bore great similarities with those of 1926–1929, both periods revealing deep structural flaws in the concept of a gold-exchange standard. The gold standard had a built-in self-equilibrating mechanism, namely that funds flowing out of one country into another increased the money supply in the receiving country and reduced it in the sending country. Not so under the gold-exchange standard, where dollars were treated as substitutes for gold. This meant that dollars sent abroad did *not* reduce the money supply in the United States, as the receiving country left the dollars on deposit in the United States, where they were loaned out to create yet more money. This factor had in the late 1920s led to the substantial credit creation that preceded the 1929 market collapse. In the late 1950s, as in the 1920s, the gold-exchange standard not only loosened the essential link between credit and gold, but severed it entirely.[53] This was one of the key factors making it inherently inflationary, contributing both to the wave of speculation that preceded the 1929 crash and to the worldwide inflation of the 1960s and 1970s, when the system finally collapsed.

This is an essential point to which we will return in chapter 7. When a central bank creates excess liquidity, wittingly or otherwise, it can show up in many different places. In the 1920s, it was in the stock market. In the 1960s and 1970s, it was in the consumer price index. In developing countries in the 1990s, it was often in foreign exchange; that is, the populace took new money printed by their central banks and used it to buy dollars, thus producing depreciation. In recent years, it appears to have shown up in house prices and, rather worryingly for the future survival of our fiat monies, gold.

Over the course of the 1960s, the U.S. gold stock dwindled to the point where, if foreigners had demanded redemption in gold for a substantial portion of their dollar holdings, they would have wiped out the stock and precipitated a collapse of the country's credit structure. The only act which could have saved a gold-based monetary system would have been for the United States to double the price of gold, reflecting the doubling of dollar prices which had taken place since 1934, when Roosevelt established the $35 an ounce parity. This would have doubled the nominal value of U.S. gold holdings, restoring the country's solvency, albeit most certainly at the cost of the dollar's credibility. Thereafter, redemptions of foreign dollar holdings in gold would have to have been made mandatory, as it is on a gold standard, to prevent the otherwise inevitable reemergence of a dangerous credit pyramid in the United States. But the United States adamantly refused to devalue the dollar, resulting in a shortage in the gold stock, a shortage in gold production, and a shortfall in the portion of production which goes into increasing monetary reserves.

The results of the operation of the deeply flawed gold-exchange standard were eminently foreseeable—and indeed were not only foreseen but loudly warned of by a few souls, such as Jacques Rueff and Robert Triffin, brave enough to call the emperor naked in public. The United States ran a persistent balance of payments deficit, which was never counteracted by a contraction in the aggregate credit supply (as it would have been under a true gold standard). The resulting inflation in the United States was spread to the creditor countries through the fixed exchange rate. The U.S. government—as with governments since time immemorial, when wishing fervently for something which contradicts the laws of supply and demand—then began paring away economic freedoms in the name of safeguarding the "national interest." In this case, the goal was to eliminate the balance of payments deficit without confronting its cause.

The Interest Equalization Tax was imposed in 1963. Designed to reduce capital outflows by offsetting higher investment returns abroad, the tax was imposed on all purchases of foreign securities (with a few exemptions) by U.S. residents. The tax failed to stem capital outflows, and instead encouraged foreign borrowers to replace securities sales in the United States with bank financing, which was exempt. This motivated introduction in 1965 of the Voluntary Foreign Credit Restraint program, which requested financial institutions to observe voluntary ceilings on lending to foreigners, and the Foreign Direct Investment (FDI) program, which requested U.S. nonfinancial corporations to restrain FDI. Though initially "voluntary," the programs involved a steadily ratcheted-up diet of government intervention into the commercial dealings abroad of individual U.S. banks and businesses. The FDI program was made mandatory in 1968, forcing U.S. companies to accept a cap on their investments or earnings abroad. In that same year, the

United States reneged on its commitment to redeem dollars for gold; the only exception being monetary authorities, toward which the United States applied extreme moral suasion to prevent redemptions.

It didn't work. By 1971, foreign official and private dollar claims had risen to over three times the U.S. gold stock. Demands by France and others to redeem their growing dollar holdings for gold finally placed the United States in an untenable position, resulting in President Nixon's decision to end convertibility. Attempts to limit exchange-rate movements among currencies over the next several years proved ineffective, leading to the world's major currencies all floating against one another by 1976. The collapse of the Bretton Woods monetary regime led Rueff to comment presciently that "as long as we do not restore a convertible-currency [i.e., gold standard] system . . . the world will be doomed to suffer balance-of-payments disequilibriums, monetary insecurity, migrations of hot money, exchange-rate instability, and all the distempers that the ignorance of men and the weakness of institutions can beget."[54] That such suffering has in fact come to pass is once again being widely blamed on a lack of economic sovereignty—this despite the fact that it was a predictable, and indeed predicted, result of a *return* to economic sovereignty in the monetary sphere.

7

THE FUTURE OF THE DOLLAR

The Emperor's Clothes

They get our oil and give us a worthless piece of paper.
—Mahmoud Ahmadinejad, OPEC summit, November 18, 2007

Unkind words about the U.S. currency from an Iranian president could normally be dismissed as political bluster, but in this case it was bluster with a disturbing kernel of truth to it. Over the course of 2007, states with large dollar holdings were becoming increasingly fearful about the dollar's long-term global purchasing power, but they simply had less incentive to sound the alarm about it.

A dollar was once redeemable for a fixed amount of precious metal, but has for four decades now been redeemable only for near-worthless metal—pennies, nickels, dimes, and quarters. It is valuable only to the extent that vast numbers of people believe that vast numbers of other people will continue, of their own volition, to exchange intrinsically valuable things for it. Should this confidence evaporate, the dollar is truly just "a worthless piece of paper."

It is hard to imagine that this confidence could be fatally undermined any time soon. History, however, does not provide kind testimony to the durability of national monies. Many dozens of them lost more than half of their purchasing power between 1950 and 1975 alone—including the dollar, which lost 57%.[1]

The Iranian president was not alone, however, in disparaging the dollar on the world stage in autumn 2007. The dollar is "losing its status as the world currency," Xu Jian, a central bank vice director, told a conference in Beijing on November 7. "We will favor stronger currencies over weaker ones, and will readjust accordingly," said Cheng Siwei, vice chairman of China's National People's Congress, at the same meeting.[2] Their concerns were echoed two weeks later by Chinese premier Wen Jiabao. "We have never been experiencing such big pressure," Wen said. "We are worried about how to preserve the value of our [$1.5 trillion in] reserves."[3]

On the same day as Xu and Cheng's comments, the price of gold climbed to $833.50 per ounce, a record high in nominal terms (though in real terms still substantially below its peak in the early 1980s). Oil prices leapt to a record high $98 a barrel. The stock market tumbled. The ABX indexes tied to high-risk mortgages fell sharply. The newswires also reported an estimate that U.S. banks would have to write down as much as $600 billion as a result of the housing market bust and the associated collapse of the Structured Investment Vehicle (SIV) markets.[4] Last but not least in the parade of worrying economic news, the dollar fell to a record low 1.46 dollars/euro, down more than 75% from its high in 2000.

Teasing out cause and effect at any given moment is never simple in financial markets, but the signs are recognizable from the 1960s. Like China and the dollar-saturated Persian Gulf states today, European governments made similar remarks in the 1960s about the reliability of the dollar as a store of value—just a few years before President Nixon demonetized gold in order to preempt a run on America's dwindling gold stock. In the private markets, Jacques Rueff noted that people were turning to "tangible goods, gold, land, houses, corporate shares, paintings and other works of art having an intrinsic value because of their scarcity or the demand for them." Sound familiar? Indeed, this is the story of our decade to date. In the 1960s, Rueff pinned the blame squarely on "the growing insolvency" of the dollar.[5] Then, as today, U.S. monetary policy was spreading inflation to countries importing such policy through fixed exchange rates, encouraging them to seek out other more reliable long-term stores of wealth.

Today, of course, foreign governments are not asking the United States for their gold back, because the country reneged on its redemption pledge long ago. But they are warning that they will begin exchanging their growing hoards of dollars for other currencies and assets. Even a gradual diversification would mark the coming of a new age in international monetary relations. It would end the age of what Rueff called "the precarious dominance of the dollar" in the global monetary markets. In its most benign form, an orderly diversification would usher in a new period of shared dominance with the euro, and possibly other currencies. In its most malignant form, a dollar rout, mirroring the collapse of a Ponzi scheme, could instigate a period of international monetary disorder that would have damaging repercussions for trade, financial globalization, and living standards worldwide.

The Dollar as Global Money

Remarkably, there is no theoretical framework in macroeconomics for analyzing the problems now besieging the international monetary system. As discussed in chapter 5, Optimum Currency Area (OCA) theory describes the world in terms of economic regions separated monetarily by domestic currencies that float against each other. It says nothing of the existence of an international currency that would be necessary to conduct cross-border transactions, much less the principles that should guide its creation.

This stands in sharp contrast with the era of the gold standard, when the international monetary system was supported by a clear theory that specified the way in which the underlying world currency should relate to other currencies. It established mechanisms that would bring about equilibrium in times of crisis, automatically or through specific central bank actions. It is not true of the current system.

The crucial role of the international currency having been left out of the script, it fell to a national currency, the U.S. dollar. The rules that should be followed to provide international liquidity, as opposed to the rules that the U.S. Federal Reserve would follow to provide liquidity to the United States, were never defined. This created a conflict of interest in the two de facto functions of the Fed: the money it creates is both a domestic currency and an international one, and the objectives of each of the aspects of this dual role can and frequently do clash. In other words, there is a principal-agent problem at the core of the international monetary system. In case of conflict, the Fed could be trusted to follow the course that would, in its perception and in accordance with domestic statute, benefit the United States, even if this would be against the interests of all the other users of the international monetary system.

The presence of this principal-agent problem is ironic because the floating-rate system was supposed to be impervious to conflicts between the needs of the international monetary system and the needs of monetary sovereignty—the latter having destroyed the gold standard and its Bretton Woods offshoot. How could this be an issue if all currencies floated against each other, allowing for the pursuit of independent monetary policies in all countries? Any excess or deficit in the creation of the world money could be compensated for with domestic monetary policies. This was, after all, the very purpose of the system.

Yet the system never operated this way. As we will illustrate shortly, only the Fed has been meaningfully "sovereign," with other central banks being obliged, to greater and lesser degrees, to accommodate their policies to conditions prevailing in the international markets. But the Fed is hardly immune to the forces of financial globalization, and could see its powers severely curtailed under the weight of growing macroeconomic imbalances.

The U.S. Imbalances

The United States has experienced three major episodes of macroeconomic imbalance in the last four decades. They manifested themselves in three different ways: high inflation, large current account deficits, and currency depreciation. These coincide with the three outcomes that excess domestic demand—the natural result of excess monetary creation—can have in an economy. If the economy is open, excess demand generates current account deficits. If the economy is closed, either because of protection or because other countries refuse to finance the current account deficits, the inflation rate goes up. In any case, the exchange rate tends to depreciate, as the value of the local currency in terms of other currencies is naturally lowered by the excess monetary creation that drives excess demand.

The first episode of serious macroeconomic imbalance marked the end of the Bretton Woods system in the 1960s and continued well into the realm of the new fiat money floating system. It manifested itself in a burst of inflation coupled with a depreciation of the dollar. Figure 7.1 portrays the origins of this first crisis. The top panel shows how the shifts in the exchange rates among major countries increased in frequency in the 1960s, after the liberalization of capital flows. Up to 1970, most of the exchange rate movements were devaluations against the dollar. Yet the dollar was weakening against gold throughout the 1960s. In that decade, the United States printed dollars well in excess of what its gold reserves could support, in an attempt to finance the Vietnam War and expanded domestic programs without raising taxes. This prompted a run against the dollar as well as demands from several countries to convert the dollars held by their central banks into gold. The figure shows how all of these currencies appreciated against the dollar when it was finally floated in 1971, evidence that the run against the dollar was justified.

In the decades since the end of the Bretton Woods system, the idea that it had to be abandoned because it had become an irrational monetary lid on world economic progress has become folklore.[6] But if this were true, the last few years of the Bretton Woods system should have been deflationary. Yet, as is visible in the lower panel of Figure 7.1, prices were not falling in the 1960s and early 1970s—they were rising in the key world economies. And liberation from the fixed exchange rate system did not result in a stabilization of the international monetary environment but, instead, in an explosion of inflation unprecedented in peace time. Like today, the complaint that countries leveled against the United States was not that the dollar was too scarce, which the Fed's decisions to slash interest rates between September 2007 and April 2008 implied, but that it was too plentiful.

With its credibility at stake, the dollar sustained its role as the international standard of value because of good fortune in two fronts. First, the Fed under chairman Paul Volcker hammered out inflation in the 1980s with a painful period of high real interest rates. It took almost a decade to reduce inflation expectations back down to moderate levels. Second, there was no viable alternative. None of the economies of the countries with strong currencies had the size and diversification needed to sustain a world currency.

The high inflation rates that marked the 1970s have not yet reemerged. However, another symptom of macroeconomic imbalance, large current account deficits, has appeared in two episodes. As shown in Figure 7.2, the U.S. current account went into deficit as the inflation rate declined in

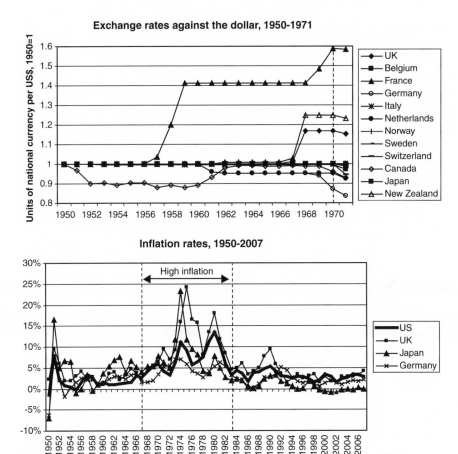

Figure 7.1. The collapse of Bretton Woods.
Data source: IMF International Financial Statistics.

the early 1980s. The deficits widened until they reached a then-record-setting 3.4% of gross domestic product (GDP) in 1985, subsequently declining to virtually zero in 1991. A second episode of imbalance started in 1991, as the current account deficit began to widen again, and kept on widening through 2007. In recent years, these deficits reached levels without precedent in the United States or other major countries, near 7% in the third quarter of 2006. They are as unprecedented as the rates of inflation of the 1970s were in their times.

U.S. macroeconomic imbalances have been mirrored in the exchange rate. As shown in Figure 7.3, the real effective exchange rate of the dollar

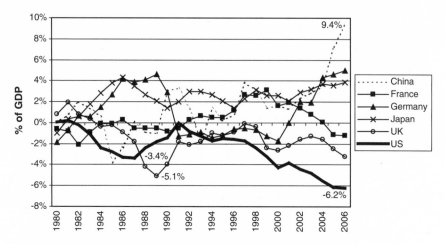

Figure 7.2. Current account balances: United States versus other major economies, 1980–2006.
Data source: IMF World Economic Outlook.

has had substantial ups and downs in the last several decades, roughly co-inciding with the turns of the tides of macroeconomic weakening and strengthening.[7] The dollar suffered substantial depreciations in the 1970s,[8] the late 1980s, and over the current decade. Yet it is during this cur-

Figure 7.3. U.S. real effective exchange rate, 1978–2007.
Data source: IMF International Financial Statistics.

rent period of depreciation that global trust in the dollar has appeared to crack, to an extent not witnessed in the previous episodes.

Is Fiscal Policy to Blame?

The current U.S. macroeconomic imbalance is frequently labeled a problem of the "twin deficits," the twins being the fiscal and current account deficits. Most simple macroeconomic models predict that these two variables will move together, in such a way that a fiscal deficit tends to lead to a current account deficit, while a fiscal surplus tends to produce a current account surplus. Yet, as is borne out in a recent study by Federal Reserve Board economists, the fiscal deficit does not seem to be a primary culprit behind the current account deficits.[9]

As shown in Figure 7.4, the twins separated from 1989 to 2000, and then again from 2003 to 2006. In the first episode, the current account deficit narrowed as the fiscal deficit worsened from 1989 to 1991. Subsequently, the current account deficit increased while the fiscal balance improved, passing from a large deficit to a substantial surplus. In the second episode, the fiscal deficit fell from almost 5% of GDP to about half this level while the current account deficit kept on increasing. Notice that the periods in which the two "twins" moved in opposite directions are too

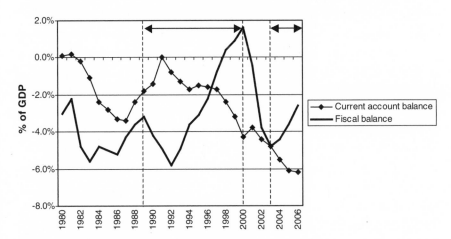

Figure 7.4. U.S. current account and fiscal balances, 1980–2006.
Data source: IMF World Economic Outlook.

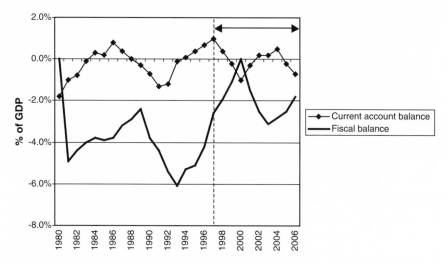

Figure 7.5. EU current account and fiscal balances, 1980–2006.
Data source: IMF World Economic Outlook.

long to be explained by lags in the fiscal effect on the current account. Notice also that even though there was a brief period in which the current account deficit declined while the fiscal deficit increased (1989–1991), for
most of the time the current account deficit widened while the fiscal deficit
declined (1991 to 2001, and then 2003 to 2006). That is, reality contradicted the established idea that reducing the fiscal deficit should significantly reduce the current account deficit.

So much for the American twins. What about their European cousins?
As is visible in Figure 7.5, the separation has taken place in Europe as well.
The two variables have moved in opposite directions since 1997.

Furthermore, the magnitudes involved suggest that variables other
than the fiscal deficit must be behind the recent current account deficits.
While the recent U.S. current account deficits are record-setting, the recent fiscal deficits have not been extraordinary by contemporary standards, or even larger than those of the other major economies. As is
visible in Figure 7.6, the worst U.S. fiscal deficit in recent years, 4.8% of
GDP in 2003, was a full percentage point lower than the 1992 deficit.
The recent deficits have also been of the same order of magnitude as
those of other major countries. If the fiscal deficits were the cause of the
weakening of the dollar and the large current account deficits, all major

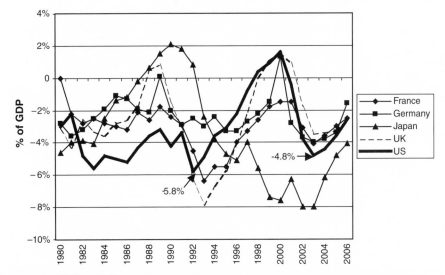

Figure 7.6. Fiscal balances in major economies, 1980–2006.
Data source: IMF World Economic Outlook.

countries should be suffering from these same problems. And this is manifestly not the case. One particular example worth noting is that of Japan, which ran fiscal deficits exceeding 4% of GDP from 1993 to 2006, while running current account surpluses from 1% to 4% of GDP during that same period. At 4.3% of GDP, the 2006 Japanese fiscal deficit was much larger than the 2.6% deficit of the United States. Yet Japan had a current account surplus of 4% of GDP, compared with a 6.5% deficit in the United States.

Some observers have directed their concern not at the most recent fiscal deficits but at their accumulated impact, the public debt level.[10] Yet the ratio of government debt to GDP has not reached excessive levels either. Figure 7.7 shows the gross and net government debt[11] of seven major economies. As is apparent in the two panels, the U.S. government debt is among the lowest by both measures. Only Canada and the United Kingdom are lower in net terms, and only the latter in gross terms. Moreover, U.S. government debt as a percentage of GDP is actually about ten percentage points lower than it was in 1993.

Thus, it is clear that neither fiscal deficits nor the accumulation of public debt can be blamed for the serious deterioration of the current account

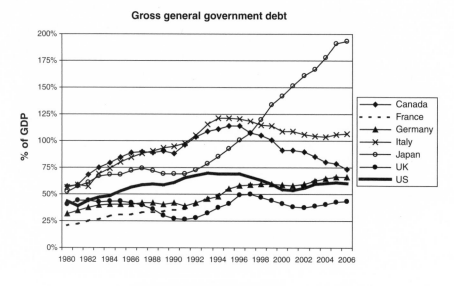

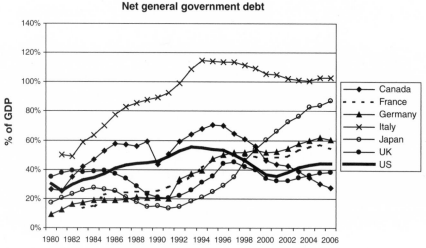

Figure 7.7. General government debt in major economies, 1980–2006.
Data source: IMF World Economic Outlook.

deficit that has taken place since 1991, or for the associated weakening of the dollar. So what is the source of these phenomena?

Figure 7.4, which charts the path of the U.S. current account deficit since 1980, provides a hint. Notice that the first episode of large current account deficit deterioration, from 1981 to 1985, took place under the Volcker

Fed, which was applying a contractionary monetary policy that successfully reduced inflation. As inflation came down under high interest rates, the current account deficit rose to then-record-setting levels. This fact illustrated a phenomenon of financial globalization that began to take hold in the 1980s: the emergence of autonomous capital flows, and the reversal of the causal link between current account balances and capital flows.

During the life of the Bretton Woods system, international capital flows were not autonomous. Capital flowed across borders mainly to settle current account deficits, in such a way that current account transactions largely determined capital flows. This has changed in recent decades with the globalization of finance.

According to the McKinsey Global Institute, the sum of international financial assets and liabilities owned and owed by residents of high-income countries leapt from 50% of aggregate GDP in 1970 to 100% in the mid-1980s to 330% in 2004.[12] We calculate that one part of the international capital flows of the United States, total trade in long-term securities, increased from $373 billion in 1982 to $52.1 trillion in 2006, while total U.S. trade in goods and services only increased from $575 billion to $3.65 trillion in the same period. Therefore, as shown in Figure 7.8, this portion of capital flows is now more than fourteen times the dollar volume of U.S. trade in goods and services. Most of these capital flow transactions are autonomous, in the sense that they are not carried out to finance current account deficits. Instead, they take place as part of an ongoing worldwide diversification of investment.

The foreign funds entering the economy increase aggregate domestic demand, pushing up the rate of inflation (for the nontradable goods and services) and opening a deficit in the current account (for the tradable goods and services). That is, the traditional causality in the relationship between current account balances and capital flows has been reversed. Autonomous capital inflows now drive current account deficits, a phenomenon that first became clear during the Volcker Fed. In those years, the Fed increased dollar interest rates to high real levels and made it clear that it would stick to this policy as long as necessary to bring down inflation. These actions increased the appeal of U.S. financial and real assets, thereby drawing in large scale capital inflows from abroad. These in turn led to current account deficits.

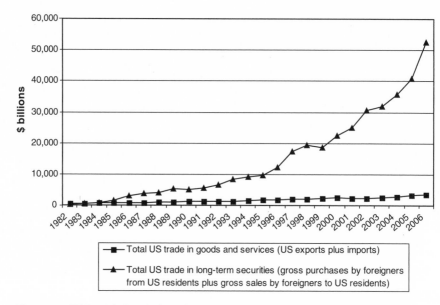

Figure 7.8. U.S. trade in goods and services versus trade in long-term securities, 1982–2006.
Source: Steil and Litan (2006), updated with data from U.S. Bureau of Economic Analysis and U.S. Department of the Treasury.

This reversed relationship between capital flows and current account deficits explains why such deficits can coexist with fiscal surpluses, as occurred in the United States between 1991 and 2001. In those years, the United States was the beneficiary of huge inflows of foreign private capital looking to take advantage of the rapid expansion of productivity and the wave of innovations associated with the advent of online business and consumer connectivity and the "New Economy." As shown in Figure 7.4, the current account deficits mirroring these capital inflows became wider as the fiscal deficit shrank and eventually became a surplus.

The fascination of foreign investors with America's New Economy ended with the collapse of the dot-coms in 2001. Private capital entering the United States declined sharply. Yet, as shown in Figure 7.9, the vacuum left by the evaporating private inflows was filled with foreign official capital inflows, most of it owned by central banks. They were invested primarily in U.S. Treasury bonds, which in terms of risk are similar to

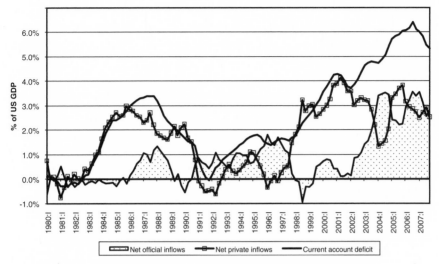

Figure 7.9. U.S. capital inflows and the current account deficit, 1980–2007.
Source: Setser (2007).
Data source: U.S. Bureau of Economic Analysis International Transactions Accounts Data.
Note: Data are rolling four-quarter sums.

those issued by governments of other major countries, such as Germany, France, or the United Kingdom. Yet the yields paid on U.S. securities, when adjusted for persistent dollar depreciation, have been consistently lower than those paid on securities issued by these other governments.

This would seem to be a paradox, yet it is the natural result of the phenomenon that Benjamin Strong, Jacques Rueff, and Friedrich Hayek expressed concern over in the 1920s, during the reign of the gold-exchange standard. When a domestic currency is used as the international currency, central banks can earn interest by depositing their reserves in the country issuing the international currency—in this case, the United States. Thus, the dollars issued by the United States to finance its current account deficits routinely come back in the form of capital inflows—if not through private transactions, then as deposits of reserves of foreign central banks. The United States thereby rests assured that the expansion of the current account deficit need not be constrained by the need for continuing capital inflows—provided it does not lose the privileges associated with issuing the international currency.

The Falling Dollar

As shown in Figure 7.10, the exchange rate of the dollar relative to the euro has, since the euro's creation in 1999, been closely associated with the geometric ratio of the nominal interest rates set by the Fed and the European Central Bank (ECB). (Note that any reading below 1.00 in the figure represents a dollar depreciation.) The same finding holds for dollar exchange rates with other major currencies, such as the pound sterling and the yen.

The figure is consistent with the structural change that the international economy has been undergoing over the last several decades; namely that capital flows, rather than trade flows, are increasingly determinant in the balance of payments and, therefore, in their macroeconomic impact. That is, when the Fed lowers (raises) dollar interest rates relative to those of, say, the eurozone, demand for dollars falls (rises) because dollar-denominated financial instruments pay lower (higher) yields relative to euro-denominated instruments.

As shown in Figure 7.11, the Fed aggressively cut interest rates in the early part of this decade, with the dollar falling substantially in tandem.

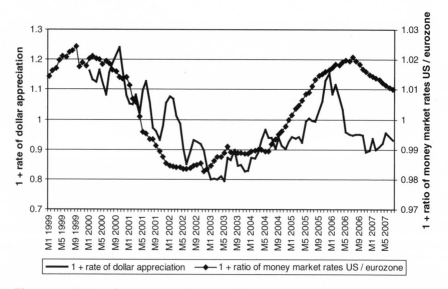

Figure 7.10. U.S. and eurozone exchange and interest rates, 1999–2007.
Source: Hinds (2006), updated with data from IMF International Financial Statistics.

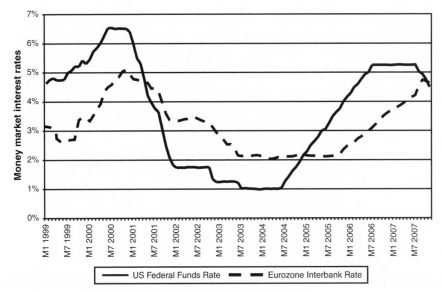

Figure 7.11. Dollar and euro money market rates, 1999–2007.
Data source: IMF International Financial Statistics.

It then raised rates between 2004 and 2006, slowing the broad trend of dollar depreciation. It then cut rates dramatically, by half a percentage point, in September 2007 as alarm spread over the credit crunch that emerged from bank exposure to deteriorating subprime mortgages and mortgage-linked assets. It followed with further quarter-point cuts in November and December, leading to a substantial further dollar weakening, and precipitating expressions of deep concern from governments, particularly in Asia and the Middle East, holding vast and rising dollar central bank reserves. "For China, what we worry about . . . is that very accommodative U.S. monetary policy could give rise to a new burst of liquidity in global markets," said Zhou Xiaochuan, governor of the People's Bank of China.[13] "If the federal funds rate continues to fall," said Hu Xiaolian, director of the Chinese State Administration of Foreign Exchange, "this will certainly have a harmful effect on the U.S. dollar exchange rate and the international currency system."[14] The rate of money creation by the Fed in recent years has clearly been excessive from the perspective of foreign holders of dollars.

The response of the Fed chairman and vice-chairman to repeated questions about the falling dollar was to state that the Fed took exchange rate movements into account insofar as they expected higher import prices to increase domestic inflation, but that the Treasury secretary was the U.S. government's spokesman on the dollar. The obvious problem with this response, from the perspective of foreigners concerned about the eroding value of the dollar, is that the Treasury secretary has no control over monetary policy, which was the clear driving force behind such erosion.

The Fed justified its aggressive rate cutting, which it accelerated in January 2008, by saying that the downside risks to growth were greater than the upside risks to inflation. (This logic reflected its so-called dual mandate to pursue both price stability and maximum employment, a trade-off that the single mandate of the ECB, price stability, presumes illusory.) U.S. inflation, as measured by the consumer price index (CPI), was not yet in deeply worrisome territory, although at 3.5% in September and 4.3% in December, up from 2.5% a year prior, was well outside the Fed's long-term comfort zone. Unfortunately, there are circumstances in which excessive monetary creation can destabilize the economy while the rate of CPI inflation remains moderate. These tend to be present when the danger of monetary destabilization is at its highest because people have lost faith in the ability of money to keep its value through time. The story of our present decade has been one in which alternatives to the dollar as a store of value have soared even while the CPI has remained relatively subdued.

This phenomenon is well known in developing countries, where asset booms combined with low CPI inflation have preceded monetary and financial crises. In Mexico, for example, share prices rose twelvefold between January 1989 and November 1994, while inflation fell from 35% to 7%. CPI inflation then soared as the Tequila crisis exploded. The prices of shares and real estate more than doubled from 1993 to 1996 in Indonesia and South Korea while CPI inflation rates were declining. In May 1997, just weeks before the currencies collapsed, inflation was only 4.5% in Indonesia and 3.8% in Korea. The same symptoms have been visible in many other monetary crises in developing countries.

And they seem to be visible today in the United States. Following the 2001 dot-com crash, resources flowed into real estate, foreign exchange, and commodities, while CPI inflation remained modest. In 2007, the housing bubble finally burst, causing credit to crunch as the market struggled to out the owners of dud mortgages and mortgage-linked contracts.

The Fed reacted with cheaper dollars, which did precisely nothing in that regard. Credit risk fears remained unabated. But the market duly dumped the dollars for harder assets, pushing the euro, shares, oil, and gold to record dollar prices (see Figure 7.12).

Gold, having been global money for the better part of 2,500 years, and therefore the commodity most sensitive to expectations of macroeconomic instability, provides the best measure of the extent of the rush toward inflation-proof hard assets. Between August 2001 and August 2007, the dollar price of gold soared 144%, while the CPI rose only 17%. The last time such a substantial and sustained appreciation of gold was observed was in the 1970s, following on the heels of America's loose-money policy and balance of payments deterioration in the 1960s, and Rueff's warnings regarding "the precarious dominance of the dollar." There were two episodes, from 1971 to 1975 and from 1977 to 1980. In both, the increase in the price of gold and other commodities presaged substantial increases in CPI inflation as well as significant falls in the international value of the

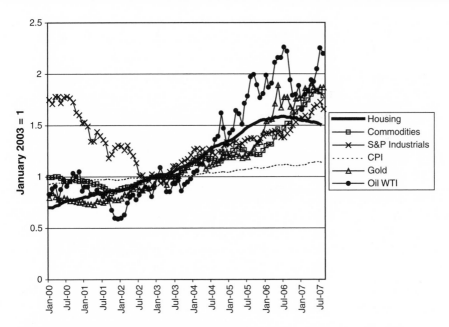

Figure 7.12. U.S. asset prices and CPI, 2000–2007.
Data source: S&P/Case-Shiller Home Price Indices for housing prices and IMF International Financial Statistics for the rest.

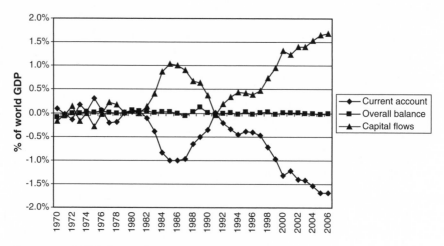

Figure 7.13. U.S. balance of payments, 1970–2006.
Data source: IMF International Financial Statistics.

dollar. Under the hawkish tutelage of the Volcker Fed, and with no viable competitor currency at the time, the dollar sustained its role as the international standard of value. It may not be so lucky this time.

Figure 7.13 shows that there are two visible differences between the recent past and the two prior episodes of dollar weakness: the magnitude of the U.S. current account imbalance in terms of world economic output, and the length of time that elapsed before the deficits were corrected. The deficits of the 1970s were not only relatively small, but were corrected within one or two years. In the 1980s, it took five years before the trend toward wider deficits was halted at a record 1% of world GDP, and five more years to reduce them back to zero. The United States has been absorbing capital inflows equivalent to more than 1% of world GDP since 1999. The deficits reached a record 1.7% of world GDP in 2005 and 2006, with the trend to widening deficits having increased virtually uninterrupted since 1991.

The top panel of Figure 7.14 shows how the level of the world's central bank reserves has risen in step with the U.S. current account deficit. The lower panel shows that the accumulation of reserves in foreign central banks, which had gone from 2% to 4% of world GDP during the previous dollar crisis in the 1970s, went from 4% to 10% of GDP from the early 1990s to 2006. That is, the injection of dollars into the world economy as-

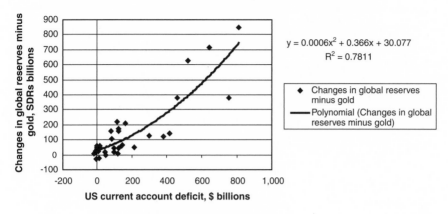

US current account deficit and changes in global reserves, 1971-2006

$$y = 0.0006x^2 + 0.366x + 30.077$$
$$R^2 = 0.7811$$

◆ Changes in global reserves minus gold
— Polynomial (Changes in global reserves minus gold)

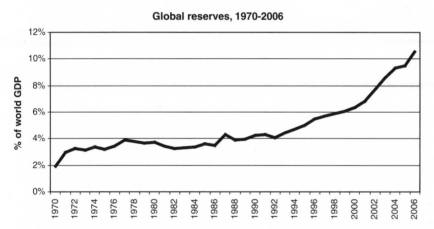

Global reserves, 1970-2006

Figure 7.14. U.S. current account deficit and changes in the world's reserves.
Data source: IMF International Financial Statistics.

sociated with the growing U.S. current account deficits over the last fifteen years has increased worldwide reserves to unprecedented levels at a remarkable pace. This is money waiting to be created in all the countries that have excess reserves. If these countries decided to create national money with these reserves, their domestic money supply would increase by the domestic equivalents of $2.3 trillion of reserves (the excess of their reserves over the normal level they held over the last two decades, which was 4% of GDP). This would roughly double their money supply. Given the enormous magnitude of the injection of currency, worldwide inflation rates would soar.

Worldwide reserves denominated in all international currencies increased from a $2 trillion equivalent to a $5.7 trillion equivalent from 2001 to 2006. About 60% of the increment, or about $2.2 trillion, was denominated in dollars.[15] The total increase in reserves was equivalent to 178% of the total level of reserves in 2001. Central banks of developing countries account for 82% of this increase, mostly owing to exports of oil, other commodities, and, in the case of Asia, noncommodity goods and services. They more than doubled their reserves between 2004 and 2007, to what the International Monetary Fund (IMF) estimates as $4.1 trillion.

Why have central banks been willing to accumulate such historically unprecedented levels of dollar assets? Two main motivations are apparent, and they are not mutually exclusive. The first is that the Asian currency crisis of 1997–1998 taught governments that they needed huge war chests of dollars to ward off potential runs on their domestic currencies. The alternative, going begging to the IMF and U.S. Treasury in times of crisis, is now considered politically and economically unacceptable. The second is mercantilism: by keeping their currencies pegged to the dollar at a rate below that which the market would establish, they believe they are helping their exporters. This strategy leads to a continuous net inflow of dollars. Both of these strategies lead to the need for the central bank to sterilize the inflow in order to keep it from generating domestic inflation, which works like this: (1) the United States sends dollars to, say, Chinese exporters for their goods; (2) the exporters send the dollars to the Chinese central bank for renminbi; (3) the central bank sends the dollars back to the United States for treasury bills, and removes the excess renminbi from the Chinese economy by selling governments bonds. If the central bank cannot sell enough bonds, inflation accelerates, as we witnessed in 2007.[16]

Over the course of this decade, the burden of keeping the global monetary markets stable has fallen on these foreign central banks, which tend to be in developing countries. And they are certainly not holding on to the dollars for the sake of global stability, but to serve their own domestic purposes. We should therefore expect a change in their calculation as to what dollar accumulation policy serves their interests as inflation and dollar depreciation continues to erode their wealth.

The Euro as Understudy

Could an alternative existing currency fill the global gap should the dollar fall victim to a crisis of confidence? No currency other than the euro enjoys the breadth of use that would be necessary to kick start such a transition.

The creation of the euro and the growth of worldwide confidence in it since 1999 is a remarkable achievement. Many prominent political and economic commentators had argued in the 1990s that the euro was either impossible or doomed to quick failure. One even suggested it could lead to war.[17] Such was the power of the belief in the economic and political importance of the bond between money and national sovereignty.

Yet the dollar has, since the euro's creation, shown remarkable resilience. One might have expected the role of the dollar in the international monetary and financial marketplace to decline in tandem with its depreciation since 2001. As shown in the top panel of Figure 7.15, the share of the dollar in central bank reserves has fallen by about 7% since 2001, yet its share in mid-2007 was still noticeably higher than in 1995. The lower panel shows that the share of the dollar in the long-term debt of developing countries has also increased in the last few years. By 2006, it was around 64%, almost the same as its share in central bank reserves. On the flip side of the ledger, the share of the appreciating euro in central bank reserves was slightly *lower* than that of its component currencies in 1995. There has been no general uptrend in noneurozone use of the euro, in trade invoicing or debt issuance, in recent years. Ten to 15% of euros in circulation are held abroad, compared with 60% of U.S. dollars.[18] These figures illustrate the considerable staying power of an international currency.

Chinese and OPEC-nation officials who have expressed public concern about the dollar's erosion might wish that their reserve holdings were more heavily euro-weighted, but they have little incentive to initiate a significant diversification. This would put further downward pressure on the dollar, thus driving down the international purchasing power of their reserves even further. Having said this, no one involved in a Ponzi scheme wants to precipitate its collapse, yet Ponzi schemes invariably do collapse. People sell when they expect others will otherwise sell first. The United

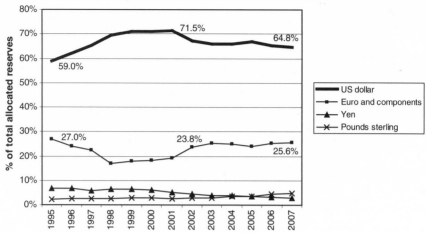

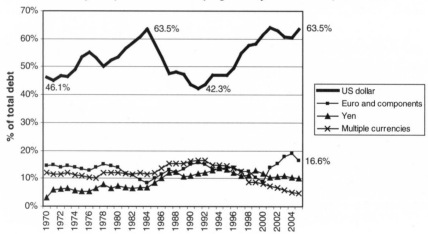

Figure 7.15. Share of main currencies in world reserves and developing country external debt.

Data source: IMF COFER database for international reserves, and World Bank GDF statistics for developing country external debt.

Note: All data in the top panel are from the fourth quarter, except for the 2007 figure, which is from the second quarter.

States cannot, therefore, afford to be insouciant regarding foreigners' views of the dollar as a long-term store of value. Whereas tremendous network externalities support an incumbent international currency (people use a currency because others use it), once a tipping point is reached the shift from one currency to another can be very rapid. As late as 1940, the level of foreign-owned liquid pound sterling assets was still double the level of foreign-owned liquid dollar assets. Yet by 1945 this statistic had reversed.[19] Sterling never regained its luster.

So, could the euro overtake the dollar as the leading international currency? Menzie Chinn and Jeffrey Frankel investigated one aspect of this question: use of the euro as a central bank reserve currency. Applying a regression analysis based on past macroeconomic data, they show, consistent with our discussion above, that the dollar's future performance in terms of inflation and depreciation are the critical variables. If the dollar were, going forward, to depreciate at the broadly measured 3.6% annual rate it experienced from 2001–2004, while the euro appreciated at the 4.6% rate of this period, the euro would overtake the dollar as the leading reserve currency around 2024. If the United Kingdom were to adopt the euro, however, the euro would overtake the dollar approximately four years earlier, around 2020.[20]

Statements from the ECB and the Fed in late 2007 also appeared to indicate a stronger commitment from the former to inflation fighting going forward: with inflation at 3.1% in the eurozone and 4.3% in the United States, the ECB was warning of higher interest rates to push down inflation while the Fed was signaling lower rates to prevent recession. (To put the inflation numbers into context, in July 1971, a month before President Nixon imposed price controls and suspended convertibility of the dollar into gold, U.S. inflation was 4.4%—only 0.1% higher than in November 2007.) For the first time since the ECB's creation, the ECB's "single mandate," price stability, stood in both stark philosophical and practical contrast to the Fed's "dual mandate," price stability and maximum employment. The ECB's stronger stance on maintaining purchasing power is apt to engender increased international confidence in the euro as a store of value, at least relative to the dollar.

There are good reasons, however, to be doubtful about the euro's prospects as a much more significant international currency.

The first is that it would require a degree of economic adaptation that eurozone members are unlikely to embrace. A growing demand for euros internationally means growing eurozone current account deficits and euro appreciation, both of which eurozone politicians are likely to counter with increased protectionism and confidence-jarring political pressure on the ECB. Recent episodes of economic stress have evoked concern in Italy and elsewhere about the euro's contributory role, raising questions about the durability of the political commitment to monetary union across the eurozone.

The second is that official European Union (EU) policy is hostile toward outsiders freely adopting the euro.[21] Non-EU members Montenegro and Kosovo euroized unilaterally, and Iceland is seriously debating the option. The economic logic of euroization for such small European statelets is impeccable. Estonia, for example, adopted a deutschmark-based currency board in 1992, which subsequently morphed into a euro-based board when the mark was eliminated. Speculative attacks on the board during the Asian and Russian currency crises led to damaging interest rate spikes, such as the surge from 8% to 19% in 1998, which would have been avoided entirely had the country been able to euroize outright.[22] The European Council of Ministers and the European Commission have nonetheless stated clearly and repeatedly that unilateral euroization is undesirable and, indeed, impermissible. According to one Council document, "It should be made clear that any unilateral adoption of the single currency by means of 'euroisation' would run counter to the underlying economic reasoning of [European Monetary Union] in the Treaty, which foresees the eventual adoption of the euro as the endpoint of a structured convergence process within a multilateral framework. Therefore, unilateral 'euroisation' would not be a way to circumvent the stages foreseen by the Treaty for the adoption of the euro."[23]

As a matter of both economics and legality, this statement is illogical. In explaining why noneurozone members "cannot" adopt the euro unilaterally, the Commission says that "the credibility of the euro rests on the economic fundamentals of the Member States belonging to the euro zone, which participate fully in the institutions defining the monetary policy and the co-ordination of the economic policies of members."[24] Yet countries adopting the euro unilaterally are not able to affect its "credibility" because they do not participate in the institutions that establish the eurozone's monetary policies. Moreover, money is a liability of the issuer that people and states buy. Why should a person, or a state, ask for permission to use an asset they have legally bought? Should the citizen of a third country that is planning to receive or make payments in euros first obtain a permit from the European Commission? And what is the economic difference between individuals and the sum of all the individuals in a country? The EU's stance is reminiscent of primitive societies in which people objected to being photographed on the grounds that the camera would steal their spirit.

If possession of a euro, bought and paid for, must be seen as a privilege that can be curtailed, or at least controlled, by the issuer of the sold obligation, the potential holder must ask what else could come down the line in terms of restrictions. Given the greater vibrancy and freedom of the U.S. marketplace overall, the dollar is, all else being equal, a more attractive form of monetary asset to store for future use. This, of course, may change in time, but the process of change will be economically and politically challenging for Europe.

Finally, if international confidence in the dollar were to be mortally compromised, it is far from clear that the euro would effectively address the world's concerns. The ECB, after all, has never in its history actually hit its inflation benchmark of "close to but below 2%." Furthermore, when Moody's in January 2008 declared the United States' triple-A credit rating "under threat,"[25] it referred to soaring government commitments on health care and retirement spending. With an aging population and comparably ominous long-term government spending commitments, the eurozone as yet offers no clear promise of superior long-term monetary and fiscal outcomes.

Spoiled Wine, New Bottles

The dollar cannot remain "someone else's problem." If we are not careful, monetary disarray could morph into economic war. We would all be its victims.
—French President Nicolas Sarkozy, before a joint session of the U.S. Congress, November 7, 2007

At the heart of the contradiction that brought down the Bretton Woods gold-exchange system was what came to be known in the late 1950s as "the

Triffin dilemma." Named for the Belgian-American economist Robert Triffin, the dilemma consisted in the need for the issuer of the de facto international currency, in this case the U.S. dollar, to run persistent balance of payments deficits in order to provide the liquidity needed to finance the world economic system. The deficits may have been necessary, but they simultaneously undermined the credibility of the dollar's gold convertibility, which was at the core of the system.

Triffin observed that the result of this system could be either that the international currency would be too scarce or too plentiful, but only by chance appropriate. It was too scarce in the late 1940s. At the time, the United States held most of the world's gold reserves and was running balance-of-payments surpluses. The country that was supposed to issue the world's liquidity was instead absorbing liquidity from the rest of the world.

The only way Europe and Japan could generate gold, represented then by the dollar, was to run balance-of-payments surpluses while simultaneously generating the current account deficits that they required to rebuild their economies. This feat required large capital inflows from abroad, which the United States helped provide through the Marshall Plan. As Europe and Japan recovered during the 1950s and 1960s, however, the situation reversed. These countries began to generate large balance-of-payments surpluses, thus accumulating enormous amounts of dollars, far exceeding the gold reserves of the United States. This threatened the ability of the United States to honor its pledge to redeem dollars with gold, and hence the credibility that the dollar needed to serve as the international currency.

Triffin wrote about this dilemma assuming that the United States created international liquidity when running balance-of-payments deficits. Yet, as we have seen, the United States creates international liquidity when running *current account deficits* balanced out by capital account surpluses — that is, where there is no deficit in the overall balance of payments. The dilemma was forgotten for many years because the post-1971 system of floating currencies seemed to be logically impregnable to disruptions from excessively expansionary or contractionary rates of monetary creation. According to OCA theory, after all, if this rate were too high (low), the currency would just depreciate (appreciate). In a world of complete currency flexibility, these fluctuations would have no effect in any of the domestic compartments into which the world money supply would be split. Yet the rate of growth of the supply of the international currency, still the U.S. dollar, has become a major issue today, long after the death of Bretton Woods.

The Triffin dilemma is quite alive because the problem it describes is not unique to a global system of fixed exchange rates. When states need to accumulate a foreign currency, they will pursue macroeconomic policies designed to attract it. But the central bank issuing that currency will pursue its own domestic monetary needs, and will not base its actions on what other states may need. Thus that currency will at any point in time be, from the world's perspective, under- or oversupplied—that is, there will either be a shortage of international liquidity or a shortage of international confidence. This was the problem in the 1960s, when Triffin wrote, and is still the problem today, nearly forty years after the international monetary system based on fixed exchange rates was abandoned.

Triffin posed his dilemma as one in which the issuer of the international currency could either fail to issue enough money for the rest of the world (as would happen if the United States ran current account surpluses) or issue too much money for the rest of the world (as would happen if it ran excessive deficits). Yet the United States only created the first problem, surpluses, right after World War II. It has been creating the second problem, however, deficits, with much greater frequency. The consequence of issuing too much money is loss of international confidence in the currency, which was in evidence in 2007 and early 2008.

There is today, therefore, as in the past, a clear and dangerous conflict between the needs of the international monetary system and the application of monetary sovereignty. This conflict destroyed the gold-backed dollar that was the basis of the Bretton Woods system, and is now threatening to undermine the credibility of the fiat dollar that is the basis of the current system. When French President Nicolas Sarkozy warned of "economic war" if the dollar's decline were not halted, he was expressing a sentiment felt widely around the world today, one with severe potential consequences for global economic and political relations—as in the 1920s. "No gold-club member," writes Jim Grant, referring to the pre–World War I gold standard, "conducted its domestic monetary affairs as if the outside world didn't exist. Today, the monetary hegemon permits itself the luxury of formulating its interest rate policy for the 50 states alone. Thus do imbalances become institutionalized."[26]

The Consequences of Excessive Imbalances

Even if the only change the international monetary system experienced were the shift from one world currency to a competition between two currencies, the consequences for the United States would be considerable. Such competition would substantially reduce the leverage that the Federal Reserve has on the world's economy, and even on the domestic U.S. economy. The impunity that the Fed has enjoyed for decades in stuffing foreign central banks with ever-growing dollar reserves would come to an end. People around the world would react more assertively to Fed actions that reduce the expected return on their dollar assets, quickly shifting their investments to an alternative denomination.

Such a change would be similar to that which most other countries experienced many decades ago, in the 1960s and 1970s, when globalization of the financial system began. Prior to that, the world's financial system was partitioned along country boundaries. This allowed interest rates to differ substantially from one country to the next, giving more freedom to central banks, as the cost of transactions to move from one currency to another, and from one country to another, was much greater than it is today. There was some capital flight toward more secure or more profitable financial markets, but only large, sophisticated investors were able to bear the costs, bypass the controls, and access the limited facilities that existed to move capital across borders.

The growth of electronic money transfer infrastructure and the eurodollar markets (holdings of dollars outside the United States) changed this radically. With the growing ease of capital movements, central banks found their ability to manipulate interest rates more and more constrained. When they lowered rates, or failed to raise them in line with foreign rates, capital flowed out of the country ever more quickly and in greater volumes. This depleted their reserves of foreign currency, at times provoking major currency crises.

This did not happen in the United States. The United States not only remained an independent monetary space in spite of its opening to the

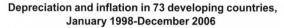

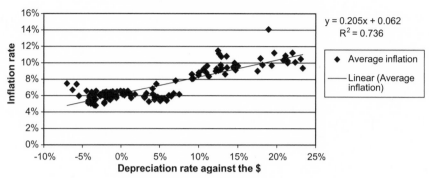

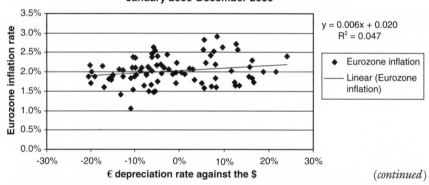

(continued)

Figure 7.16. Currency depreciation and inflation: The world versus the United States.
Source: Hinds (2006), updated with data from IMF International Financial Statistics.

rest of the world, but became the global monetary space of reference. This independence was evident along two main dimensions: the substantial independence of the rate of inflation and the rate of interest from the rate of change of the exchange rate.

Figure 7.16 illustrates the first of these dimensions of independence: U.S. inflation has not generally been driven up by the rate of dollar depreciation. One would expect a positive relationship between the two variables. Depreciation pushes up the prices of tradeables (things that can be imported or exported), which pushes up the general price level if the prices of nontradeables (such as wages) do not fall. As shown in the first

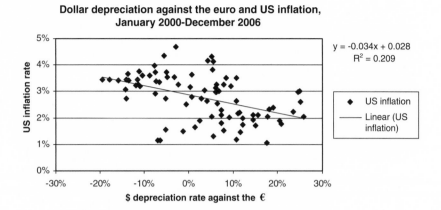

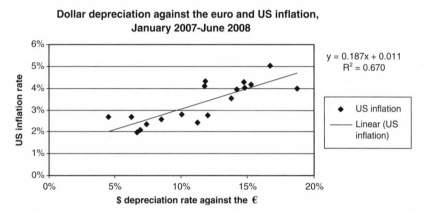

Figure 7.16. (*continued*)

two panels of the figure, this is what tends to happen around the world: inflation increases when the currency depreciates. The third panel shows that this relationship was generally absent in the United States for the first seven years of this decade.

Imports account for only about 15% of U.S. GDP, and the economy is sufficiently diverse that it can substitute quickly with internal production (some of it by foreign companies invested there) for most of what it imports. The broad upward resistance of U.S. inflation to dollar depreciation is therefore due to a feature not of the dollar, but instead of the size and diversity of the U.S. economy.

The mildly *negative* relationship we found between U.S. inflation and depreciation may be explained by higher U.S. inflation leading to market expectations of higher U.S. interest rates, thus encouraging a shift toward dollar assets. Those expectations were entirely absent in early 2008, when the Fed, diverging from practice over the previous twenty-five years, made clear that it would continue to cut interest rates to ward off recession in spite of elevated inflation levels. Of course, even an economy the size of the United States is not immune from imported inflation when depreciation is so large that the opportunities for substitution are not sufficient to suppress it. And indeed, as the fourth panel of the figure shows, U.S. inflation and dollar depreciation began moving in tandem as the dollar fell sharply in 2007 and early 2008.

The second dimension of independence that the Fed retained was the setting of dollar interest rates without regard to those of other currencies. This was easy for central banks to do when they operated in closed monetary markets, but became far more difficult as financial markets globalized. As we showed in Figure 5.8, interest rates in developing countries tended to increase as their currencies depreciated against the dollar.

Broadly speaking, interest rates around the world are pushed upwards by inflation and currency depreciation, and downwards by disinflation and currency appreciation. Figure 7.17 shows that the Fed has not been similarly constrained in its setting of interest rates.

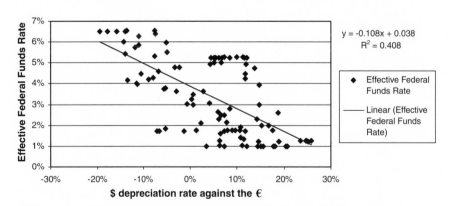

Figure 7.17. U.S. dollar interest rates and depreciation against the euro, January 2000–June 2008.
Data source: IMF International Financial Statistics.

The fact that the United States has been able to conduct monetary policy independently of interest rates in other currencies is a reflection of the fact that investors in the United States and elsewhere, particularly central banks, have accorded a remarkable premium to dollar-denominated assets. Yet there is little basis for presuming that this premium will persist, that investors will indefinitely sacrifice yield vis-à-vis investments denominated in other credible currencies. In the 1950s, the same presumption was made regarding cars, television sets, and many other industrial products that are now dominated by Asian suppliers. If the dollar's global standing as a reliable store of value continues to weaken, investors should be expected to react exactly as U.S. consumers have in recent decades, in blissful ignorance of "Buy American" sloganeering. Internet shopping for financial products issued by credible institutions has never been easier. If investors begin treating the choice between dollar and foreign-currency assets as a form of arbitrage, the powers of the Federal Reserve would be greatly diminished. The signs are already there: in early 2008, the *Wall Street Journal* reported that investors were reacting to dollar weakness by pouring money into U.S.-managed foreign bond funds, assets in which had nearly doubled since two years prior.[27] This is consistent with the March 2008 observation of the president of the Federal Reserve Bank of Dallas, Richard Fisher, that "in today's world, where investors can move their funds instantly from one currency to another to avoid depreciation, the price central bankers pay for high inflation is much higher than in the past."[28]

Suppose, for example, that in an environment of much greater U.S. investor sensitivity to foreign asset yields the Fed pursues an expansionary monetary policy by lowering interest rates. This would depreciate the dollar and reduce the relative yield of U.S. financial instruments. Up to this point, nothing would be new. The new element would be that an enormous mass of people, controlling most of the world's dollar financial assets, would have a greater awareness of alternatives and feel impelled to take defensive action, selling dollars and driving down their value further. Market rates on dollar assets would have to rise in order to attract investment back, thus nullifying the Fed's easing. The Fed will have lost its ability to set dollar interest rates and determine the rate of dollar creation. It will have become dependent on the decisions of the other major central banks, especially the ECB. It will, in essence, have become a mortal central bank like all the others.

In such circumstances, the Fed would also lose its ability to act as a lender of last resort in cases of financial crisis. Expanding credit rapidly to bail out banks would immediately raise fears of dollar depreciation, which would in turn feed a run on dollar deposits in order to buy euros. Just as in developing countries, the United States would be subject to a "reverse liquidity trap," wherein printing more domestic money just finances the stampede into foreign money.[29]

Of course, the ECB would operate under the same limitations. Any deviation from prudent monetary policy would lead to a flight of capital to the dollar. In this way, the competition between two major currencies would strictly limit the scope for truly independent action by any central bank. Developing countries would tend to align with one of the two major currencies, for reasons explained in chapter 5. Currency consolidation is woven into the logic of globalization. Most countries already try to maintain a fixed, or at least stable, exchange rate with the dollar or the euro, and more can be expected simply to adopt one or the other in place of their domestic currencies.

The clearest danger in this setting would be collusion between the two largest central banks, the Fed and the ECB. Collusion would allow them to engage in simultaneous monetary expansions without triggering corrective mechanisms tending to restore sound money. This may seem farfetched, but there are historical precedents. The debauching of the gold standard into the gold-exchange system in the 1920s is the clearest example, with excessive monetary creation having been facilitated by central bank collusion to prevent the normal operation of market constraints.

Alternatives to Monetary Sovereignty

Much has been written about the potential for information technology to render central banks irrelevant by creating "e-monies" that will progressively take the place of central bank currencies, like dollars and euros, in commercial transactions. Indeed, we have all experienced templates for such a world in our use of subway "MetroCards" and the like. It is possible to imagine a world in which MetroCards became so widely used that merchants accepted them in payment for items, receiving balances on the books of the MetroCard issuer, rather than balances on the books of banks (which is how credit cards operate at present).

The unit of account in any fiat money system, however, is defined in terms of the liabilities of the central bank—in the case of the United States, the dollar. So even if MetroCards were to become widely used as a means of payment, and did not involve transfers across central-bank settlement accounts, the Federal Reserve would still control monetary policy in the United States. In short, the march of information technology is not, on its own, a threat to national monetary sovereignty.

The chain of causation which explains this conclusion is complex, but operates in the following manner. The Federal Reserve holds exclusive power to dictate the nominal interest yield on Federal Reserve settlement balances. Provided that banks, including e-money issuers, ultimately continue to finance themselves in dollars, the Fed retains the ability effectively to set the shortest-term (overnight) nominal interest rates for the market as a whole, which in turn determines how interest rates are set in the market for longer maturities.

Noted monetary economist Michael Woodford explains the durability of central banking this way:

> Under present circumstances, it is quite costly for most people to attempt to transact in a currency other than the one issued by their national government, and under these conditions, the central bank's responsibility for maintaining a stable value for the national currency is a grave responsibility. In a future in which transactions costs of all sorts have been radically reduced, that might no longer be the case, and if so, the harm that bad monetary policy can do would be reduced. Nonetheless, it would surely still be convenient for contracting parties to be able to make use of a unit of account with a stable value, and the provision and management of such a standard of value would still be a vital public service. Thus central banks that demonstrate both the commitment and the skill required to maintain a stable value for their countries' currencies should continue to have an important role to serve in the century to come.[30]

Yet there is no *necessary* reason for e-money issuers to continue to adopt central-bank currencies, like the dollar, as their monetary standard. If central banks, which are frequently hampered by fiscally reckless legislators, fail to perform their "vital public service," it may well become a private one. If e-money issuers can persuade users to move to an alternative monetary standard, the domain of central-bank economic control will shrink. The most plausible such alternative standard is the world's oldest and most durable—gold.

Back to the Golden Future?

Fiat money, in extremis, is accepted by nobody. Gold is always accepted.
—Alan Greenspan, in testimony before the House Committee on Banking and Financial Services, May 20, 1999

Nearly four decades after the death of the Bretton Woods system, the gold market continues to show signs of gold's bond with monetary matters. Gold still serves as a global store of value. Figure 7.18 shows how the price of oil, which has soared in dollar terms this decade, has remained stable when measured in terms of gold. Figure 7.19 shows how in the last fifteen years the real price of gold (that is, the price of gold deflated by the U.S.

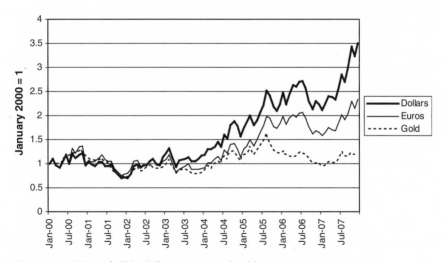

Figure 7.18. Price of oil in dollars, euros, and gold, 2000–2007.
Data source: Bloomberg.

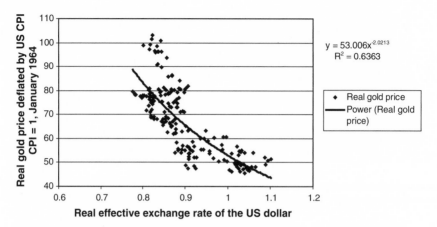

Figure 7.19. Gold prices and the real effective exchange rate of the dollar, January 1992–August 2007.
Data source: IMF International Financial Statistics.

consumer price index) has tended to move inversely with the real effective exchange rate of the de facto international currency, the dollar, such that the value of gold has tended to increase when the dollar depreciated relative to other currencies, and vice-versa.

As shown in Figure 7.20, the real price of gold peaked back in 1980, at the height of the dollar's inflationary troubles. Its fairly steady decline through the end of the 1990s corresponded with a return to low inflation and, as a consequence, lower inflation expectations.

As inflation in the developed world fell over the course of the 1980s, the gold price fell from $615 to $381 an ounce. Central banks added a modest net 344 tons of gold to their reserves. Yet over the 1990s, as gold fell further to $279 an ounce, central banks sold a net 3,148 tons. In one year alone, 1992, central bank sales amounted to nearly a quarter of the annual gold supply, depressing the price by an estimated 8.27%.[31] As shown in Figure 7.21, central bank net gold sales continued at an annual rate of about 500 tons in the early years of this decade. If the dollar's recent woes were to persist, however, central banks might well start accumulating gold again. This would, of course, further drive up the price of gold. Yet since a rising gold price would not be experienced on the central bank ledgers as a depreciation of their dollar assets (which are measured against other currencies), diversification into gold would actually

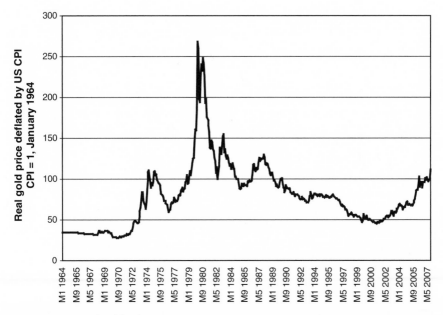

Figure 7.20. Real gold price, 1964–2007.
Data source: IMF International Financial Statistics.

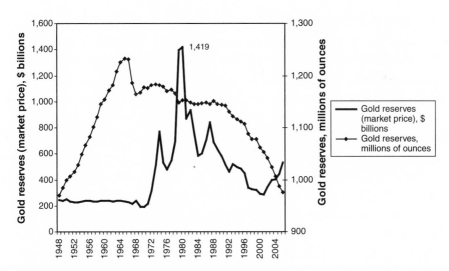

Figure 7.21. Central bank gold reserves, 1948–2006.
Data source: IMF International Financial Statistics.
Note: The market price of central bank gold reserves is measured in 2000 dollars.

be more politically palatable than diversification into euros and other currencies.

Might such a process of central bank gold reaccumulation herald a return to a formal monetary role for gold? A revived gold standard, we should emphasize, is politically infeasible—not merely its establishment, given the political power of contemporary independent central banks, but its sustainability were it to be established. The nineteenth-century gold standard operated in a world in which governments spent less than 10% of national income. "Fiscal policy" was almost meaningless in such a world. In our world, in which governments spend half or more of national income, the government sector is simply too large to be capable of subordinating its money flows to an international commodity rule. Furthermore, political systems have evolved enormously since the late nineteenth century, such that the voting masses now expect government institutions to intervene actively to protect current incomes and employment. They are highly unlikely to tolerate indefinitely a government institution with a monopoly on currency production that appeared to be operating as a passive observer of a self-regulating system.

A private gold-based monetary system, however, is a very different proposition, particularly given advances in computer, telecommunications, and smartcard technology over the past ten years. In recent decades, Americans and non-Americans alike have been happy to receive international payments in dollars because they have had confidence that dollars would, relative to other transaction vehicles, retain their value well in future commercial transactions. Particularly given the recent turmoil in financial, commodity, and foreign exchange markets, however, it is hardly science fiction to imagine a tomorrow in which this is no longer the case.

Some have already imagined it, and are living it. There already exist e-money firms that manage investment accounts denominated in gold and intermediate payments in gold across account holders. These "gold banks" hold physical gold bars in a vault, and account holders acquire and exchange digitized legal claims to fractions of these bars. Of course, clients must bear the cost of storing the gold. But at generally less than 1% a year, this cost compares favorably with the inflation cost imposed by almost all the world's central banks.

Whereas digital gold has grown dramatically over the past several years, in tandem with the dollar's decline against gold, it is a still a small niche business.[32] As of March 2008, the two largest digital gold companies, GoldMoney.com and e-gold.com, which appear to dominate the industry, reported a combined $419 million of digital currency in circulation. At the same date, the liquid liabilities of the U.S. banking system were nearly 25,000 times larger; those of the Peruvian banking system were nearly seventy-five times larger.

Could the masses come to trust a privately managed gold money system? To date, they have never been asked to trust a publicly managed fiat money system; they have merely been obliged to live with it since 1971, often at the cost of having their savings and livelihoods repeatedly decimated by inflation and devaluation. As French economist Charles Rist wrote in 1934, the move away from gold was accomplished in the face of considerable public resistance:

> A wider and wider gap is opening every day between this deep-rooted conviction [in gold as the only safe store of wealth] on the part of the public and the disquisitions of those theoretical economists who are representing gold as an outworn standard. While the theorizers are trying to persuade the public and the various governments that a minimum quantity of gold—just enough to take care of settlements of international balances—would suffice to maintain monetary confidence, and that anyhow paper currency, even fiat currency, would amply meet all needs, the public in all countries is busily hoarding all the national currencies which are supposed to be convertible into gold.[33]

Contract law and competition can provide some security against fraud or mismanagement in a private digital gold system, whereas contract law is nonexistent in the case of inflation-racked fiat systems, and competition has generally been feasible only for the wealthy elites who have access (frequently illegal) to foreign assets.

An organic transition to a system of private money would obviously face enormous hurdles. First, people do not change their mental accounting easily. People forgetting about the dollar and thinking only in terms of "goldies" is only imaginable with a complete collapse of confidence in the dollar, something we have heretofore seen only with developing country currencies. Tracking price changes in an economy still dominated by the dollar as the standard of value would be tremendously challenging for businesses and their customers, as the dollar price of gold varies substantially from day to day, and even within the day. For example, on November 15, 2007, gold closed at $787.00 per ounce, 3.3% lower than the $813.86 closing price the day before. Yet during the day the price actually went up as high as $819.40 before heading sharply south. Such severe price movements would make goldie transaction costs prohibitive in a world in which people still think in terms of fiat currencies. Of course, if you think that gold has absolute value, you will say that it is the *dollar* that changes relative to that absolute value. Yet given that people are currently using dollars and digital gold in a proportion of 9.4 million to one, conventional wisdom will attribute the volatility to gold.

There are, secondly, huge transition costs in establishing a private system that would back each and every transaction with gold. Gold would have to soar to dramatically higher prices, many multiples of the $1,000 an ounce it reached in early 2008, in order to accommodate the new monetary demand. The rise in U.S. inflation expectations that would justify such a costly flight to gold would therefore also have to be dramatic.

A third major hurdle for "goldies" would be the development of a commercial banking and credit system. Digital gold companies now in operation work like banks with a 100% reserve requirement—that is, they cannot multiply money through credit extension because they hold 100% of their deposits in reserves. They do this to boost public confidence that their digital gold certificates are solidly backed by real gold. A system based on such institutions exclusively would be perfect in terms of ensuring the convertibility of gold certificates, but it would mean that the economy would have to work without credit.

This problem could be addressed through the emergence of a commercial bank structure to complement the existing digital gold companies. The commercial banks would logically be specialized in goldies, to avoid the problems of asset and liability mismatch that would arise in their balance sheets if they operated in both goldies and dollars. A new problem arises, however, when such banks begin lending out their goldie deposits. If the original issuer of the goldies were seen as a sort of "central bank," ready to act as a lender of last resort when commercial banks got into trouble, there would emerge a risk of a dangerous pyramiding of the credit superstructure, as Bank A loaned out a goldie deposit to Mr. X, who would deposit it in Bank B, which would loan it out to Miss Y, and so on. The credibility of goldies could be fatally undermined, just as with government monies when the public fears overissue.

The basic problem for a private goldie issuer, as with a government money issuer, is therefore one of credibility. A goldie issuer would naturally wish to short circuit a spiraling of unbacked goldie credit by making it explicit that it did not stand behind goldie deposits at other banks, which would thereby discourage people from depositing goldies at banks that lend without their own 100% gold backing. Competition among issuers would help in establishing and sustaining credibility. But such competition is on the rise among today's issuers of government money, fueled by computer and communications technologies that allow ever cheaper and more rapid transitions from one currency denomination to another. To the extent, then, that central banks do continue to maintain control over the money we use in the future, either their room for discretion will be so tightly constrained by competition from foreign central bank monies, or emerging privately managed commodity monies, that they will be little more than seigniorage vehicles for their governments, or governments will have to apply ever more repressive techniques to prevent their citizens from using alternatives (witness postdevaluation Argentina). This is another way of saying that globalization and monetary sovereignty are incompatible.

8

THE SHIFTING SANDS OF SOVEREIGNTY

"There exists perhaps no conception the meaning of which is more controversial than that of sovereignty," wrote L. F. L. Oppenheim, one of the founding figures of the discipline of international law at the turn of the twentieth century.[1] Sovereignty is a powerful and deeply emotive word. It has for centuries been invoked to defend inalienable powers of the state, internally and externally, even as the political organization of states has been turned on its head.

The idea of sovereignty was first enunciated in rigorous form by the sixteenth-century political thinker Jean Bodin, whose aim was to bolster the supreme power of the French ruler in the hierarchical organization of society.[2] Certainly, he never explicated the idea with the aim of giving voice to popular aspirations. It is a curious phenomenon, then, that the legitimacy of economic globalization is today being so passionately challenged by so many prominent voices claiming to speak for the interests of both a common humanity and national sovereignty.

The transformation of the concept of sovereignty reflects the evolution over centuries of the dominant system of government from monarchy to democracy, with the mythology of the king as the embodiment of the popular will being substituted for by the elected executive or legislature. The shift is redolent of Nietzsche's account of the genealogy of morals, with concepts such as "good" and "bad" having no fixed meaning through time, but instead reflecting changes in the locus of political power. Thus the moral status of absolute monarchy shifts from supreme in one epoch to abominable in a later one, as power ebbs from the monarch's allies toward the masses opposed to him. Yet sovereignty retains its warm glow even as its center of gravity shifts dramatically.

There is a deep internal tension in contemporary challenges to the legitimacy of globalization, which are typically grounded in two political ideas that are frequently at odds: the idea of popular sovereignty, that the state should be created by and subject to the will of its people, and the idea that organs of state are naturally empowered to divine and enforce a "general will," banning forms of consensual exchange they dislike.[3] Bodin, interestingly, believed neither. Though a defender of absolute monarchy, he insisted that political power in a well-ordered state was exercised in accordance with natural law.[4] This included the right of persons to own and transfer private property.[5] Legitimate political power, therefore, was not, even to the mind of an absolutist like Bodin, the same as the will of the sovereign.

Contrast this with a contemporary assertion of the right of the state to override any and all norms of consensual exchange. Former Clinton Administration Labor Secretary Robert Reich writes that

> The idea of a "free market" apart from the laws and political decisions that create it is pure fantasy. . . . The market was not created by God on any of the first six days (at least, not directly), nor is it maintained by divine will. It is a human artifact, the shifting sum of a set of judgments about individual rights and responsibilities. What is mine? What is yours? . . .
>
> In modern nations, government is the principle agency by which the society deliberates, defines, and enforces the norms that organize the market. Judges and legislators, as well as government executives and administrators, endlessly alter and adapt the rules of the game.[6]

Reich is surely correct that God did not create, and logically cannot create, reified social constructs like "the market," nor is His will sufficient to maintain them. Markets are a form—indeed, the most historically consequential form—of spontaneous social order, created and maintained by human beings, but without any one of them intending it. Reich is simply wrong, however, in stating that it is *government* that "defines and enforces the norms that organize the market." This is a prime example of the ancient intentionalist fallacy, which sees any form of persistent social institution or practice as having necessarily been designed by a thinking authority that must have willed it. Property and trade are much older than states. Judges and legislators that would "endlessly alter and adapt the rules" of property and exchange would have been seen throughout Western history as *destroyers* of law, not creators. The essence of natural law, the international Lex Mercatoria, and common law is that these rules are *discovered*[7] based on the expectations the parties would reasonably have brought to their interactions. The norms of that social construct we call "the market" are inferred by us based on the repeated interactions of people voluntarily acquiring and parting with private property. Judges and legislators do indeed enunciate rules. But it is only where such rules are consistent with sufficiently widespread notions of natural just conduct that they are enforceable by convention rather than repeated use of force.

Reich's view of the natural relationship between state sovereignty and the market, so widely shared in today's popular consciousness, is a distinctly twentieth-century one—one that is increasingly invoked as a fundamental challenge to the legitimacy of *globalization*, the extension of consensual economic exchange across borders. This challenge finds little support in the history of Western legal and political thought. Confronting it, however, is not merely a matter of defending old ideas. It is of great practical importance. Rolling back economic liberalism in the cause of reclaiming "sovereignty" is a well-documented recipe for stifling wealth creation, entrenching poverty, and ratcheting up international conflict.

Of all the various doctrines of economic sovereignty, that of the right of the state to monopolize the issuance and circulation of money is certainly the most confused. Defenders of monetary sovereignty typically believe that the state must be able to control the internal and external price (the interest rate and exchange rate) of the money used within its borders. Yet when foreign providers of goods, services, and capital have no want of such money, monetary sovereignty is only compatible with ever-increasing state control of trade.

When in 2002 Argentina did not have enough foreign money to satisfy creditors, local as well as foreign, its economy went into a tailspin, creating enormous social and political unrest. The years since have seen a massive resurgence of economic populism, marked by robust popular support for a political project built around reclaiming sovereignty. In concrete terms, this has meant repudiation of state debt, restrictions on citizens' access to foreign money, price controls, and ever-widening import and export taxes and bans. Meanwhile, the internal value of the now-sovereign peso declines by over 20% a year, while the value of the country's annual production measured in international money, U.S. dollars, remains 20% below its peak nearly a decade ago. Political relations with creditor countries have swooned.

Our current period of international economic relations is as unusual as it is precarious. Eras of economic protectionism have historically coincided with monetary nationalism; eras of liberal international trade, on the other hand, have coincided with a universal monetary standard. Today, we are witness to an unprecedentedly liberal global trade and investment regime operating side by side with the most extreme doctrine of monetary nationalism governments have ever contrived. This is a recipe for periodic crisis, both economic and political.

It is an admirable intention of governments that interest rates in their country should be low so as to facilitate investment. It is also an admirable intention of governments that the exchange rate of their currency be stable, so as to facilitate foreign trade and investment. But as a deputy to the French National Assembly said in 1790, in response to a proposal that the government issue more fiat revolutionary currency—with the admirable intention of providing the people with more wealth: "It is necessary to be gracious as to intentions; one should believe them good, and apparently they are; but we do not have to be gracious at all to inconsistent logic or to absurd reasoning. Bad logicians have committed more involuntary crimes than bad men have done intentionally."[8] Likewise, we do no good in being gracious to bad logicians with good intentions. Where governments grant themselves the right to print money in the future, interest rates will rise proportionally with people's expectations of future exchange rate depreciations. Speculation ceases to be stabilizing, as it is when such sovereign discretion is foresworn, and becomes highly destabilizing—a one-way bet that depreciation and inflation are coming. The governments and the supporters of their good intentions then reflexively malign the intentions of those who notice the faulty logic and act to protect their financial interests.

The mythology of monetary sovereignty is of considerably more political and economic consequence today than it was in earlier times. In the long-ago days of pure commodity monies, the exercise of monetary sovereignty was largely limited to the resolution of conflicts between debtors and creditors based on changes in relative prices between the time of contracting and the time of settlement. The power of a ruler to cancel all or part of a particular debt was indeed an important one, but it was not the stuff of which nations were formed or lost. Monetary power essentially lay with individuals, who created money which was valuable only to the extent that others esteemed the substance it was made from. Monetary sovereignty only took on great political significance where money became, in Mundell's terminology, "overvalued," or in Keynes's more polite terminology, "representative"—that is, its value exceeded its intrinsic commodity value. This could be achieved by numerous means, from debasing precious-metal coins to lowering the redemption value of paper money, but only sustained by stopping others from offering better quality money—money that retained its value better through time. Thus over time we have witnessed the elevation of the act of challenging a ruler's monetary sovereignty to the level of serious crime—often high treason, meriting the most severe punishment.[9] Only when money is overvalued does the sole right to produce it bestow great power on a monetary sovereign, which can use it as a fiscal resource.

It is not surprising that the principle of unlimited monetary sovereignty today provokes such great popular nationalist passions, almost certainly far greater than at any other time in human history. Money has never been of less intrinsic value than it is today (that is, zero), and governments routinely invoke traitorous and foreign forces to explain historically unprecedented inflation and capital flight. Since paper monies began proliferating in the eighteenth century, governments have zealously exploited overvaluation to tax without consent. Having done away with the entire idea of redeemable money in 1971, however, governments have since tested the outer limits of their sovereign powers. As Milton Friedman observed, there appears to be no historical record of hyperinflation outside of wartime, with the exception of the post-1971 period, which has witnessed many.[10] Over the past two decades, Argentina, Brazil, Bolivia, Bulgaria, Peru, Russia, Ukraine, and Zimbabwe, among others, have experienced annualized inflation rates of around 1,000% or more. Those who believe that these are just teething pains along the way to the inexorable spread of responsible central banking need only look at Argentina, Iran, and Venezuela, where the political response to recent spiraling inflation has not been to curtail monetary growth but to raise the level of jingoistic rhetoric. All have expanded laws and regulations restricting their citizens from acquiring alternative monies. In so doing, they act in line with the tradition of rulers going back to the ancient Lydian tyrants, who first faced the challenge of enforcing usage of overvalued coins.

Money and nationalism are condemned to remain fatally intertwined. Commodity monies have, throughout history, always been nationalized by governments. State currencies have always come to lose their commodity backing and become fiat monies. And when a state currency emerges as the dominant international money, it inexorably teeters under the weight of the Triffin dilemma (that is, the trade-off in supplying foreigners with both liquidity and confidence). There is no permanent way out of this trap. There are only better and worse ways for governments to manage the political pressures steering policy toward ruinous economic nationalism.

The period of the 1990s through the early years of the new millennium was a golden age for the fiat U.S. dollar. Following on the heels of the Volcker Fed's defeat of inflation expectations in the 1980s, investors around the globe bought up dollar-denominated assets and central banks sold off their gold reserves, believing they were no longer necessary or desirable. This allowed not only the United States, but the world, to enjoy the fruits of a sustained period of low interest rates and low inflation.

The soaring commodities prices which accompanied the Bernanke Fed's slashing of interest rates in late 2007 and early 2008 reflected rising concerns of a collapsing fiat currency bubble. People were looking, as they have for the better part of human history, to hard assets as a store of wealth. Monetary psychology was reverting to its historic norm. Once the transatlantic banking and credit crisis eases, this shift, if not short-circuited by a sustained period of Fed monetary tightening, will become entrenched and globally traumatic. A further soaring euro cannot fill the breach without provoking a major European protectionist backlash that will undermine the euro's political sustainability. And emerging private monetary alternatives, like digital gold, will clash head on with ever more intrusive state efforts to criminalize them.

The best hope for salvaging financial globalization, then, is a renewed statutory framework for the Fed, one which explicitly acknowledges the global role of the dollar and the dependence of the U.S. economy on foreign confidence in it. This would no doubt lead to very different Fed behavior when faced not only with rising inflation, but with evidence of persistent dollar selling in favor of alternative monetary assets, like gold. Many in the United States will see this as undermining U.S. monetary sovereignty. Yet without foreign confidence in a dollar which is used globally, the Fed's ability to guide interest rates, control inflation, and contain financial crises *domestically* will all dissipate to the point where its sovereignty is meaningless. What Charles de Gaulle once called America's "exorbitant privilege," printing the world's reserve asset, is one which America will in the future have to do far more to sustain.

1. Thinking about Money and Globalization

1. See, for example, *Financial Times* (2006).
2. Stewart (2004).
3. Quoted in Rothschild (1999: 108).
4. See, for example, Milanovic (2005).
5. Russell (1945: xiv).
6. "Hellenic" refers to ancient Greece; "Hellenistic" to the wider Greek-inspired eastern Mediterranean and Middle East between the death of Alexander the Great in 323 BC and the Roman conquest of Egypt in 30 BC.
7. Russell (1945).
8. Hont (2005: 4–5).
9. Indeed, the Greek biographer Plutarch (AD 46–ca. AD 119) explicitly connected the ideas of the Stoic founder, Zeno (ca. 335 BC–ca. 263 BC), in his *Republic* with the exploits of Alexander, who consciously attempted to obliterate cultural differences in his conquered territories, although there is no evidence that his conquests were in any sense Stoicism in practice (Schofield 2005).
10. Russell (1945: xxii).
11. Russell (1945) singles out in particular early Calvinism and Anabaptism.
12. See, for example, Schofield (2005).
13. Muller (2002: 4).
14. See, for example, Berman (1983).
15. Quoted in Berman (1983: 34).
16. Quoted in Hont (2005: 23).
17. Simmel (1978 [1900]: 191).

2. A Brief History of Law and Globalism

1. Micklethwait and Wooldridge (2000: 336).
2. Wolf (2004).

3. Lal (2006).

4. Friedman (2005: 8).

5. Friedman (1999: 469–470).

6. Regarding Mill, this would be the Mill represented by "On Liberty," rather than the Mill reflected in the more statist "Principles of Political Economy."

7. Translated by R. C. Jebb. http://classics.mit.edu/Sophocles/antigone.html.

8. Cary (2000).

9. The Middle Ages, nominally beginning in 312 AD with Constantine's conversion to Christianity, may be likened to the torso, or the conjunction of the traditions of Jerusalem and Athens. Scholastic thought may be said broadly to represent the intellectual merging of theology and philosophy, commonly dated from the early sixth century with the ascendance of the scholar Boethius and his injunction "as far as you are able, [to] fuse faith with reason," and ending in the fourteenth century, represented by the thinking of William of Ockham, who rejected this conflation, and insisted instead on a radical logical separation between matters of fact and faith. The Renaissance, reclaiming and renovating the classical tradition, may then be likened to the left arm, and the Reformation, reclaiming and renovating the biblical tradition, to the right arm. Finally, modernity, the head, positions reason and faith as antagonists: with the Enlightenment, reason comes to despise faith, while in the Romantic epoch faith reemerges as an elemental, prerational, human-centered truth, beyond and prior to reason.

10. Sabine (1937).

11. From *On Law*, quoted in Sabine (1937: 150).

12. Mattli (2001: 919–947).

13. *The Economist* (1992: 17).

14. Cited in Irwin (1996: 21).

15. Suarez (1934: 347).

16. Cited in Irwin (1996: 22–23).

17. It is interesting to note that the one area where the Romans drew a firm distinction between ius gentium and ius naturale is that of slavery, which the Romans recognized as something common to all ancient societies but not in any way supported by "natural reason." See, for example, Stein (1999).

18. Sabine (1937).

19. From *Laws*, III, 1, 2, quoted in Sabine (1937: 166).

20. Aquinas (1989: 90.1).

21. Hayek (1973: 82).

22. Sabine (1937: 433).

23. In spite of Gray, in his recent anti-globalist incarnation, expressing profound contempt for Enlightenment thinkers such as Thomas Jefferson, it is notable that he shares with Jefferson a respect only for law determined and imposed from above, by an empowered legislature, with a precise social end in mind. Jefferson loathed common law (see, for example, Jefferson's letter to Edmund Randolph, August 18, 1799, http://odur.let.rug.nl/~usa/P/tj3/writings/brf/jefl128.htm).

24. Hunter and Saunders (2002).

25. From *Prolegomena*, sect. 6, quoted in Sabine (1937: 423).

26. Quoted in Sabine (1937: 424).

27. Sabine (1937: 424).

28. Hunter and Saunders (2002).

29. Quoted in Wight (1977: 127).

30. Condliffe (1951: 832).

31. Sabine (1937: 158).

32. Bennett (2004: 250).

33. *Bonham's Case* of 1610, as quoted in Malcolm (1999, 1: xlvi).

34. Védrine (2001: 17).

35. Condliffe (1951: 23).

36. See, for example, Berman and Kaufman (1978).

37. Schmitthoff (1968: 105).

38. Wiener (1999).

39. Berman (1983).

40. See, for example, Berman (1983) and Mather (2001).

41. Quoted in Berman (1983: 342).

42. Berman (1983).

43. See, for example, Benson (1989: 644–661).

44. Benson (1989).

45. Trakman (1983: 34).

46. See, for example, Volckart and Mangels (1999).

47. See, for example, Carbonneau (1990).

48. Wiener (1999).

49. See, for example, Ruggie (1993: 154–155).

50. Clive Schmitthoff is the primary advocate for this positivist view of the Lex Mercatoria. See Wiener (1999) for a literature review.

51. Gray (1998: 199–200).

52. Gray (1998: 199).

53. Mattli (2001: 920).

54. See, for example, Volckart and Mangels (1999).

55. Data from ICA and Mattli (2001).

56. Mitchell (1904: 20).

57. Craig, Park, and Paulsson (1990) and David (1985).

58. *Swift v. Tyson*, 16 Peters (41 U.S.) 1, 19 (1842).

59. International Swaps and Derivatives Association, http://www.isda.org.

60. For an overly sanguine perspective, see this statement of the Financial Economists Roundtable, http://www.stanford.edu/~wfsharpe/art/fer/fer94.htm.

61. http://www.isda.org/.

62. To be sure, the utility of the ISDA Master Agreement could be diminished in jurisdictions that refused to confirm the enforceability of certain of its provisions. Dozens of countries, however, have given assurances that its provisions would, if challenged, be enforced as law, with some countries, such as France and Mexico, passing legislation drafted by ISDA itself (Partnoy 2002).

63. Frank Partnoy is perhaps alone in calling attention to its importance. See Partnoy (2002).

64. Berman (1983: 38).

65. See, for example, Hayek (1988: 38–47) and Leakey (1981: 212).

3. The Anti-philosophy of Anti-globalism

1. Stern (1961: 276).

2. Gray (1998: 71).

3. Marx and Engels (1969 [1848]: 5).

4. Gray (1998: 71).

5. Gray (1998: 235).

6. Nader and Wallach (1996: 94).

7. Marx and Engels (1969 [1848]: 4).

8. Gray (1998: 195).

9. Gray (1998: 124).

10. Stern (1961: xvii).

11. Russell (1945: 683).

12. Stiglitz (2005: 235).

13. Stiglitz (2002: 247).

14. Stiglitz (2005: 235).

15. Scholte (2000: 157).

16. See Krasner (1995–1996).

17. Stiglitz (2005: 235).

18. Krasner (1995–1996).

19. Nader and Wallach (1996: 104).

20. Krasner (1995–1996).

21. Krasner (1995–1996).

22. Feis (1930).

23. Stiglitz (2005: 235)

24. *Oxford English Dictionary* online, http://dictionary.oed.com/.

25. Sabine (1937: 423).

26. Rabkin (2004: 23).

27. Mill (1909 [1848]: 581–582).

28. As quoted in Rothschild (1999: 107).

29. Stiglitz (2005: 236).

30. Justi (1760: 555–558 and 636) as translated in Walker (1971: 169).

31. Modern lending got its start in the fourteenth-century Italy. Using a bill of exchange, a bank could lend money, designate from among dozens of currencies, and transport it safely over poorly guarded highways. Even if it was stolen, it could not be cashed by the robber. Thus, 100 gold coins in a bank in Venice could be used in Florence. The bill of exchange was then able to be used as currency among merchants and lenders, further increasing the value of the initial gold coins (http://www.ihatedebt

.com/ALookatDebt/TheHistoryofDebt.html). The long-alleged role of Jews in their development may be apocryphal, although Montesquieu provides a footnote documenting his account.

32. Montesquieu (1748), as translated in Hirschman (1977: 72).

33. Stiglitz (2002).

34. Muller (2002: 97).

35. Möser (1990 [1772]: 23–24), as translated in Muller (2002: 86).

36. Stern (1961: 131).

37. Klein (2000: 129).

38. Greider (1997: 81).

39. Cowen (2002: 146).

40. Stiglitz (2005: 236).

41. Yardley (2006).

42. Micklethwait and Wooldridge (2000: 339).

43. Rousseau (1920 [1762]: 18).

44. Smith (1853 [1759]: 342–343).

45. Muller (2002).

46. See Barber (1995).

47. Krasner (1999: 36).

48. Krasner (1999: 36).

49. Muller (2002).

50. Milanovic (2005: 156).

51. Milanovic (2005: 155).

52. Lindert and Williamson (2003: 1).

53. Hayek (1960: 87).

54. Hayek (1960: 93).

55. Sen (2002).

56. Nader and Wallach assert that globalization leads to "lowering standards of living for most people in the developed and developing world" (1996: 94).

57. *Financial Times* (2006).

58. See Lindert and Williamson (2003).

59. See the review of the empirical evidence in Wolf (2004).

60. "Despite repeated promises of poverty reduction made over the last decade of the twentieth century, the actual number of people living in poverty has actually increased by almost 100 million" (Stiglitz 2002: 5). Stiglitz cites World Bank data as his source, data that have been shown by Bhalla (2002) to be fatally flawed owing to a change in methodology in the early 1990s.

61. See Bhalla (2002). See also Lal (2006).

62. Milanovic (2005).

63. Hayek (1976).

64. Stiglitz (2005: 236).

65. See in particular Lindert and Williamson (2003).

66. Nuffield Council on Bioethics (2003).

67. Chua (2003: 125).

68. Chua (2003: front inside cover).

69. "The relationship between free market democracy and ethnic violence around the world is inextricably bound up with globalization. . . . To a great extent, globalization consists of, and is fueled by, the unprecedented worldwide spread of markets and democracy" (Chua 2003: 7).

70. Chua (2003: back inside cover).

71. Chua (2003: 14).

72. Chua (2003: 224).

73. "Just as the United States should not promote unrestrained laissez-faire capitalism (a form of markets that the West itself has repudiated) throughout the non-Western world, so too the United States should not promote unrestrained, overnight majority rule (a form of democracy the West has repudiated)" Chua (2003: 274). In Afghanistan and Iraq, where the United States imposed democracy, constitution-building was made the first essential task. "Unrestrained, overnight majority rule" was never even considered.

74. "In other words, to a surprising extent Weimar Germany shared both the basic background conditions prevalent in many developing countries today and the standard policy package being pursued by these countries. In conditions of widespread economic distress and a (perceived) economically dominant minority, Weimar Germany pursued intensive market liberalization and widespread democratization" (Chua 2003: 205).

75. Muller (2002: 355).

76. Muller (2002).

77. Wieser (1983 [1926]: 373–374).

78. Chua (2003: 206).

79. Chua (2003: 266–267).

80. Chua (2003: 270).

81. Saul (2005: 269).

82. Rousseau, quoted in Russell (1945: 693).

83. Byron (1905 [1817]).

84. Consider this quote: "Barbarism can be thought of as violence done to the individual's understanding of herself as a citizen. That violence arises from the belief that truth has revealed itself. A religious truth, a racial truth, an economic truth. Even a scientific truth. The adjective hardly matters. In the false light of truth, history withers and seems to come to an end. Destiny, it seems, is inextricably at work. And leadership shrinks to less than choice or citizenship. Instead it is centered on the sophisticated exercise of power, which can be gained and held by skillfully riding the wave of inevitability" (Saul 2005: 11). Huh?

85. Saul (2005: 278).

86. Saul (2005: 51).

87. Irwin (1996: 8).

88. Russell (1945: 687).

89. Bodanis (2006).

90. Dobbs (2004: 150).

91. See, for example, Hont's account of this debate (2005: 58–68).

92. CNN (2005).

93. Samuelson (1969: 9).

94. Dobbs (2004: 67).

95. See, for example, Hufbauer and Goodrich (2003).

96. Domowitz and Steil (2002).

97. Korten (1996: 28).

98. Rousseau (1769).

99. Russell (1945: 15–16).

100. Greider (1997: 471).

101. Krugman (1997a).

102. François-Rene de Chateaubriand as quoted in Rothschild (1999: 107).

103. Gray (1984: 27).

104. Hayek (1988: 91).

4. A Brief History of Monetary Sovereignty

1. Burns (1927).

2. Burns (1927).

3. Mundell (1997).

4. Burns (1927).

5. Burns (1965 [1927]: 81–82).

6. Ure (1922: 2).

7. Cited in Parsons (2001: 68).

8. Quoted in Burns (1927: 84).

9. Burns (1927: 112).

10. Burns (1927: 465).

11. Sargent and Velde (2002: 91).

12. Sargent and Velde (2002: 92).

13. Sargent and Velde (2002: 75).

14. Innocent IV (1570 reprint), as translated by Sargent and Velde (2002: 96).

15. Sargent and Velde (2002: 96).

16. Bartolo (1570–1571 reprint), as translated by Sargent and Velde (2002: 95).

17. Sargent and Velde (2002).

18. Oresme (ca. 1360), as translated by Johnson (1956: 32).

19. Buridan (1637 reprint: 432), as translated by Sargent and Velde (2002: 97).

20. Sargent and Velde (2002: 98).

21. Sargent and Velde (2002: 98).

22. Parsons (2001: 64).

23. Parsons (2001: 64).

24. From Swift's satirical poem "The Bank's Thrown Down," on early notes issued by the Bank of England (quoted in Poovey 2008: 45).

25. Sargent and Velde (2002: 103).

26. Dumoulin (1681 [1612]), as translated by Sargent and Velde (2002: 106).

27. Dumoulin (1681 [1612]), as translated by Sargent and Velde (2002:107–108).

28. In particular, the gold écu was not made sole legal tender, instead sharing this status with silver and certain billon coins. A fixed rate between gold and silver coins combined with free minting of silver led to the melting down and ultimate disappearance of the undervalued gold coins. See Sargent and Velde (2002), chapter 11, for a fascinating discussion.

29. Butigella (1608 reprint), as translated by Sargent and Velde (2002: 108).

30. Hotman (1610 [1573]: 121–123), as translated by Sargent and Velde (2002: 110).

31. Sargent and Velde (2002).

32. González Téllez (1715 [1673]: 554), as translated by Sargent and Velde (2002: 112).

33. Montanari (1804 [1683]: 104), as translated by Sargent and Velde (2002: 113).

34. Poullain (1709 [1612]: 67), as translated by Sargent and Velde (2002: 113).

35. Montanari (1804 [1683]: 109), as translated by Sargent and Velde (2002: 115–116).

36. Cited in Parsons (2001: 63).

37. Ricardo (1817), as quoted in Angell (1929: 236).

38. Sargent and Velde (2002: 6).

39. Sargent and Velde (2002) back both explanations.

40. Redish (2000).

41. Sargent and Velde (2002).

42. See Sargent and Velde (2002), chapter 18.

43. The United States has never used a formal, stated inflation target, but it is widely accepted that the Federal Reserve seeks a core inflation rate of roughly 1–2% over the long term.

44. Cannan (1935: 40).

45. Weatherford (1997: 129).

46. Redish (2000).

47. American farmers of the late nineteenth century, backed by 1896 and 1900 Democratic presidential candidate William Jennings Bryan, supported free coinage of silver in order to increase the money supply and counteract the relentless decline in commodity prices against gold. The parallels with coffee bean farmers in contemporary Latin America, who back continuous depreciation to counteract the persistent decline in coffee bean prices, are precise.

48. Redish (2000: 246).

49. Nurkse (1944); Cesarano (2006).

50. Eichengreen (1996).

51. Hawtrey explained the logic of Britain applying the restoration rule thus: "Well, some people would argue that there is no very great harm in devaluing the pound. There is no special virtue in the pre-war gold value of 113 grains of fine gold. It might be reduced to 100 grains or thereabouts, and in a way it is true there is no great

virtue in pre-war parity. But there is one fundamental advantage in getting back to pre-war parity if we can: that is, that if we have got back there with a certain amount of struggle, have regarded it as an end for several years, and finally achieve it, everybody believes we shall stay there. If we devalued, though we started with 100 grains, it might be convenient to change it to 85 grains later, and there would not be that confidence in the gold value of the currency which is so valuable in great financial affairs" (Hawtrey 1924: 165).

52. Mundell (2000: 331).

53. There are brief prior instances of fiat monies, such as in Britain's North American colonies and in France during the Revolution, but otherwise only China offers an example of a deliberate paper currency economy (Cesarano 2006).

54. This process has been eloquently captured by Jacques Rueff. See, for example, Rueff (1972).

55. Mundell (2000).

56. Keynes (1960: 383).

57. Mill (1894 [1848]: 544).

58. Quoted in Weatherford (1997: 123).

59. Bordo (1995).

60. Bordo and Schwartz (1997).

61. De Long (1996).

62. Cesarano (2006: 201).

63. Bordo and Schwartz (1997).

64. De Long (1996: 36–37). See also political memoirs about the Nixon era, such as Ehrlichman (1982).

65. As quoted in Wells (1994: 199).

66. Mlynarski (1937: 269–308).

67. Cesarano (2006).

68. Schumer and Graham (2006).

69. O'Rourke and Williamson (1999: 2).

70. Weatherford (1997: 265).

71. On the positive side of the debate is Lundgren (1996). On the negative side is Hummels (1999).

72. See Bordo, Eichengreen, and Irwin (1999).

73. O'Rourke and Williamson (1999).

74. McKinnon (1993).

75. McCloskey and Zecher (1976).

76. Bordo and Rockoff (1996).

77. Polanyi (1944: 193).

78. McKinnon (1993).

79. Hayek (1937: 64).

80. Hayek (1937: 63–64).

81. Nurkse (1944: 29).

82. See, for example, Cesarano (2006).

83. See, for example, Stiglitz (2002) and Stiglitz (2005).

84. Hayek (1937: 65–66).

85. Hayek (1937: 67).

86. *Financial Times* (2004).

87. *The Economist* (2005).

88. Hayek (1937: 71–72).

89. Independent Strategy (2006) and Williams (1968).

90. Cesarano (2006: 194–195).

91. Eichengreen (2005: 20).

92. Chinn and Frankel (2007).

93. Rueff and Hirsch (1965: 2–3).

94. See Bloomberg (2007) for the comments of Xu Jian, a Chinese central bank vice director, at a Beijing conference on November 7, 2007.

95. Rueff and Hirsch (1965: 2–3).

96. As quoted in Weatherford (1997: 11).

97. Mill (1894 [1848]: 176).

98. Simmel (2004 [1900]: 181–182).

99. Simmel (1978 [1900]: 181–182).

100. Simmel (1978 [1900]: 175).

5. Globalization and Monetary Sovereignty

1. See, for example, Price (2001: 88).

2. Cox and Alm (1995). Available at: http://www.reason.com/news/show/29783
.html.

3. See Goldin and Katz (2007).

4. Bureau of Labor Statistics (2006).

5. Wacziarg and Welch (2003). The other three were Papua New Guinea, Syria, and Iran.

6. As U.S. Senator John Taylor of South Carolina said in 1811, "No man who has attentively considered the rise, progress, and growth of these States, from their first colonization to the present period, can deny that foreign capital, ay, British capital, has been the pap on which we first fed; the strong ailment which supported and stimulated our exertions and industry, even to the present day." As quoted in Mead (2002: 15).

7. *Wall Street Journal* (2007).

8. International Monetary Fund (2001). The regions are South America (56% of total deposits in foreign currencies), formerly communist (48%), the Middle East (42%), Africa (33%), Asia (28%), and Central America and Mexico (34%).

9. Rodrik (1998: 68).

10. Obstfeld (1998).

11. Obstfeld and Taylor (1998: 359).

12. Hausmann (1999: 67).

13. Moody's Investors Service (2007) and Hinds (2006).

14. See, for example, Hinds (2006).

15. See Bank for International Settlements (2007).

16. Tirole (2002: 104).

17. Steil (2007).

18. European Central Bank (2007: 44, 55).

19. See McKinnon (2004: 691). This paper provides a marvelous historical analysis of OCA theory and Mundell's role in its evolution.

20. Mundell (1961: 637).

21. Some prominent economists working within the OCA framework, such as Eichengreen (1992b) and Krugman (1993), actually came to worry that existing currency areas, like the United States, were becoming, or would become, less optimum over time. But none to our knowledge has made a case for subnational currencies.

22. Eichengreen (1997), while not himself an opponent of EMU, provides some useful examples of such work.

23. Alesina and Barro (2002: 409).

24. *Financial Times* (2000).

25. Their combined current account surplus in 2005 exceeded $157 billion and their combined fiscal surplus was on the order of $95 billion (Hanna 2006).

26. Hanna (2006: 3).

6. Monetary Sovereignty and Gold

1. The balance of payments has two main components: the current account and the capital account. The current account measures the flows of goods and services into and out of the country. The capital account records international capital transfers and the acquisition and disposal of nonproduced, nonfinancial assets (such as rights to natural resources, or intangible assets like patents). Countries experiencing a payments deficit must make up the difference by exporting gold or "hard currency" reserves, such as the U.S. dollar, that are accepted currencies for settlement of international debts.

2. Keiley (1900).

3. Kenwood and Lougheed (1999).

4. Robinson (1954: 460).

5. Mill (1965 [1848]: 515).

6. Bordo and White (1991).

7. The details of the Act can be found at http://www.ledr.com/bank_act/1844032.htm.

8. Eichengreen (1992a: xii).

9. For further details on the policy tools of the Bank of England, see Dutton (1984).

10. The banking system as a whole can multiply money through its intermediation of deposits. The process works like this. A bank receives a deposit of one currency unit and lends a portion of it, say 60%. The recipient of the loan spends its proceeds. The people receiving the proceeds in turn deposit them in banks, which in turn lend out 60% of them, and so on. The system continues to multiply the original deposit until it

converges to a number equal to 1 divided by the quantity 1 minus the percentage of deposits that banks lend in each iteration. In this particular example, the banking system would multiply the original deposit 2.5 times (that is, 1/0.4).

11. Dornbusch and Frenkel (1984: 244).

12. See Dutton (1984). Another view can be found in Pippenger (1984). Pippenger also finds that the Bank of England engaged in monetary policy, although he believes this was motivated not by monetary reasons but by profit seeking (during the time covered by his study the Bank of England was a private institution).

13. Notice how similar the gold standard was in this respect to the current international system based on the dollar, particularly when seen from the perspective of the developing countries—where, as noted in chapter 5, people dissatisfied with trends in the value of their currency can buy dollars with their pesos, etc.

14. The rate of inflation could differ between countries, but only as a result of shifts in relative prices that affected the price index asymmetrically. The gold standard also left a certain leeway for shifts in exchange rates across currencies, the size of which were determined by the cost of transporting gold from one country to another.

15. The distinction between total exports and exports of British products at the time is essential because London was world's transportation hub, so that a very large portion of the exports and imports went through London just to be resent to their ultimate destination.

16. Iliasu (1971).

17. The Zollverein was the customs union of all the states that eventually created Germany in 1871.

18. See Kenwood and Lougheed (1999: 65–66).

19. Morys (2007: abstract).

20. Meissner (2002).

21. López-Cordova and Meissner (2000).

22. This period certainly envelops the end of the gold standard, which some observers mark as 1933, the year when the United States abandoned it (Britain and others abandoned it over the prior two years). It is difficult to specify definitively the year in which the standard was ended because the United States returned to it in 1934 at a devalued rate for the dollar. The restored regime, however, violated a basic principle of the standard: it eliminated the right of citizens to exchange their dollars for gold and export it. Still, many observers such as Eichengreen (1992a) believe that, even if the standard had been formally abandoned early in the decade, central banks kept on applying some of its principles up until the outbreak of World War II.

23. Temin (1989: 56); emphasis in original.

24. Friedman (1994 [1992]: 113).

25. Friedman discusses the deflationary pressures exerted by the purchase of gold by the countries joining the gold standard. Speaking of the United States, he says: "In preparation for resumption [of the gold standard after the Civil War] the U.S. Treasury began accumulating gold; by 1879 the stock of monetary gold in the United

States, both in the Treasury and in private hands, already amounted to nearly 7 percent of the world's stock. By 1889, the U.S. share had increased to nearly 20 percent. Even more dramatically, the increase from 1879 to 1899 in the U.S. stock of monetary gold exceeded the increase in the world's stock" (1994 [1992]: 67).

26. Johnson (1997).

27. Bordo and Redish (2003: abstract).

28. Hayek (1999 [1932]: 156).

29. Eichengreen (1992a: 215).

30. Kindleberger (1986).

31. Temin (1989: 38).

32. France's 1939 GDP was only 3.4% higher than that of 1929, while U.S. GDP was 1.2% higher. Between 1929 and 1936, France's prices fell 23% while those of the United States fell by 19%. France went into an inflationary period after abandoning the gold-exchange standard in 1936. As a result, its prices were 23% higher in 1939 than in 1929, while those of the United States were 19% lower. (Data are from Maddison 1991: 212–215, 300–302.)

33. See Temin (1989: 60).

34. Hayek (1999 [1932]: 165).

35. See, for example, Moggridge (1972: 171–187).

36. Kindleberger (1986).

37. Hayek (1999 [1932]: 164–165).

38. Hayek (1999 [1932]: 168).

39. Kurihara (1949: 162, 165); emphasis in original.

40. Kurihara (1949: 164–165, 168).

41. Shlaes (2007).

42. See Johnson (1997: 739–741).

43. Kindleberger (1986: 92–93).

44. Kindleberger (1986).

45. Kindleberger (1986).

46. A good account of these valorization schemes all over the world can be found in Kindleberger (1986).

47. U.S. Bureau of the Census (1975).

48. If the events had been related only to a Keynesian liquidity trap, people would have moved their resources to a liquid form that included current accounts in the banks. The fact that they withdrew their currency from the banks evidences not just a desire for liquidity but a mistrust of the banks.

49. Bagehot (1991 [1873]: 97).

50. Kindleberger (1986).

51. See Eichengreen (1992a: 16–17).

52. Rist (1934: 251–252).

53. See, for example, Rueff (1972).

54. Rueff (1972: 202).

7. The Future of the Dollar

1. See Hayek (1990 [1976]).

2. Bloomberg (2007).

3. *Financial Times* (2007b).

4. SIVs use short-term funding, such as asset-backed commercial paper, to buy longer-term assets, such as bank debt and asset-backed securities. They issue commercial paper, medium-term notes, and capital and invest the proceeds in a portfolio of diversified assets, aiming to generate returns from the spread between the yield on the portfolio and the cost of funding. More on SIVs is available at http://www.reuters .com/article/bondsNews/idUSL145069320071014.

5. Rueff (1972: 167).

6. For example, in 1996 Paul Krugman wrote: "The United States abandoned its policy of stabilizing gold prices back in 1971. Since then the price of gold has increased roughly tenfold, while consumer prices have increased about 250 percent. If we had tried to keep the price of gold from rising, this would have required a massive *decline* in the prices of practically everything else—deflation on a scale not seen since the Depression. This doesn't sound like a particularly good idea."

7. The real exchange rate of one currency against another is a measure of the changes in the real purchasing power of the two currencies, which declines when a currency depreciates in real terms and increases when it appreciates in real terms. To estimate these changes, the indicator of the real exchange rate is calculated taking into account not just the changes in the nominal (observable) exchange rate, but also the relationship between the domestic rates of inflation in each of the countries. The real *effective* exchange rate of one currency provides this measure against the currencies of all its partners in trade and capital flows taken together.

8. The IMF real effective exchange rate data in Figure 7.3 only go back to 1978.

9. See Erceg, Guerrieri, and Gust (2005).

10. See, for example, *Christian Science Monitor* (2006).

11. Net government debt is debt that is not held by government institutions.

12. See Wolf (2007).

13. *Financial Times* (2007a).

14. Associated Press (2007).

15. There is no certainty about the share of the dollar in the total reserves of central banks because (1) the IMF does not publish data by country, but only aggregate figures for the world as a whole, for industrial and for developing countries; and (2) some countries (classified as developing countries by the IMF) report to the IMF their total level but not the currency composition of their reserves. Thus, there is a difference between the total reserves and the total of the reserves classified by currency (called the "allocated reserves"). The difference between these two magnitudes was equivalent to $1.6 trillion, or 36% of the total reserves, in June 2007, which suggests that the countries not reporting the currency composition command a huge portion of the total reserves and of their increment. The estimate of the 60% share of the dol-

lar in the increase is an extrapolation from the share of the dollar in the allocated reserves. One could suspect that China, which commands an independently estimated level of $1.5 trillion dollars in dollar-denominated reserves, is one of the nonreporting countries. If this were true, the share of the dollar in the increment would be even higher.

16. It is interesting to note that whereas China is today routinely accused by the United States of pursuing motivation two, mercantilism, China actually began pegging its currency firmly to the dollar back in 1994, and sustained the peg during the Asia crisis in spite of enormous downward pressure on the renminbi at that time.

17. Feldstein (1997).

18. European Central Bank (2007).

19. Chinn and Frankel (2007).

20. Chinn and Frankel (2007).

21. See Steil and Litan (2006).

22. See, for example, Sulling (2002: 469–490).

23. See ECOFIN (2000).

24. European Commission (2000).

25. *Financial Times* (2008).

26. *Grant's Interest Rate Observer* (2007).

27. *Wall Street Journal* (2008).

28. Fisher (2008). Fisher was the lone dissenter on the Fed's interest rate setting body, the Federal Open Market Committee, at the January 30, 2008, meeting, voting against an interest rate cut.

29. See Hinds (2006).

30. Woodford (2000: 258–259).

31. M. Murenbeeld & Associates (2002: 7).

32. See, for example, *Wall Street Journal* (2005). The article focuses on one such company, GoldMoney.com.

33. Rist (1934: 251–252).

8. The Shifting Sands of Sovereignty

1. Oppenheim (1905: 103).

2. "Majesty or Sovereignty is the most high, absolute, and perpetual power over the citizens and subjects in a Commonwealth" (Bodin 1606 [1583]: 84). Spelling modernized by Beaulac (2004: 107).

3. Such bans are widely called for even when they involve no "negative technological externalities," or third-party effects occurring outside the pricing system.

It is critical to draw a distinction between "pecuniary" externalities and "technological" externalities, as only the latter have public policy implications. As an example, a Staples store opening up next to an Office Depot may lower the profits at the Office Depot, but such pecuniary externalities involve no market failure—quite the reverse, in fact. If the Staples store were to burn its garbage and pollute the Office Depot premises, on the other hand, these technological externalities would indeed involve a market failure—Staples would not be bearing the cost of the damage to a common resource, air. This would justify some form of government intervention to force Staples to internalize this cost.

Likewise, if you cease buying from me and start buying from someone else, this will certainly affect me negatively but, as a pecuniary externality, will not constitute a market failure, and hence not in itself justify government intervention to prevent you changing your buying behavior.

4. "But as for the laws of God and nature, all princes and people of the world are unto them subject: neither is it in their power to impugn them" (Bodin 1606 [1583]: 92). Spelling modernized by Beaulac (2004: 100).

5. See Bodin (1583: 152–154 and 156–157).

6. Reich (1991: 186).

7. See, for example, Kern (2006 [1939]: 151).

8. Pierre S. du Pont, September 25, 1790, quoted in Friedman (1977: 471).

9. See, for example, Mundell (2002).

10. Friedman (1994 [1992]).

REFERENCES

Alesina, Albert, and Robert J. Barro. 2002. "Currency Unions." *Quarterly Journal of Economics*, Vol. 117, No. 2, May.

Angell, Norman. 1929. *The Story of Money*. Garden City, NY: Garden City Publishing.

Aquinas, Thomas. 1989. *Summa Theologiae: A Concise Translation*. Edited by Timothy McDermott. Westminster, MD: Christian Classics.

Associated Press. 2007. "Chinese Official Says More U.S. Rate Cuts Will Have 'Harmful Effect' on Dollar." December 27.

Bagehot, Walter. 1991 [1873]. *Lombard Street: A Description of the Money Market*. Reprinted as *Lombard Street: A Description of the Money Market, with "the Currency Monopoly."* Philadelphia: Orion Editions.

Bank for International Settlements. 2007. "Financial Stability and Local Currency Bond Markets." Committee on the Global Financial System, CGFS Papers No. 28, June.

Bank of England. "About the Bank: History." Available at: http://www.bankofengland .co.uk/about/history/.

Barber, Benjamin. 1995. *Jihad vs. McWorld: How Globalism and Tribalism Are Reshaping the World*. New York: Ballantine Books.

Bartolo da Sassoferrato. 1570–1571. *Opera*. Venice: Giunta.

Beaulac, Stéphane. 2004. *The Power of Language in the Making of International Law*. Leiden, The Netherlands: Martinus Nijhoff Publishers.

Bennett, James C. 2004. *The Anglosphere Challenge: Why the English-Speaking Nations Will Lead the Way in the Twenty-First Century*. Lanham, MD: Rowman and Littlefield.

Benson, Bruce L. 1989. "The Spontaneous Evolution of Commercial Law." *Southern Economic Journal*, Vol. 55, No. 3, January.

Berman, Harold J. 1983. *Law and Revolution*. Cambridge, MA: Harvard University Press.

Berman, Harold J., and Colin Kaufman. 1978. "The Law of International Commercial Transactions (Lex Mercatoria)." *Harvard International Law Journal*, Vol. 19, No. 1.

Bhalla, Surjit. 2002. *Imagine There's No Country: Poverty, Inequality and Growth in the Age of Globalization*. Washington, DC: Institute for International Economics.

Bloomberg. 2007. "Dollar Slumps to Record on China's Plans to Diversify Reserves." By Ming Zeng and Agnes Lovasz. November 7. Available at: http://www.bloomberg.com/apps/news?pid=20601087&refer=home&sid=alGVN031e30s.

Board of Governors of the Federal Reserve System. 2007. Press release, October 31. Available at: http://www.federalreserve.gov/newsevents/press/monetary/20071031a.htm.

Bodanis, David. 2006. "Scientists Have No Chance against Spin Doctors." *Financial Times*, May 24.

Bodin, Jean. 1583. *Les six livres de la republique*. Paris: Iacques du Puys.

———. 1606 [1583]. *The Six Bookes of a Commonweale*. Translated by Richard Knolles. London: Impensis G. Bishop.

Bordo, Michael. 1995. "Is There a Good Case for a New Bretton Woods International Monetary System?" *American Economic Review*, Vol. 85, No. 2, Papers and Proceedings, May.

Bordo, Michael D., Barry Eichengreen, and Douglas A. Irwin. 1999. "Is Globalization Today Really Different than Globalization a Hundred Years Ago?" NBER Working Paper 7195, June.

Bordo, Michael D., and Angela Redish. 2003. "Is Deflation Depressing? Evidence from the Classical Gold Standard." NBER Working Paper 9520, February.

Bordo, Michael D., and Hugh Rockoff. 1996. "The Gold Standard as a 'Good Housekeeping Seal of Approval.'" *The Journal of Economic History*, Vol. 56, No. 2, June.

Bordo, Michael D., and Anna J. Schwartz, eds. 1984. *A Retrospective on the Classical Gold Standard, 1821–1931*. Chicago: University of Chicago Press.

———. 1997. "Monetary Policy Regimes and Economic Performance: The Historical Record." NBER Working Paper 6201, September.

Bordo, Michael D., and Eugene N. White. 1991. "A Tale of Two Currencies: British and French Finance during the Napoleonic Wars." *The Journal of Economic History*, Vol. 51, No. 2, June.

Budé, Guillaume. 1514. *De Asse et partibus ejus libri quinque*. Paris.

Bureau of Labor Statistics. 2006. "Employment Status of the Civilian Noninstitutional Population, 1940 to Date." Current Population Survey. Available at: http://www.bls.gov/cps/table.htm.

Buridan, Jean. 1637. *Quaestiones in decem libros ethicorum Aristotelis ad Nicomachum*. Oxford: H. Cripps.

Burns, A. R. 1927. *Money and Monetary Policy in Early Times*. New York: Alfred A. Knopf.

———. 1965 [1927]. *Money and Monetary Policy in Early Times*. New York: Augustus M. Kelley, Bookseller.

Butigella, Girolamo. 1608. "Repetitiones in legem cum quid." In Pompeius Limpius, ed., *Repetitionum in varias iuris civilis leges*. Venice: sub signo aquilae renovantis.

Byron, Lord. 1905 [1817]. "Manfred." In Paul Elmer, ed., *The Poetical Works of Byron*. New York: Houghton Mifflin.

Cannan, Edwin. 1935. *Money: Its Connexion with Rising and Falling Prices*. London: P. S. King & Son.

Carbonneau, Thomas E., ed. 1990. *Lex Mercatoria and Arbitration*. New York: Transnational Juris Publications.

Cary, Phillip. 2000. "Lecture 13." In *Great Minds of the Western Intellectual Tradition: Part 2*. Chantilly, VA: The Teaching Company.

Cesarano, Filippo. 2006. *Monetary Theory and Bretton Woods: The Construction of an International Monetary Order*. Cambridge: Cambridge University Press.

Chinn, Menzie, and Jeffrey Frankel. 2007. "Will the Euro Eventually Surpass the Dollar as the Leading International Reserve Currency?" In Richard Clarida, ed., *G7 Current Account Imbalances: Sustainability and Adjustment*. Chicago: University of Chicago Press.

Christian Science Monitor. 2006. "Is Rising US Public Debt Sustainable?" *Christian Science Monitor*, March 14.

Chua, Amy. 2003. *World on Fire: How Exporting Free Market Democracy Breeds Ethnic Hatred and Global Instability*. New York: Doubleday.

CNN. 2005. "Lou Dobbs Tonight." May 12. Transcript available at: http://transcripts .cnn.com/TRANSCRIPTS/0505/12/ldt.01.html.

Condliffe, J. B. 1951. *The Commerce of Nations*. New York: George Allen & Unwin.

Cowen, Tyler. 2002. *Creative Destruction: How Globalization Is Changing the World's Cultures*. Princeton, NJ: Princeton University Press.

Cox, W. Michelle, and Richard Alm. 1995. "The Good Old Days Are Now." *Reason*, Vol. 27, No. 7, December.

Craig, W. Laurence, William W. Park, and Jan Paulsson. 1990. *International Chamber of Commerce Arbitration*. 2nd ed. New York: Oceana Publications.

David, Reneé. 1985. *Arbitration in International Trade*. Boston: Kluwer Law and Taxation Publishers.

De Long, J. Bradford. 1996. "America's Only Peacetime Inflation: The 1970s." NBER Historical Paper 83, May.

Dobbs, Lou. 2004. *Exporting America: Why Corporate Greed Is Shipping American Jobs Overseas*. New York: Time Warner Book Group.

Domowitz, Ian, and Benn Steil. 2002. "Securities Trading." In Benn Steil, David G. Victor, and Richard R. Nelson, eds., *Technological Innovation and Economic Performance*. Princeton, NJ: Princeton University Press.

Dornbusch, Rudiger, and Jacob A. Frenkel. 1984. "The Gold Standard and the Bank of England in the Crisis of 1847." In Michael D. Bordo and Anna J. Schwartz, eds., *A Retrospective on the Classical Gold Standard, 1821–1931*. Chicago: University of Chicago Press.

Dumoulin, Charles. 1681 [1612]. *Omnia quae extant opera*. Paris: Charles Osmont.

Dutton, John. 1984. "The Bank of England and the Rules of the Game under the International Gold Standard: New Evidence." In Michael D. Bordo and Anna J. Schwartz, eds., *A Retrospective on the Classical Gold Standard, 1821–1931*. Chicago: University of Chicago Press.

ECOFIN. 2000. "Press Release: 2301st Council Meeting, Exchange-Rate Strategies for Accession Countries." Brussels: ECOFIN, November 7.

The Economist. 1992. "Survey on the Legal Profession." *The Economist*, July 18–24.

———. 2005. "After Lavagna, an Uncertain Tilt towards Populism." *The Economist*, December 3.

Ehrlichman, John. 1982. *Witness to Power: The Nixon Years*. New York: Simon and Schuster.

Eichengreen, Barry. 1992a. *Golden Fetters: The Gold Standard and the Great Depression, 1919–1939*. New York: Oxford University Press.

———. 1992b. "Should the Maastricht Treaty Be Saved?" *Princeton Studies in International Finance*, No. 74, December.

———. 1996. *Globalizing Capital: A History of the International Monetary System*. Princeton, NJ: Princeton University Press.

———. 1997. *European Monetary Unification: Theory, Practice, and Analysis*. Cambridge, MA: MIT Press.

———. 2005. "Sterling's Past, Dollar's Future: Historical Perspectives on Reserve Currency Competition." NBER Working Paper 11336, May.

Erceg, Chirstoper J., Luca Guerrieri, and Christopher Gust. 2005. "Expansionary Fiscal Shocks and the U.S. Trade Deficit." *International Finance*, Vol. 8, No. 3, Winter.

European Central Bank. 2007. "Review of the International Role of the Euro." June. Available at: http://www.ecb.int/pub/pdf/other/reviewoftheinternational roleoftheeuro2007en.pdf.

European Commission. 2000. "Exchange Rate Strategies for EU Candidate Countries (Note for the Economic and Financial Committee)." August 22. European Commission, ECFIN/521/2000-EN.

Feis, Herbert. 1930. *Europe: The World's Banker: 1870–1914*. Published for the Council on Foreign Relations. New Haven, CT: Yale University Press.

Feldstein, Martin. 1997. "EMU and International Conflict." *Foreign Affairs*, November/December.

Financial Economists Roundtable. 1994. "Statement on Derivative Markets and Financial Risk." September 26. Available at: http://www.stanford.edu/~wfsharpe/ art/fer/fer94.htm.

Financial Times. 2000. " 'Father of the Euro' Stirs Up Currency Debate in South American Family." *Financial Times*, May 9.

———. 2004. "Argentina to Raise Tax on Crude Oil Exports." *Financial Times*, August 5.

———. 2006. "Obituary: Theodore Levitt, Harvard Professor Who Coined the Term Globalization." *Financial Times*, June 30.

———. 2007a. "China Turns the Tables on U.S. with Lecture on Effects of a Weak Dollar." *Financial Times*, December 13.

———. 2007b. "China Voices Alarm at Dollar Weakness." *Financial Times*, November 20.

———. 2008. "US's Triple-A Credit Rating 'Under Threat.' " *Financial Times*, January 11.

Fisher, Richard. 2008. "Comments on Stylized Facts of Globalization and World Inflation." Remarks for a panel discussion at the International Symposium of the Banque de France on Globalisation, Inflation and Monetary Policy, March 7. Available at: http://www.dallasfed.org/news/speeches/fisher/2008/fs080307.cfm.

Flood, Robert P., and Michael Mussa. 1994. "Issues Concerning Nominal Anchors for Monetary Policy." IMF Working Paper 94/61.

Friedman, Milton. 1977. "Nobel Lecture: Inflation and Unemployment." *The Journal of Political Economy*, Vol. 85, No. 3, June.

———. 1994 [1992]. *Money Mischief: Episodes in Monetary History.* New York: Harcourt Brace Jovanovich.

Friedman, Milton, and Anna J. Schwartz. 1963. *A Monetary History of the United States, 1857–1960.* Princeton, NJ: Princeton University Press.

———. 1982. *Monetary Trends in the United States and the United Kingdom.* Chicago: University of Chicago Press.

Friedman, Thomas L. 1999. *The Lexus and the Olive Tree.* New York: Anchor Books.

———. 2005. *The World Is Flat: A Brief History of the Twenty-First Century.* New York: Farrar, Straus and Giroux.

Goldberg, Linda S., and Cédric Tille. 2005. "Vehicle Currency Use in International Trade." NBER Working Paper 11127, February.

Goldin, Claudia, and Lawrence F. Katz. 2007. "The Race between Education and Technology: The Evolution of U.S. Educational Wage Differentials, 1890 to 2005." NBER Working Paper 12984, March.

González Téllez, Manuel. 1715 [1673]. *Commentaria perpetua in singulos textus quinque librorum Decretalium Gregorii IX.* Lyon, France: Anisson & Posuel.

Grant's Interest Rate Observer. 2007. "End of the Honor System." *Grant's Interest Rate Observer*, December 14.

Gray, John. 1984. "The Road to Serfdom: 40 Years On." In Norman Barry et al., eds., *Hayek's "Serfdom" Revisited.* London: Institute of Economic Affairs.

———. 1998. *False Dawn: The Delusions of Global Capitalism.* New York: The New Press.

Greider, William. 1997. *One World, Ready or Not: The Manic Logic of Global Capitalism.* New York: Simon and Schuster.

Hanna, Daniel. 2006. "A New Fiscal Framework for GCC Countries Ahead of Monetary Union." Chatham House Briefing Papers. London: Chatham House.

Hausmann, Ricardo. 1999. "Should There Be Five Currencies or One Hundred and Five?" *Foreign Policy*, No. 116, Autumn.

Hawtrey, Ralph G. 1924. "Discussion on Monetary Reform." *Economic Journal*, Vol. 34, No. 134, June.

———. 1947. *The Gold Standard in Theory and Practice*. 5th ed. London: Longmans, Green.

Hayek, Friedrich. 1937. *Monetary Nationalism and International Stability*. London: Longmans, Green,

———. 1960. *The Constitution of Liberty*. London: Routledge.

———. 1973. *Law, Legislation and Liberty*. Vol. 1. Chicago: University of Chicago Press.

———. 1976. *Law, Legislation and Liberty*. Vol. 2. Chicago: University of Chicago Press.

———. 1988. *The Fatal Conceit: The Errors of Socialism*. London: Routledge.

———. 1989. *Monetary Nationalism and International Stability*. Fairfield, NJ: Augustus M. Kelley.

———. 1990 [1976]. *Denationalisation of Money: The Argument Revised*. 3rd ed. London: Institute of Economic Affairs.

———. 1999 [1932]. "The Fate of the Gold Standard." Reprinted in Stephen Kresge, ed., *The Collected Works of F. A. Hayek*. Vol. 5, *Good Money, Part I: The New World*. Chicago: University of Chicago Press.

Hinds, Manuel. 2006. *Playing Monopoly with the Devil*. New Haven, CT: Yale University Press.

Hirschman, Albert O. 1977. *The Passions and the Interests: Political Arguments for Capitalism before Its Triumph*. Princeton, NJ: Princeton University Press.

Hont, Istvan. 2005. *Jealousy of Trade*. Cambridge, MA: Belknap Press of Harvard University Press.

Hotman, François. 1610 [1573]. *Liber quaestionum illustrium*. Hanover, Germany: Wilhelm Anton.

Hufbauer, Gary Clyde, and Ben Goodrich. 2003. "Next Move in Steel: Revocation or Retaliation?" *International Economics Policy Briefs*. Washington, DC: Institute for International Economics, October.

Hummels, David. 1999. "Transportation Costs and International Integration in Recent History." Unpublished manuscript, University of Chicago.

Hunter, Ian, and David Saunders. 2002. "Introduction." In Ian Hunter and David Saunders, eds., *Natural Law and Civil Sovereignty*. New York: Palgrave Macmillan.

Iliasu, A. A. 1971. "The Cobden-Chevalier Commercial Treaty of 1860." *The Historical Journal*, Vol. 14, No. 1, March.

Imlah, A. H. 1958. *Economic Elements in the Pax Brittanica: Studies in British Foreign Trade in the Nineteenth Century*. Cambridge, MA: Harvard University Press.

Independent Strategy. 2006. "New Monetarism and the Currency Accelerator." November 1. Available at: http://www.instrategy.com/pdf/NM011106.pdf.

Innocent IV. 1570. *Commentaria super quinque libros Decretalium*. Frankfurt-am-Maim: Sigmund Feyerabend.

International Monetary Fund. 2001. *Financial Stability in Dollarized Economies*. Washington, DC: International Monetary Fund, Monetary and Exchange Affairs Department.

———. 2007. *World Economic Outlook: Spillovers and Cycles in the Global Economy*. Washington, DC: International Monetary Fund.

International Swaps and Derivatives Association. "ISDA Market Survey Historical Data." Available at: http://www.isda.org/statistics/pdf/ISDA-Market-Survey -historical-data.pdf.

Irwin, Douglas A. 1996. *Against the Tide: An Intellectual History of Free Trade*. Princeton, NJ: Princeton University Press.

Jefferson, Thomas. 1799. Letter to Edmund Randolph. August 18. Available at: http:// odur.let.rug.nl/~usa/P/tj3/writings/brf/jefl128.htm.

Johnson, Charles, ed. 1956. *The "De Moneta" of Nicholas Oresme and English Mint Documents*. London: Nelson.

Johnson, Paul. 1997. *A History of the American People*. New York: HarperCollins.

Justi, Johann Gottlob von. 1760. *Die Grundfeste der Macht und Glükseligkeit der Staaten*. Vol. 1. Koenigsberg: J. H. Hartungs.

Keiley, A. M. 1900. "Bills of Exchange." *The Virginia Law Register*, Vol. 6, No. 2, June.

Kenwood, A. G., and A. L. Lougheed. 1999. *The Growth of the International Economy 1820–2000: An Introductory Text*. 4th ed. New York: Routledge.

Kern, Fritz. 2006 [1939]. *Kingship and Law in the Middle Ages*. Translated by S. B. Chrimes. Clark, NJ: The Lawbook Exchange.

Keynes, John Maynard. 1960. *The General Theory of Employment, Interest and Money*. New York: Harcourt, Brace and Company.

Kindleberger, Charles P. 1986. *The World in Depression, 1929–1939*. Revised and enlarged edition. Berkeley: University of California Press.

Klein, Naomi. 2000. *No Logo: No Space, No Choice, No Jobs*. New York: Picador.

Korten, David C. 1996. "The Failures of Bretton Woods." In Jerry Mander and Edward Goldsmith, eds., *The Case against the Global Economy*. San Francisco: Sierra Club Books.

Krasner, Stephen D. 1995–1996. "Compromising Westphalia." *International Security*, Vol. 20, No. 3, Winter.

———. 1999. "Globalization and Sovereignty." In David A. Smith et al., eds., *States and Sovereignty in the Global Economy*. New York: Routledge.

Kresge, Stephen, ed. 1999. *The Collected Works of F. A. Hayek*. Vol. 5. Chicago: University of Chicago Press.

Krugman, Paul. 1993. "Lessons of Massachusetts for EMU." In F. Torres and F. Giavazzi, eds., *Growth and Adjustment in the European Monetary Union*. Cambridge: Cambridge University Press.

———. 1996. "The Gold Bug Variations: The Gold Standard—and the Men Who Love It." *Slate*, November 23. Available at: http://www.slate.com/id/1912/.

———. 1997a. "The Accidental Theorist: All Work and No Play Makes William Greider a Dull Boy." *Slate*, January 24. Available at: http://www.slate.com/id/1916.

———. 1997b. *The Age of Diminished Expectations: U.S. Economic Policy in the 1990s.* Cambridge, MA: MIT Press.

Kurihara, Kenneth K. 1949. "Toward a New Theory of Monetary Sovereignty." *The Journal of Political Economy*, Vol. 57, No. 2, April.

Lal, Deepak. 2006. *Reviving the Invisible Hand: The Case for Classical Liberalism in the Twenty-First Century.* Princeton, NJ: Princeton University Press.

League of Nations. 1934. "Monthly Bulletin of Statistics." Geneva: League of Nations, February.

Leakey, Richard E. 1981. *The Making of Mankind.* New York: Dutton.

Le Blanc, François. 1703. *Traité historique des monnoyes de France.* Paris.

Levitt, Theodore. 1983. "The Globalization of Markets." *Harvard Business Review*, May/June.

Lindert, Peter H., and Jeffrey G. Williamson. 2003. "Does Globalization Make the World More Unequal?" In Michael D. Bordo, Alan M. Taylor, and Jeffrey G. Williamson, eds., *Globalization in Historical Perspective.* Chicago: University of Chicago Press.

López-Cordova, J. E., and Christopher Meissner. 2000. "Exchange Rate Regimes and International Trade: Evidence from the Classical Gold Standard Era." Institute of Business and Economic Research, Paper 118.

Lundgren, Nils-Gustav. 1996. "Bulk Trade and Maritime Transport Costs: The Evolution of Global Markets." *Resources Policy*, Vol. 22, No. 1–2, March–June.

Maddison, Angus. 1991. *Dynamic Forces in Capitalist Development: A Long-Run Comparative View.* New York: Oxford University Press.

Malcolm, Joyce Lee, ed. 1999. *The Struggle for Sovereignty: Seventeenth-Century English Political Tracts.* 2 vols. Indianapolis: Liberty Fund.

Marx, Karl, and Fredrich Engels. 1969 [1848]. *Manifesto of the Communist Party.* From *Karl Marx and Frederick Engels: Selected Works.* Vol. 1. Moscow: Progress Publishers. Available at: http://www.marxists.org/archive/marx/works/download/manifest.pdf.

Mather, Henry. 2001. "Choice of Law for International Sales Issues Not Resolved by the CISG." *Journal of Law and Commerce*, Vol. 20, Spring. Available at: http://www.cisg.law.pace.edu/cisg/biblio/mather1.html.

Mathias, Peter. 1969. *The First Industrial Nation: An Economic History of Britain, 1700–1914.* London: Methuen & Co.

Mattli, Walter. 2001. "Private Justice in a Global Economy: From Litigation to Arbitration." *International Organization*, Vol. 55, No. 4, Autumn.

McCloskey, Donald, and Richard Zecher. 1976. "How the Gold Standard Worked: 1880–1913." In Jacob A. Frenkel and Harry G. Johnson, eds., *The Monetary Approach to the Balance of Payments.* London: Allen and Unwin.

McKinnon, Ronald I. 1993. "The Rules of the Game: International Money in Historical Perspective." *Journal of Economic Literature*, Vol. 31, No. 1, March.

———. 2004. "Optimum Currency Areas and Key Currencies: Mundell I versus Mundell II." *Journal of Common Market Studies*, Vol. 42, No. 4, November.

Mead, Walter Russell. 2002. *Special Providence: American Foreign Policy and How It Changed the World*. New York: Routledge.

Meissner, Christopher M. 2002. "A New World Order: Explaining the Emergence of the Classical Gold Standard." NBER Working Paper 9233, October.

Menger, Carl. 2007 [1871]. *Principles of Economics*. Corrected edition of the 1976 reprinting by New York University Press. Auburn, AL: Ludwig von Mises Institute. Available at: http://www.mises.org/Books/Mengerprinciples.pdf.

Micklethwait, John, and Adrian Wooldridge. 2000. *A Future Perfect: The Challenge and Hidden Promise of Globalization*. New York: Random House.

Milanovic, Branko. 2005. *Worlds Apart: Measuring International and Global Inequality*. Princeton, NJ: Princeton University Press.

Mill, John Stuart. 1871 [1848]. *Principles of Political Economy*. 7th ed. Book 3. London: Parker and Company.

——. 1894 [1848]. *Principles of Political Economy*. Vol. 2. London: Macmillan.

——. 1909 [1848]. *Principles of Political Economy*. Edited by William Ashley. New York: Augustus M. Kelley. Available at: http://www.econlib.org/library/Mill/mlP46.html.

——. 1965 [1848]. *Principles of Political Economy*. Books III–V and Appendices. London: Routledge & Kegan Paul.

Mishel, Lawrence, Jared Bernstein, and Sylvia Allegretto. 2007. *The State of Working America 2006/2007*. The Economic Policy Institute. Ithaca, NY: ILR Press. Available at: http://www.stateofworkingamerica.org/.

Mitchell, W. 1904. *An Essay on the Early History of the Law Merchant*. Cambridge: Cambridge University Press.

Mlynarski, Feliks. 1937. "Proportionalism and Stabilization Policy." In Arthur D. Gayer, ed., *The Lessons of Monetary Experience: Essays in Honor of Irving Fisher*. London: George Allen and Unwin.

M. Murenbeeld & Associates. 2002. "An Analysis of Central Bank Gold Sales and Its Impact on the Gold Mining Industry in Canada." Prepared for the Joint Working Group on Gold, May. Available at: http://www.nrcan.gc.ca/mms/mmc/2002/rmf.pdf.

Moggridge, E. D. 1972. "Policy in the Crises of 1920 and 1929." In Charles P. Kindleberger and Jean-Pierre Lafarge, eds., *Financial Crises: Theory, History and Policy*. Cambridge: Cambridge University Press.

Montanari, Geminiano. 1804 [1683]. *Della moneta: Trattato mercantile*. In *Scrittori classici italiani di economia politica, parte antica*. Vol. 3. Milan: G. G. Destefanis.

Montesquieu, Charles de. 1989 [1748]. *The Spirit of the Laws*. Translated by Anne M. Cohler, Basia Carolyn Miller, and Harold Samuel Stone. Cambridge: Cambridge University Press.

Moody's Investors Service. 2007. "Moody's Statistical Handbook: Country Credit." New York: Moody's Investors Service, May.

Morys, Mathias. 2007. "The Emergence of the Classical Gold Standard." Paper presented at the Economic History Society Annual Conference, University of

Exeter, Exeter, U.K., March 31. Abstract available at: www.york.ac.uk/res/cherry/docs/AbstractMatthiasMorys.doc.

Möser, Justus. 1990 [1772]. "Der jetzige Hang zu allgemeinen Gesetzen und Verordnungen ist der gemeinen Freiheit gefahrlich." In *Justus Mösers Sämtliche Werke: Historisch-kritische Ausgabe in 14 Bänden*. Vol. 5. Oldenburg/Berlin: Gerhard Stalling Verlag.

Muller, Jerry Z. 2002. *The Mind and the Market: Capitalism in Western Thought*. New York: Anchor Books.

Mundell, Robert A. 1961. "A Theory of Optimum Currency Areas." *American Economic Review*, Vol. 51, No. 4, September.

———. 1997. "The International Monetary System in the 21st Century: Could Gold Make a Comeback?" Lecture given at St. Vincent College, Letrobe, PA, March 12.

———. 2000. "A Reconsideration of the 20th Century." *The American Economic Review*, Vol. 90, No. 3, June.

———. 2002. "Monetary Unions and the Problem of Sovereignty." *Annals of the American Academy of Policy and Social Science*, Vol. 579, January.

Nader, Ralph, and Lori Wallach. 1996. "GATT, NAFTA, and the Subversion of the Democratic Process." In Jerry Mander and Edward Goldsmith, eds., *The Case against the Global Economy*. San Francisco: Sierra Club Books.

Nuffield Council on Bioethics. 2003. "The Use of Genetically Modified Crops in Developing Countries: A Follow-Up Discussion Paper." Available at: http://www.agbios.com/docroot/articles/03-363-001.pdf.

Nurkse, Ragnar. 1944. *International Currency Experience: Lessons of the Inter-War Period*. Geneva: League of Nations.

Obstfeld, Maurice. 1998. "The Global Capital Market: Benefactor or Menace?" *The Journal of Economic Perspectives*, Vol. 12, No. 4, Autumn.

Obstfeld, Maurice, and Alan M. Taylor. 1998. "The Great Depression as a Watershed: International Capital Mobility over the Long Run." In Michael D. Bordo, Claudia D. Goldin, and Eugene N. White, eds., *The Defining Moment: The Great Depression and the American Economy in the Twentieth Century*. Chicago: University of Chicago Press.

Oppenheim, L. F. L. 1905. *International Law: A Treatise*. Vol. 1, *Peace*. London: Longmans, Green, and Co.

Oresme, Nicole. ca. 1360. *Tractatus De Origine, Natura, Jure et Mutationibus Monetarum*.

O'Rourke, Kevin H., and Jeffrey G. Williamson. 1999. *Globalization and History*. Cambridge, MA: MIT Press.

Panagariya, Arvind. 2006. "The Pursuit of Equity Threatens Poverty Alleviation." *Financial Times*, May 31.

Parsons, Jotham. 2001. "Money and Sovereignty in Early Modern France." *Journal of the History of Ideas*, Vol. 62, No. 1, January.

Partnoy, Frank. 2002. "ISDA, NASD, CFMA, and SDNY: The Four Horsemen of Derivatives Regulation?" *Brookings-Wharton Papers on Financial Services*. Washington, DC: The Brookings Institution.

Pippenger, John. 1984. "Bank of England Operations, 1893–1913." In Michael D. Bordo and Anna J. Schwartz, eds., *A Retrospective on the Classical Gold Standard, 1821–1931*. Chicago: University of Chicago Press.

Polanyi, Karl. 1944. *The Great Transformation*. Boston: Beacon Press.

Poovey, Mary. 2008. *Genres of the Credit Economy: Mediating Value in Eighteenth- and Nineteenth-Century Britain*. Chicago: University of Chicago Press.

Poullain, Henri. 1612. *Traitez des monnoyes*. Paris: Frédéric Léonard. Reprinted in 1709. As translated in Thomas J. Sargent and Francois R. Velde, *The Big Problem of Small Change*. Princeton, NJ: Princeton University Press, 2002.

Price, Victoria Curzon. 2001. "Some Causes and Consequences of Fragmentation." In Sven W. Arndt and Henryk Kierzkowski, eds., *Fragmentation: New Production Patterns in the World Economy*. Oxford: Oxford University Press.

Rabkin, Jeremy. 2004. *The Case for Sovereignty: Why the World Should Welcome American Independence*. Washington, DC: AEI Press.

Redish, Angela. 2000. *Bimetallism*. Cambridge: Cambridge University Press.

Reich, Robert B. 1991. *The Work of Nations: Preparing Ourselves for 21st Century Capitalism*. New York: Vintage Books.

Rist, Charles. 1934. "Gold and the End of the Depression." *Foreign Affairs*, Vol. 12, No. 2, January.

Robinson, Austin. 1954. "The Changing Structure of the British Economy." *The Economic Journal*, Vol. 64, No. 255, September.

Rodrik, Dani. 1998. "Who Needs Capital-Account Convertibility?" In Stanley Fischer et al., eds., *Should the IMF Pursue Capital Account Convertibility?* Essays in International Finance, No. 207. Princeton, NJ: Princeton University Press.

Rothschild, Emma. 1999. "Globalization and the Return of History." *Foreign Policy*, No. 115, Summer.

Rousseau, Jean-Jacques. 1769. *Emile*. 4th Book: "The Confessions of Faith of a Savoyard Vicar."

———. 1920 [1762]. *The Social Contract*. Translated by G. D. H. Cole in *Rousseau's Social Contract, Etc*. New York: E. P. Dutton & Co.

Rueff, Jacques. 1972. *The Monetary Sin of the West*. Translated by Roger Glément. New York: The Macmillan Company.

Rueff, Jacques, and Fred Hirsch. 1965. *The Role and the Rule of Gold: An Argument*. Essays in International Finance, No. 47. Princeton, NJ: Princeton University Press.

Ruggie, John Gerard. 1993. "Territoriality and Beyond: Problematizing Modernity in International Relations." *International Organization*, Vol. 47, No. 1, Winter.

Russell, Bertrand. 1945. *A History of Western Philosophy*. New York: Simon and Schuster.

Sabine, George H. 1937. *A History of Political Theory*. New York: Holt.

Saint-Etienne, Christian. 1984. *The Great Depression 1929–1938: Lessons for the 1980s*. Stanford, CA: Hoover Institution Press.

Samuelson, Paul A. 1969. "The Way of an Economist." In Paul A. Samuelson, ed., *International Economic Relations: Proceedings of the Third Congress of the International Economic Association*. London: Macmillan.

Sargent, Thomas J., and François R. Velde. 2002. *The Big Problem of Small Change*. Princeton, NJ: Princeton University Press.

Saul, John Raulston. 2005. *The Collapse of Globalism: And the Reinvention of the World*. Woodstock, NY: Overlook Press.

Schmitthoff, Clive M. 1961. "International Business Law: A New Law Merchant." *Current Law and Social Problems*, Vol. 129.

———. 1968. "The Unification of the Law of International Trade." *Journal of Business Law*, April.

Schofield, Malcolm. 2005. "Epicurean and Stoic Political Thought." In Christopher Rowe and Malcolm Schofield, eds., *The Cambridge History of Greek and Roman Political Thought*. Cambridge: Cambridge University Press.

Scholte, Jan Aart. 2000. *Globalization: A Critical Introduction*. New York: Palgrave Macmillan.

Schumer, Charles E., and Lindsey O. Graham. 2006. "Play by the Rules." *Wall Street Journal*, September 25.

Sen, Amartya. 2002. "Globalization and Poverty." Lecture given at Santa Clara University, October 29.

Setser, Brad. 2007. "Yes, Virginia, the World's Central Banks Are Financing Most of the U.S. Current Account Deficit." RGE Monitor, December 18. Available at: http://www.rgemonitor.com/blog/setser/233036.

Shlaes, Amity. 2007. *The Forgotten Man: A New History of the Great Depression*. New York: HarperCollins.

Simmel, Georg. 1978 [1900]. *The Philosophy of Money*. 2nd ed. London: Routledge.

———. 2004 [1900]. *The Philosophy of Money*. 3rd enlarged ed. London: Routledge.

Smith, Adam. 1776. *The Wealth of Nations*. London: Printed for W. Strahan and T. Cadell.

———. 1853 [1759]. *The Theory of Moral Sentiments*. London: H. G. Bohn.

Sophocles. *Antigone*. Translated by R. C. Jebb. Available at: http://classics.mit.edu/Sophocles/antigone.html.

Steil, Benn. 2007. "The End of National Currency." *Foreign Affairs*, May/June.

Steil, Benn, and Robert E. Litan. 2006. *Financial Statecraft: The Role of Financial Markets in American Foreign Policy*. New Haven, CT: Yale University Press.

Stein, Peter. 1999. *Roman Law in European History*. Cambridge: Cambridge University Press.

Stern, Fritz. 1961. *The Politics of Cultural Despair*. Berkeley: University of California Press.

Stewart, Rory. 2004. *The Places in Between*. Orlando, FL: Harcourt.

Stiglitz, Joseph. 2002. *Globalization and Its Discontents*. New York: Norton.

———. 2005. "The Overselling of Globalization." In Michael Weinstein, ed., *Globalization: What's New?* New York: Columbia University Press.

Suarez, Francisco. 1934. *De Legibus, Ac Deo Legislatore* (1612). In *Selections from Three Works of Francisco Suarez, S.J.* Vol. 2. Oxford: Clarendon Press.

Sulling, Anne. 2002. "Should Estonia Euroize?" *Economics of Transition*, Vol. 10, No. 2.

Swift v. Tyson, 16 Peters (41 U.S.) 1, 19 (1842).

Temin, Peter. 1989. *Lessons from the Great Depression: The Lionel Robbins Lectures for 1989*. Cambridge, MA: MIT Press.

Timoshenko, Vladimir P. 1953. *World Agriculture and the Depression*. Ann Arbor: University of Michigan Press.

Tirole, Jean. 2002. *Financial Crises, Liquidity, and the International Monetary System*. Princeton, NJ: Princeton University Press.

Trakman, Leon E. 1983. *The Law Merchant: The Evolution of Commercial Law*. Littleton, CO: Fred B. Rothman and Co.

Ure, P. N. 1922. *The Origin of Tyranny*. Cambridge: Cambridge University Press.

U.S. Bureau of the Census. 1975. *Historical Statistics of the United States: Colonial Times to 1970*. Bicentenial Edition. Washington, DC: U.S. Government Printing Office.

Védrine, Hubert. 2001. *France in an Age of Globalization*. Translated by Philip H. Gordon. Washington, DC: Brookings Institution Press.

Volckart, Oliver, and Antje Mangels. 1999. "Are the Roots of the Modern *Lex Mercatoria* Really Medieval?" *Southern Economic Journal*, Vol. 65, No. 3, January.

Wacziarg, Romain, and Karen Horn Welch. 2003. "Trade Liberalization and Growth: New Evidence." NBER Working Paper 10152, December.

Walker, Mack. 1971. *German Home Towns: Community, State and General Estate, 1648–1871*. Ithaca, NY: Cornell University Press.

Wall Street Journal. 2005. "Would You Like to Pay by Check, Cash—or Gold?" *Wall Street Journal*, October 8.

———. 2007. "Cashing Out: Venezuelans Chase Dollars amid Worries over Economy." *Wall Street Journal*, August 27.

———. 2008. "Investors Flock to Foreign Bonds." *Wall Street Journal*, February 13.

Weatherford, Jack. 1997. *The History of Money*. New York: Three Rivers Press.

Wells, Wyatt C. 1994. *Economist in an Uncertain World: Arthur W. Burns and the Federal Reserve, 1970–1978*. New York: Columbia University Press.

Wiener, Jarrod. 1999. *Globalization and the Harmonization of Law*. London: Pinter.

Wieser, Fredrich von. 1983 [1926]. *The Law of Power*. Translated by W. E. Kuhn. Lincoln, NE: Bureau of Business Research.

Wight, Martin. 1977. *Systems of States*. Leicester, U.K.: Leicester University Press.

Williams, David. 1968. "The Evolution of the Sterling System." In C. R. Whitesey and J. S. G. Wilson, eds., *Essays in Money and Banking*. Oxford: Oxford University Press.

Wolf, Martin. 2004. *Why Globalization Works*. New Haven, CT: Yale University Press.

———. 2007. "Unfettered Finance Is Fast Reshaping the Global Economy." *Financial Times*, June 18.

Woodford, Michael. 2000. "Monetary Policy in a World without Money." *International Finance*, Vol. 3, No. 2, July.

Yardley, Jim. 2006. "Fired Editors of Chinese Journal Call for Free Speech in Public Letter." *New York Times*, February 18.

INDEX

Note: Page numbers followed by *f* and *t* indicate figures and tables.